DIVINE RESPONSE
TO FALLEN MANKIND

DIVINE RESPONSE
TO FALLEN MANKIND

EMANUEL ESH LAPP

Copyright © 2021 by Emanuel Esh Lapp

All rights reserved. No part of this publication may be reproduced, distributed, or transmitted in any form or by any means, including photocopying, recording, or other electronic or mechanical methods, without the prior written permission of the publisher.

VPD Studio
307 S Main St
Milbank, SD 57252
www.vpdstudio.com

All scripture quotations contained herein come from the King James Version of the Bible.

ISBN: 978-1-7363226-0-4 (Hardback)
ISBN: 978-1-7363226-1-1 (Ebook)

Library of Congress Control Number: 2020924681

Printed in the United States of America
First Edition

To our precious children and children's children,
for whom this writing was begun that became a book.

Contents

Reviews | ix
Preface | xi
Acknowledgments | xiii
Introduction | xv

Chapter 1	Man Became a Living Soul	1
Chapter 2	Fallen Man Risen Lord	19
Chapter 3	Total Depravity of Man (Part I)	33
Chapter 4	Total Depravity of Man (Part II)	45
Chapter 5	Unmerited Favor	55
Chapter 6	Love Manifested (Part I)	71
Chapter 7	Love Manifested (Part II)	80
Chapter 8	Immutable Counsel of Almighty God	97
Chapter 9	Promises to Persevering Saints	110
Chapter 10	Sabbath Rest Messiah	126
Chapter 11	It is Finished	143
Chapter 12	The Empty Tomb	159
Chapter 13	Legalism (Part I)	172
Chapter 14	Legalism (Part II)	183
Chapter 15	Culture and the Bible	199
Chapter 16	Behold Thy King Cometh	214
Chapter 17	Meanwhile Back on the Earth (Part I)	230
Chapter 18	Meanwhile Back on the Earth (Part II)	246

Reviews

"*Divine Response to Fallen Mankind* is a very well written book of God's desire that all men be saved. I especially appreciate how the author lifts up Jesus Christ as the only all-sufficient means for our salvation. Also very much appreciate how scripture intertwines with his thoughts. May God Bless."

—*John Lapp*
Preacher, River of Hope Fellowship, Vaughn, MT

"Very profound Truth can be simply stated: 'In the beginning God...' Here you will find the most profound Bible Truths simply stated for all to understand and live by. Biblically correct, not politically correct, is this author's wise and honest commitment. With this perspective the Holy Bible answers even the most controversial social ills of our day. From falling off a house roof to an attempt to fly off a shop roof, all of life is seen as having an eternal perspective. These writings reveal not only the deliberate exercising of the head after Brother Emanuel's fall from a house roof, but even more, the exercising of the heart to seek after God and godliness. If the author's aspirations of nine billion people reading this book are realized, it will be a world-changer!"

—*Leroy Lapp*
Retired Bishop, Summitview Christian Fellowship, New Holland, PA

"In his book *Divine Response to Fallen Mankind*, Brother Emanuel gives us a welcome reprieve from the weak theology and pop psychology of our day. Interweaving keen biblical insight with relevant history, original poetry, and personal life experiences, he offers a read that is both entertaining and inspirational. While originally written for the benefit of his children, Emanuel has, in allowing his writings to be published in this book, benefited us all. I heartily recommend it."

—*David Lapp*
Pastor, New Hope Christian Fellowship, Bear Lake, MI

"From Brother Emanuel Lapp's book, we have the account of fallen man and risen Lord. A powerful message of hope, and from the chapters on man's depravity with its subtle tendency to legalism and self-righteousness, we have a much needed warning. We do well to consider the fragmentation of churches and ask with the troubled apostle, "Lord, is it I?" Only as our Lord Jesus sheds his divine Light on our dark paths can we see ourselves as He does. And say with the penitent publican, "Lord, be merciful unto me a sinner." (Psalm 51:17) Yes, within any of us is the potential to be a Nero, or a Hitler, but then also an Ambassador for Jesus Christ. May God bless this book. I recommend it to anyone."

—*Amzie Troyer*
Deacon, Living Hope Christian Church. Fulton, MO

"In my opinion, a very well thought out writing. I found it easy to understand and read. Doctrinally I found it to be spot on with what I consider correct. The devil's tactics, with the dangers and pitfalls in the world, are very well portrayed; then also God's plan for redemption and provision."

—*Ryan Tschetter*
Milbank Christian Fellowship, Milbank, SD

"Emanuel has written, by God's grace, a solid theological book, intermingled with history, science, nature, and personal tragedy and triumph. Though his heart was to pen these words for his children and grandchildren, every reader will find here a wealth of sound doctrine to edify both young and old in the Christian faith. Christ-centered and heartfelt, this book is a great read for all."

—*Jerry Mawhorr*
Pastor, Remnant Christian Fellowship, Utica, OH

"If you enjoy sound doctrine but fall asleep reading most doctrinal books, then this one may be for you. The combination of Scripture, personal testimony, poetry, and real life illustrations are refreshing. Read it and let the timeless truths of the Bible refresh your spirit and your soul."

—*Daniel Esh*
Pastor, Fulton Christian Fellowship, Fulton, SD

Preface

THIS WRITING WAS BEGUN with a father-heart desire to help our beloved children, and children's children, keep their focus on Jesus Christ and His teachings recorded in The Holy Bible, and thus to escape the snare of the devil in this 21st century, as he, through the people under his control and through tools never before available, increases his attack against every good and sacred institution, even against nature itself. It is ever needful, as we face the spiritual vertigo tossing and floating amidst the whirlwind of confusion in these last days, to live in the light of reality, to discern both good and evil, to put on the whole armor of God, (Ephesians 6:10-18) and so with the stabilizing peace of Jesus and the never-failing courage that He gives, to resist the enemy of our souls. (James 4:7) And to not only succeed in protecting ourselves and our families but to be on the offense for the sake of Christ and the increase of His Kingdom.

As that father-heart desire kept this pen moving, the writing of it eventually morphed into a book. A book that I hope can draw sinners and back-sliders to Christ and encourage Believers to "look up for your redemption draweth nigh." (Luke 21:28)

I was asked one day how many copies of this book I hope to publish and sell, and I said, "I'm hoping to reach at least a million people with its message, so I guess a million copies." Later I came across an article about the "baby boomer" era from 1946 to 1964 and learned there are approximately 27 million of us. So the next time I saw Craig I said, "I have a new goal; I want to see 27 million copies published, sold, and its message in the hands of every baby boomer plus." I later learned that there are over 69 million baby boomers in the US. But the goal doesn't even slow down there as the projected estimate is 9 billion people on planet Earth by 2050.

The goal, however, is not so much appreciation for this book, but to spark and/or refresh an appreciation for God the Father, God the Son, and Holy Spirit, together with appreciation for the record of our Creation and God's Divine Response to our fall, in His Word, The Holy Bible.

It is with this heart-felt desire that I humbly present this book to the world whom God so loved "that he gave his only begotten Son, that whosoever believeth in him should not perish, but have everlasting life. For God sent not his Son into the world to condemn the world; but that the world through him might be saved." (John 3:16-17)

There is hope. God's way. Jesus Lives!

> Gottes sege dazu winscha
> (May God add His blessing)
>
> ~Emanuel Lapp

Acknowledgments

THE WRITING OF THIS book was only possible because of the grace of God. It is my heartfelt desire that God, the Author of all that is Upright, Good, and True, receive all glory for all that is good and helpful to Christ-likeness in this book, and I the fault if any is not.

Though my parents have gone on to Glory, I wish to honor them here for their unyielding exhortations to a good and upright life, never giving up on their son who today grieves at the unnecessary grief he caused them, for their ready forgiveness, assuring me they already had forgiven when I asked, and their obvious pleasure when they sensed God working good in my life. That is love. I am grateful.

Thank you to our children. To our sons, Caleb, Steve, Jeremy, and Kenny for picking up where your dad left off in September of 2011, and for your invaluable support through the "tough" years. Thank you for being real men who persevere. To our lovely daughters, Linda, Laura, Erma, Joy, Carolyn, and Katrina for the joy you have been, and are, to us. For being the music of our home. (And I think I can relearn how to wash dishes!) Children, I am so grateful that you have given your hearts and lives to Christ. I have no greater joy. I love you all.

I have every reason to be thankful for the family I was raised in. A special thank you to my brothers and sisters for the love, loyalty, and laughter of family life. And for correcting me when you "think" I need it.

Thank you brother Paul, for your interest, your encouragement, your unwavering support; for believing that God can use this broken vessel for His glory; and for your proofreading and help along the way. I appreciate it.

Thank you Teacher Eleanor Martin for not giving up on this unruly youngster, for your patient teaching, for instilling in me the love of learning, for not bending the rules, and yes, for discipline such as writing "I will nots" hundreds of times.

Many are the friends, family members, and Church leaders who have had an impact for good in my life, providing much needed direction at times; including my Kentucky and Tennessee church brothers, I am grateful for those refining years together.

Thank you to the Christian brothers who reviewed this manuscript. I needed men whom I could trust to give me sincere, constructive feedback. Thank you for being such trustworthy men.

Thank you Barb Livingston and Jane Popowski. Thank you Barb for transforming my hand-written pages with their scribbles and side-notes into typewritten coherency. Thank you Jane for your encouraging support and for introducing me to the expertise of your sisterly friend, Barb.

Thank you to Jennifer Burdge and Dusti Johnson for taking the time needed for the proof-reading and copy-editing of this manuscript. It is much appreciated.

Thank you Craig Weinberg, at VPD Studio, for guiding the publication of this manuscript into a tangible reality.

And to the love of my life, my dear wife, Sadie Ann. Thank you for your love when we were young and that your love was still present years later, when I lay in a hospital bed, my body a broken shell of what it had been. Thank you for being with me as I recovered and as I continue recovery. I appreciate the daily ways you show me love, and your support of this completed manuscript. I love you.

Introduction

On a cold winter night in 1982, holding a restless infant in his arms, the author of this book, Emanuel Lapp, came under deep conviction that he did not have the wherewithal to impart truth, even to his posterity. Out of that deep conviction came a quest and a defense for truth that resulted in a radical change of heart and life, personally to the author, and now 38 years later has resulted in the publication of this book.

From childhood and marriage in Pennsylvania, to a time in the hills of Kentucky and North Carolina, Emanuel is currently at home in Milbank, South Dakota with his wife Sadie and their four youngest children. He has six married children and nineteen grandchildren. Father and Grandpa continues to have no greater joy in life than to hear this one thing—that his children and grandchildren are walking in that same Truth that he himself first embraced in 1982.

In 2011, Emanuel suffered from a serious accident which resulted in a three-week long coma, out of which he miraculously recovered. Receiving an extension of life at fifty-one years of age, the need to redeem the time that was given to him was impressed on Emanuel's heart as never before.

In *Divine Response to Fallen Mankind*, Emanuel offers to every culture in the world clear and concise answers to the spiritual problems facing humanity in every generation.

~Paul Lapp

1

MAN BECAME A LIVING SOUL

On day six of creation God did something very special.

Our Almighty, Omnipotent God had created light, the sun and moon, the stars and constellations, all plant life, the birds of the air, all creatures of the seas, and all land animals. And then He turned His attention to the crowning glory of His creation. And we may call it the "crowning glory of His creation," methinks, without doing violence to the Scriptures. For God said, "Let us make man in our image, after our likeness: and let them have dominion over the fish of the sea, and over the fowl of the air, and over the cattle, and over all the earth, and over every creeping thing that creepeth upon the earth. So God created man in his own image, in the image of God created he him; male and female created he them." (Genesis 1:26-27)

Genesis 2 gives us a brief explanation of how God went about forming this creature that was to resemble Himself. Verse 7, "And the Lord God formed man of the dust of the ground." This forming of man from the dust of the ground was not so different from the way God had formed the land animals, for Genesis Chapter 2 also gives us a brief description of how God went about forming the animals. Verse 19, "And out of the ground the Lord God formed every beast of the field, and every fowl of the air." So far what set man apart from the animal kingdom was that "God created man in His own image, in the image of God created He him."

Then to that very special form God added a very special touch … God stooped. Did He not?

For into that lifeless form the Lord God "breathed into his nostrils the breath of life, and man became a living soul." While the physical similarities with the animals were and are many, yet there are these three characteristics that are unique to mankind and set him (and her) apart and above the animal kingdom:

1. We are made in the image of God.
2. God gave us of His own breath.
3. Man became a living soul.

In these three respects we are very different from the animal kingdom.

Though our bodies function very much like the animals that God created; of which the obvious similarities are that they and we have bone, muscle, skin, hair, eyes, mouth, nostrils, lungs, blood, heart pumping blood, with life (nourishment) being in the blood. (Leviticus 17:11)

We may not like to think of ourselves as being similar to rats, but there are, in fact, so many similarities that rats are being—and have been for a long time—used in laboratories to test the effects that a wide variety of drugs (being developed for the cure of ailments) may or may not have on the human body.

Multitudes of these rats, guinea pigs, and mice have lost their lives for the benefit of mankind, for which we can be very thankful, for it means that they can be the "guinea pigs" and not us. So even in the similarities, we see and experience God's providential care and His keeping hand upon the human race, for without these tests the knowledge of human biology would be quite limited. And the tests would be useless without the biological similarities.

Despite all the similarities in the way our bodies function in comparison to the way an animal body functions, that is where the similarities end, and yes, even with the Anthropoid family which includes the gorilla, the ape, the chimpanzee, and the monkey. For as Dr. David Menton and others have sufficiently shown at the Creation Museum, even the visual similarities of humans with the Anthropoid family are very superficial and virtually disappear upon closer study of the skeletal structure.

For "God created man in his own image, in the image of God created he him; male and female created he them." (Genesis 1:27) And then he commissioned them (us) to subdue—to rule over—the earth and the animal kingdom; Verse 28; "And God blessed them, and God said unto them, Be fruitful, and multiply, and replenish the earth, and subdue it: and have dominion over the fish of the sea, and over the fowl of the air, and over every living thing that moveth upon the earth."

MAN BECAME A LIVING SOUL

God had created Adam before He created Eve and had brought the animals to Adam "to see what he would call them; and whatsoever Adam called every living creature, that was the name thereof." (Genesis 2:19) But among these animals there was not a helpmeet found for Adam. (Genesis 2:20) "And the LORD God caused a deep sleep to fall upon Adam, and he slept: and he [God] took one of his ribs and closed up the flesh instead thereof; And the rib, which the LORD God had taken from man, made he a woman, and brought her unto the man. And Adam said, This is now bone of my bones, and flesh of my flesh: she shall be called Woman, because she was taken out of Man. Therefore shall a man leave his father and his mother, and shall cleave unto his wife: and they shall be one flesh." (Genesis 2:21-24)

A helpmeet had not been found for Adam among the animals (Verse 20), so God provided one for him through the special process of taking a rib from Adam, (close to his heart) and making of it a woman. (Verse 22)

Many years later, God, through the Apostle Paul, likened this husband/wife relationship to the relationship of Jesus Christ with the Church, His Bride. The church is also likened to His Body, for the church proceeds from Christ and is now "bone of His bone, flesh of His flesh" and is called woman because she was taken out of Christ, for He is, individually and corporately "made unto us wisdom, and righteousness, and sanctification, and redemption: That, according as it is written, He that glorieth, let him glory in the Lord." (I Corinthians 1:30-31) And those whom God foreknew to be His children, "He also did predestinate to be conformed to the image of his Son." (Romans 8:29) For the image of God was marred by the fall; from perfection to imperfection, from very good to aging, from life to death, when the forbidden fruit was looked upon, reached out for, and partaken of.

Man became a living soul when God breathed into his nostrils the breath of life and his body came alive. Adam was then, as we are now, made up of three parts: spirit, soul and body. (I Thessalonians 5:23) All three together make up the whole man, and when first created all three were in perfect harmony with each other and with God. Harmony flowed and so there was perfect peace resting upon, and in, the breasts of the first man and woman.

Their spirit, which is the mind and will, was so one with God that there was no distinguishable difference.

Their soul, which is the mind and emotions, was at peace, at rest with God and love flowed between them, rich and deep.

Their body also, made in the image of God, was glorious in its perfection, health, and vitality.

And then they fell. They fell from God's favor and grace when they partook of that forbidden fruit.

And when they fell from God's favor, their spirit changed, their soul changed, and their body changed.

God had warned that they would "surely die."

Though their bodies didn't immediately fall over and die, yet on that day, at that very instant, their bodies began that slow, relentless march that ultimately led to their demise; for the fountain of youth was gone and their bodies began, from that moment of time, to age until the end came. As bodies do, ever since, for us all.

Their soul also fell. Their mind and emotions that had been so at peace and at rest in God, with love flowing rich and deep between them, now changed. Anxious thoughts filled their minds and as they became aware of their nakedness, they sewed fig leaves together for aprons to cover the nakedness of their bodies. Also the "perfect love" that casts out fear (1 John 4:18) was no longer there, and when God came looking for them they were so overcome with fear that they hid themselves. Despite their fig leaf aprons they still felt naked when in the presence of God. Despite all their self-efforts, they still felt naked when God came. So God slew an animal and made coats of animal hide for them, which was then sufficient, for God did it and it took the shedding of blood to cover them.

Their spirit also fell. They now had a mind and will out of sync, separated and distinct from God's, for they had now departed from Him in spirit and taken their own way. They now had a self-willed mind and spirit that found surrender to God's way extremely difficult and needed the discipline of thorns, thistles, and the sweat of the brow for the man and the discipline of child-bearing pain for the woman till they returned to dust, "for dust thou art, and unto dust shalt thou return," God told them. (Genesis 3:16-19)

They had now fallen from the grace of God. Death had overtaken them, for the pure, open relationship that they'd had with their maker, had died. Their bodies also were now mortal.

Death had come upon them. Death in spirit, soul, and body.

Death in the spirit, as the harmonious relationship with God was severed and their minds and wills were no longer willingly subject. A willfulness set in that was to glaringly show itself in their posterity, of whom we are a part.

Death in the soul, as the mind and emotions were severely affected by the disharmony of the spirit. So severely, in fact, that only a generation later, brother rose up against brother, because of envy, and killed him. And then tried lying to God about it.

Death in the body, as it immediately began aging, and in that sense, dying.

It would seem as if they had become one with the animal kingdom, to be destined to a soul-less death, ceasing to exist at all when their bodies went back to the dust from whence they came.

But, no! What do we hear? What do we hear but the voice of God, now speaking to Cain, admonishing him to not give in to the wicked emotions now raging in his heart and mind. Which emotions were beckoning his will to take action against his brother.

"And the LORD said unto Cain, Why art thou wroth? and why is thy countenance fallen? If thou doest well, shalt thou not be accepted? and if thou doest not well, sin lieth at the door." (Genesis 4:6-7) And then God ended with this instruction, "and unto thee shall be his desire and thou shalt rule over him."

While God created the animals with a survival instinct that serves them well and they instinctively care for their young, they are not conscious of moral right and wrong. Unlike mankind, they do not have a conscience guiding their moral choices of right and wrong, for they know nothing about moral choices, having no such intimate connection with their Creator.

Not so with mankind, who are often more keenly aware of what they should be doing or not doing than they wish to be. For doing or not doing what we deep down know we should be doing or not doing if we would only stop and face up to it, is a troublesome business for the conscience, which in turn brings misery to the soul, especially in the most quiet moments of reflection.

It follows then that mankind is not totally cut off from the spirit world. Unlike the animals, we have a conscience that attaches itself to the highest moral good that we know. That highest good is revealed to us by God Himself through natural law woven into the very fabric of nature, through His written word, and through His Holy Spirit, that is always in harmony with His written Word.

It is of utmost importance that our conscience be formed by being receptive to what we know to be good, and most especially that it be ultimately formed by God's Word, enlightened and made alive to us by His Holy Spirit.

That we have our "senses exercised to discern both good and evil." (Hebrews 5:14) For if we receive the witness of God against our sins, we acknowledge our sin in repentance before Him, and He in turn receives us as we receive Him, then we have a solid basis from which to understand God's word and to have our "senses exercised to discern both good and evil."

But if we do not, we are yet without excuse. "For the invisible things of him from the creation of the world are clearly seen, being understood by the things that are made, even his eternal power and Godhead; so that they are without excuse: Because that, when they knew God, they glorified him not as God, neither were thankful; but became vain in their imaginations, and their foolish heart was darkened. Professing themselves to be wise, they became fools." (Romans 1:20-22)

Fools.

That is a strong word.

But yes, it is a form of insanity, a spiritual insanity, to turn away from God to the pleasures of this world. For God, while He is the provider of pleasure, also puts a healthy restraint upon us by giving us rules to live by in regards to the pleasure He gives.

In going against those restraints, the world—while professing wisdom in its advertisement of pleasures—is in reality becoming more and more desensitized to pleasure.

So while the slow but insistent removal of restraints appear to open the door to more and more "pleasure," the reality of the situation is that there is less and less real pleasure as sensitivity becomes more and more dulled by its own over-indulgence. The end result is not unlike the alcoholic wasting his life away in a drunken stupor, desensitized to all that formerly gave him pleasure.

God—in His desire that we know pleasure in this life as a foretaste of the "pleasures forevermore," (Psalms 16:11) that he offers through Jesus Christ—has, in His wisdom, placed restraints on our drinking, our eating, our listening, where we go, what we do with our time and our money. He has placed restraints on our sexual activities, inciting the rebellion of those already deceived into thinking that the rejection of restraints leads to more pleasure.

When in reality the rejection of restraints causes one to become more and more desensitized to pleasure, explaining the rise of sexual perversions—even to the flaunting of them—in a promiscuous society. (Romans 1:18-32)

When persons or a society keep pushing along this course too long, it will eventually lead them to anarchy, a rejection of any and all restraints.

Such a society is dangerous to all persons, and indeed, dangerous to itself. "Professing themselves to be wise, they became fools." (Romans 1:22)

God, on the other hand, "who giveth us richly all things to enjoy," (I Timothy 6:17) wants us to experience pleasure and puts restraints upon us that keep us sensitive to the lawful enjoyment of pleasure. Pleasure is heightened and enhanced by true genuine love; it is dulled by an over-indulgence of the five senses.

God's concern for our pleasure doesn't stop with this life, but He sees beyond this life and allows trials for the purpose of weaning us from the temporary riches here and to motivate us to looking forward with heart-felt desire for the greater riches there. (Ephesians 2:7) So intense is His desire for our eternal welfare that He allows trials into our lives when He sees it will be an eternal benefit, either to ourselves or perhaps our trial can benefit someone else, as was the case with Fannie Crosby, whose song-writing and poetry has blessed and inspired millions and continues to do so. The inspiration that this blind lady has been is truly incalculable. Her blindness, far from being a hindrance to the kingdom of God, has only served to cause her life and poetry to be all the more inspiring, even to this day.

God is so concerned that we experience "pleasures forevermore" that He is willing to allow trials and even catastrophes (He does not cause them but does allow them) in the lives of even His children as a means of purification. So that we may come forth as "gold, tried in the fire." (Revelation 3:18) He even goes so far as to tell us that if we do not endure chastening, "then are ye bastards, and not sons." (Hebrews 12:8)

Christians are certainly not exempt from temporal suffering, but have endured it cheerfully because of the "hope we have as an anchor of the soul...which entereth into that within the veil; Whither the forerunner is for us entered, even Jesus." (Hebrews 6:19-20)

Perhaps Christian Believers are not exempt from temporal suffering so that, when we "come forth as gold, tried in the fire," our lives can then be a greater witness of God's grace to the Unbelievers and be a catalyst for them to also become Believers.

For God leaves no stone unturned in His effort to bring all to salvation, despite our free will that He will not force anyone against. He leaves no stone unturned that will yet leave our free will intact. God is "not willing that any should perish," (II Peter 3:9) but that all should "come unto the knowledge of the truth." (I Timothy 2:4) And that "Truth" is Jesus Christ, who said of Himself, "I am the way, the truth, and the life: no man cometh unto the Father, but by me." (John 14:6)

Of temporal suffering He said that, "In the world ye shall have tribulation: but be of good cheer; I [Jesus] have overcome the world." (John 16:33) And truly, one of the hallmarks of the true church of Jesus Christ in history has been its patient endurance of temporal suffering through persecution.

Persecution so severe that they were stretched on the rack and on the wheel, beheaded, drowned, or worse. Including, but not limited to, being flayed alive, burned alive, or dragged alive through the streets until their bodies succumbed to the knife, the fire, or to the cobblestones.

Why does not God intervene when His children are so horribly mistreated?

Is it not because He sees that "our light affliction, which is but for a moment, worketh for us a far more exceeding and eternal weight of glory?" (II Corinthians 4:17) And so that when the Unbelievers suffer, they may well remember the afflictions that the Believers suffered with an unwavering faith in God. When their own "faith" wavers, staggers, and topples, the Unbeliever may well be "provoked to jealousy" and begin to search—and finally experience—the same unwavering faith in God for him or her own self.

For God does everything He can, short of using force, to redeem us to Himself and eternal bliss. He wants that for us, yearns after us, desiring with heartfelt desire that we yield to His Love that is seeking His lost ones, that He may lead them into His fold and eternal bliss.

The alternative, that scripture refers to as "the second death," is excruciatingly horrible. And God knows best how horrible it really is. As we consider the Biblical references to hell and its horrors, and then heaven and its bliss, there are only two options left open to us. To continue in our three-fold dead condition, to finally die physically still in that dead condition, and go to the place "prepared for the devil and his angels;" (Matthew 25:41) or, to accept the death of our own willful mind-set and be renewed in the spirit of our minds (Ephesians 4:23) by the in-dwelling of Jesus Christ, and when we physically die, to discover that our "whole spirit and soul and body be preserved blameless unto the coming of our Lord Jesus Christ." (I Thessalonians 5:23)

Which leaves us with only one reasonable option; that of a wholehearted surrender to "serve God with reverence and godly fear." (Hebrews 12:28) A fear evoking reverence and respect, not the sort that seeks an escape route, which fear is so unreasonable as to be a form of insanity, for there is no escape; we are enjoined to have a sound mind. (II Timothy 1:7)

In the well-said words of Blaise Pascal, (AD 1642) "There are two kinds of people one can call reasonable; Those who serve God with their whole heart because they <u>know Him</u>, and Those who seek God with their whole heart because they <u>do not know Him</u>." (Emphasis added).

We should be either serving God or seeking God, anything else is so unreasonable, considering what we have to gain or lose, that "unreasonable" is hardly the word for it; "insane" is more like it.

Why does God give us such a sharp contrast of choices? Why isn't there a middle ground, a gray area? After all, most would fit into that category. Or not?

Jesus is the Lamb that was slain from the foundation of the world. It follows then that He had given His word to give His life for the sins of mankind "from the foundation of the world." To resolve the war in the spirit world.

And when He gave His word, the deed was as good as done for "he cannot deny himself." (II Timothy 2:13) What He promises, will happen. What He says will happen, does happen. Always.

When He gave His life, He gave it for all of mankind, that we might live. That action, of giving His life for all, indicted all of mankind of being dead. "The love of Christ constraineth us; because we thus judge, that if one died for all, then were all dead." (II Corinthians 5:14) And all still means all. That means you, him, her, myself, and all the hims and hers worldwide that live, have ever lived, or will live.

Except One.

That One is Jesus Christ, who gave His life for the sins of mankind. The sinless for the sinner. The perfect for the fallen. The righteous for the unrighteous. (Romans 5:7) That we might live. And since all really means all, then all of us were and are lost sinners without Christ. For "without shedding of blood there is no remission [of sins]." (Hebrews 9:22)

And without remission of sins there is no admission into Heaven. Which leaves only one other option, for there are only two destinations possible as presented to us in the word of God.

Heaven, where Jesus is.

Or Hell. Prepared for the devil and his angels.

Hell. Where all will go whose names are not written in the Book of Life. (Revelation 20:15)

Hell. Where all will go who have the mark of the Beast upon them. (Revelation 19:20)

Hell. Where the smoke of their torment goeth up forever and ever. (Revelation 14:11)

Hell. Where their worm dieth not and the fire is not quenched. (Mark 9:43-48)

Hell. A place so horrible that Jesus said, "And if thy hand offend thee, cut it off: it is better for thee to enter into life maimed, then having two hands to go into hell, into the fire that never shall be quenched: Where their worm dieth not, and the fire is not quenched. And if thy foot offend thee, cut it off: it is better for thee to enter halt into life, than having two feet to be cast into hell, into the fire that never shall be quenched: Where their worm dieth not, and the fire is not quenched. And if thine eye offend thee, pluck it out: it is better for thee to enter into the kingdom of God with one eye, than having two eyes to be cast into hell fire: Where their worm dieth not, and the fire is not quenched." (Mark 9:43-48)

Though Christians are not in the habit of plucking eyes and cutting off limbs, yet we understand the seriousness of the implications, that hell is a place to be avoided at all costs; and if dismembering parts of the body would make the difference, then the body parts should be sacrificed in order to save the whole from such an awful fate.

The certain rich man in Luke 16, who fared sumptuously every day while Lazarus ate of the crumbs that fell from the rich man's well-stocked table, and the dogs came and licked his sores, is an example that Jesus gave, exposing the horrors of hell and a reason that people go there.

For the rich man died and went to hell.

Lazarus died also and was carried by angels to Abraham.

The rich man lifted up his eyes in torment, and seeing Lazarus with Abraham, begged for Lazarus to dip his fingers into water "for to cool my tongue," he said, "for I am tormented in this flame." That little bit of water was denied him as he was reminded of his life on earth in comparison to the life of Lazarus. "And besides" he was told, "between us and you is a great gulf fixed, so that there can be no going back and forth." (Paraphrased)

The outstanding characteristic of this rich man was his lack of compassion for the poor, as within reach of the beggar, he fared sumptuously every day. The dogs came and licked the beggar's sores so it is reasonable to believe that in order to eat at all, Lazarus had to get to the rich man's crumbs before the dogs did, for dogs have no sense of sharing. Neither, sadly, did the rich man. (Luke 16:19-21)

Which is a lesson from Jesus, that when mankind becomes self-absorbed we begin on a downward trend of self-absorption that takes us to the level of—and we become like—the beasts that God created rather than like the one who created us "in His image." And really, worse than beasts, because unlike the beasts, we know better.

Rather than become more and more "conformed to the image of Christ" we become more and more like the devil who led the way into self-absorption when he rebelled and led rebellion in Heaven in his doomed bid to "become like the Most High." (Isaiah 14:14; Ezekiel 28)

Though these two scripture chapters begin in reference to the Kings of Tyre, Sidon, and Babylon, they go on without interruption to speak of a wicked spiritual being whose description best fits the devil.

It seems one of the stoutest obstacles to our own salvation and regeneration is so often our exalted opinion of ourselves, for we tend to be comforted by our good intentions to become better and better. Better than our dads, our moms, our grandparents, our siblings, the "other" Christians around us, and/or our neighbor across the way. And because we have and trust our good intentions we tend to feel better than others and become exalted in our minds.

Which leads into a self-exalted state of self-righteousness which in turn leads into a state of self-justification and legalism, a personal tragedy of deciding right and wrong for ourselves rather than allowing the full weight of God's directives to bring us to our knees in repentance and ultimately to the saving knowledge of Christ.

From Hitler to the self-righteous church-goer, self-justification has taken—and continues to take—its toll on mankind to the increase of misery and the increase of lost souls. From the drunk to the successful, but lost, business person he buys from, self-justification continues its steady slide into a lost eternity.

God in His mercy is not willing that any should perish but that all should come to the knowledge of the truth. All are redeemable. But all need to repent. And trust alone in Jesus Christ for salvation and regeneration. For "of him are ye in Christ Jesus, who of God is made unto us wisdom, and righteousness, and sanctification, and redemption: That, according as it is written, He that glorieth, let him glory in the Lord." (I Corinthians 1:30-31)

Only in Christ Jesus are we saved and made righteous.

The Old Testament saints had not yet received the promise, but their faith was in the Promise of God, which was yet future. "And these all, having obtained a good report through faith, received not the promise: God having provided some better thing for us [the fulfillment of His Promise], that they without us should not be made perfect." (Hebrews 11:39-40)

Divine Response

After the crucifixion when Jesus was three days and three nights in the heart of the earth, He went and "preached unto the spirits in prison; Which sometime were disobedient, when once the longsuffering of God waited in the days of Noah, while the ark was a preparing, wherein few, that is, eight souls [for people can be referred to as souls] were saved by water." (I Peter 3:19-20)

What all happened there and where this prison was, is best left to God, who was there, witnessed and experienced it and has promised that someday, though "now we see through a glass, darkly; but then face to face: now I know in part; but then shall I know even as also I am known." (I Corinthians 13:12) In the meantime we need to—and can—trust God who is Omniscient, Omnipresent, and Omnipotent, to judge righteous judgment. We tend not to trust His judgment and to somehow soften our ideas of hell to fit our finite ideas of justice. We need to trust God and allow His Word to say what it does. For the preponderance of Biblical reference to hell describes it as a horrible place, and a forever place. (Matthew 5:22, 29, 30; 10:28, 18:9, 24:51; Mark 9:43, 45, 47; Luke 12:5, James 3:6, II Peter 2:4, Revelation 14:11, 19:20, 21:8) And the preponderance of historical faith believed the same. As difficult as it is at times to lay down our own finite ideas of justice and to trust God to judge righteous judgment; lay down our own ideas and trust God we must.

Leading up to the idea of soul-annihilation or that the soul does not have a natural eternal existence is the idea of "soul sleep;" the two fit together like hand and glove. For if the soul can "not know anything" then the possibility of forever "not knowing anything" follows.

When our spiritual soul and body separate, the body will not know anything until judgment day, but the spirit goes back to "God who gave it." (Hebrews 12:23; Ecclesiastes 12:7)

"Today," Jesus told the repentant thief on the cross next to His own, "shalt thou be with me in paradise." (Luke 23:43) If "today" doesn't mean "today" then neither can we say that the six day creation week was an actual six days. And from there the possibilities of reinterpreting scripture are truly endless.

When Jesus "preached to the spirits in prison," (I Peter 3:19) it is unreasonable to believe that He preached to a sleeping audience. It is reasonable to believe that His preaching was to spirits that were awake, alert, and able to comprehend.

The rich man in hell, Jesus telling the thief on the cross, "today shalt thou be with me in paradise," Jesus preaching to the spirits in prison, and the Apostle Paul's testimony when he was "(whether in the body... or whether out of the body, I cannot tell: God knoweth;) ... caught up to the third heaven" (II Corinthians 12:2), are evidence that both Jesus and Paul believed that when our bodies die we remain conscious in spirit and soul.

We have much reason to believe, from the tenor and the clear statement of scripture, that death to our body simply means that our souls are transported out of full awareness of this temporal realm to a full awareness of the spirit realm.

From the realm of time into the realm of timelessness.

When Jesus said the word "today" to the repentant thief, he spoke in the realm of time which means that on Friday when he (the thief) died, he met Jesus, who was already gone, in Paradise.

Is Paradise an intermediate place? Is there also an intermediate place with degrees of despair? The possibility of such places seems very likely from the accounts of the afterlife we have already considered, and the Word of God being very clear about the separation of body and soul upon death of the body.

When Jesus died His body was laid in the tomb while His spirit was set free into the spirit realm. When His spirit came back into His body again, His body still had the spear and nail print scars and yet was so transformed that though He ate of the fish the disciples had prepared just before He appeared and stood in the midst of them, He soon led them out as far as Bethany, blessed them, and was carried up into heaven. (Luke 24: 36-53)

At the resurrection of Jesus, His body and soul united again in a glorified body, and we have much reason to believe God for the same at His coming for His Bride, the New Testament Church.

That at the resurrection our soul and now glorified body will unite again. A glorious hope for Believers who upon repentance have received the glorious gift of eternal life.

To the Unbeliever the thought of body and soul uniting only to be cast into hell is so fearful that it has caused many an Unbeliever to become a sincere seeker and eventually become a Believer. A Believer who, instead of having a "fearful looking for of judgment and fiery indignation," (Hebrews 10:27) now has hope for the future and assurance of eternal life. (John 3:17)

While salvation is not in what we know, it is in Who we know.

And what we know of Truth directs us to Who we know for salvation. "In which are some things hard to be understood, which they that are unlearned and unstable wrest, as they do also the other scriptures, unto their own destruction ... But grow in grace, and in the knowledge of our Lord and Savior Jesus Christ." (II Peter 3:16-18)

Concerning the eternal existence of the soul, some of the unstable say "it's not a salvation issue" and others, "it's not about doctrine." To which we may answer that if "today" no longer means today (Luke 23:43), "everlasting punishment" no longer means everlasting punishment (Matthew 25:46), and "the smoke of their torment ascendeth forever and ever" no longer means what it obviously says, (Revelation 14:11) then we open the door for all of scripture to be reinterpreted, including scriptures concerning the righteous judgment of God upon the unbeliever as well as teachings about the fruit of the Spirit, the works of the flesh, and the all-sufficiency of Jesus Christ. When all words become (in our minds) subjective to what we read into the context, how can there be any objective truth left (in our minds)?

It has been said by some, that only God is immortal, therefore man does not, and never did have, "natural immortality." The references pointed to are: "Our Savior Jesus Christ, who hath abolished death, and hath brought life and immortality to light through the Gospel," (II Timothy 1:10) "who only hath immortality, dwelling in the light which no man can approach unto; whom no man hath seen, nor can see: to whom be honor and power everlasting. Amen." (I Timothy 6:16)

Yes, only God has immortality. And only God has the breath of life. And when He breathed that breath of His into Adam, the "man became a living soul." (Genesis 2:7) A personal life-giving breath from God, which leads us to believe from God's word—in the first book of the Bible, Genesis, to the last, Revelation—that when man became a living soul, that soul became eternally existent.

If man is believed to have been created mortal, then the question needs to be asked, "was the whole man mortal?" For if the whole man was mortal, it must needs include the spirit, soul, and body of man. And if the whole spirit, soul, and body were created mortal, then it would follow that God created a corruptible being and not only called it good, but also did so after saying, "Let us make man in our image, after our likeness." And then proceeded to do so, for, "God created man in His own image, in the image of God created he him." (Genesis 1:26-27) If man was made part mortal and part immortal then the question arises, "who of us is able to discern which had which?"

If the soul became void of eternal existence at the Fall in the Garden, then the scriptures we have already reviewed have no explanation that allows for a continuity of Biblical understanding. For in "comparing Scripture with Scripture" we have too much evidence that our souls are eternally existent to believe otherwise. Unless, of course, we choose to believe otherwise, for God has allowed us that choice. But only for a time. When time comes to an end, is "folded up as a vesture," God's word, despite our believing this or not believing that, will come to pass. For God only is Almighty. All Life and Immortality are an extension of Himself. And separation from Him is the definition of death. "The soul that sinneth," He warns us, "it shall die." (Ezekiel 18:20)

Though our finite ideas of justice could well be satisfied with the annihilation of lost souls, yet God, in His infinite understanding of right, wrong, and justice, does—from the evidence of scripture—give the historical view of the church, that of eternal torment. "Now we see through a glass, darkly" and now we "know in part." (I Corinthians 13:12) We can, and must, trust God to judge righteous judgment.

Of our redeemed bodies the word of God says, "So when this corruptible shall have put on incorruption, and this mortal shall have put on immortality, then shall be brought to pass the saying that is written, Death is swallowed up in victory. O death, where is thy sting? O grave, where is thy victory? The sting of death is sin; and the strength of sin is the law. But thanks be to God, which giveth us the victory through our Lord Jesus Christ." (I Corinthians 15:54-57)

That this scripture is referring to the resurrection of the body is evident in the entire context of Chapter 15 emphasized in verse 44. "It is sown a natural body; it is raised a spiritual body. There is a natural body, and there is a spiritual body." The context of the chapter is the body, not the soul. To say that our souls only become eternally existent upon being saved does not fit with the account of Jesus preaching to the souls in prison who sometime were disobedient, nor to the account of the rich man in hell, nor to the prophecy of the final judgment in Revelation, nor to the overall context of Scripture. Nay, our own finite ideas of justice only create confusion and God is not the author of confusion. We must and can trust Him to judge righteous judgment. To trust both the "goodness and severity of God." (Romans 11:22)

It is noteworthy that God does not call us to reason with ourselves, but with Him. "Come now, let us reason together," He says, "though your sins be as scarlet, they shall be as white as snow; though they be red like crimson, they shall be as wool." (Isaiah 1:18)

DIVINE RESPONSE

I love that word come. For I needed to come when God called. And when I came, God came. Like the prodigal son's father eagerly going out to meet his son when he came home, so God comes to us when we come to Him. God stays where He is until we draw nigh to Him (James 4:8) unmovable and rock solid, for which we can be very thankful because it means we have Someone, and a place, to come home to when we become done with ourselves.

He calls the lonely with persistent kindness,
Offering His friendship.
He calls the lost with compassion
Offering His salvation.
He calls the needy sinner
Offering His cleansing.
And then; With our will surrendered
Our mind renewed
Our emotions sanctified
Our body quickened to serve, we may "serve God acceptably with reverence and Godly fear: For our God is a consuming fire." (Hebrews 12:28-29) Consuming all that is not of Him. (Matthew 3:12; Luke 3:17)

That we may have continual, refreshing, otherworldly courage because of hope that we have as an "anchor of the soul, both sure and steadfast..." Our hope being in Jesus.

"And I pray God your whole spirit and soul and body be preserved blameless unto the coming of our Lord Jesus Christ." (I Thessalonians 5:23)

In II Corinthians 5, starting in Verse 1, God tells us through the Apostle Paul, "For we know that if our earthly house of this tabernacle were dissolved, we have a building of God, an house not made with hands, eternal in the heavens.

For in this we groan, earnestly desiring to be clothed upon with our house which is from heaven:

If so be that being clothed we shall not be found naked. For we that are in this tabernacle do groan, being burdened: not for that we would be unclothed, but clothed upon, that mortality might be swallowed up of life.

Now he that hath wrought us for the selfsame thing is God, who also hath given unto us the earnest of the Spirit. Therefore we are always confident, knowing that, whilst we are <u>at home in the body</u>, we are <u>absent</u> from the Lord:

(For we walk by faith, not by sight:)

MAN BECAME A LIVING SOUL

We are confident, I say, and willing rather to be <u>absent</u> from the body, and to be <u>present</u> with the Lord. (Emphasis added) Wherefore we labour, that, whether present or absent, we may be accepted of him.

For we must all appear before the judgment seat of Christ; that every one may receive the things done in his body, according to that he hath done, whether it be good or bad.

Knowing therefore the terror of the Lord, we persuade men …" Verse 17, "Therefore if any man be in Christ, he is a new creature: old things are passed away; behold, all things are become new." Verse 21, "For he hath made him to be sin for us, who knew no sin; that we might be made the righteousness of God in him." (II Corinthians 5:1-11,17,21)

A LIVING SOUL

When man became a living soul,
God had breathed in his nostrils the breath of life.
God gave to man the leadership role,
And a womanly helpmeet to be his wife.

God placed them both in a beautiful garden,
He'd made the two a perfect fit.
All was perfect harmony in Eden,
They were to dress it, and to keep it.

God had placed a tree in the garden,
And said, if you eat of it, ye shall surely die.
From that death no hope was given,
Did they look upon it and then wondered why?

The devil took on the form of a serpent,
How he did it, we are not told.
He succeeded in deceiving the woman,
She ate of the fruit, it looked so good.

She gave to her man, 'n he did eat,
Who knew, but chose her above his Lord.
The fruit, at first, had seemed so sweet,
Now aware they were naked, they hid from God.

Divine Response

In the Garden, in the cool of the day,
God came searching, Adam, where art thou?
He to Adam had become so frightening,
They who'd loved God, were fearful now.

Futuristic fear has marked man's course,
All struggling along on this way called life.
Knowing ahead are unknown shores,
Between here and there is much toil and strife.

God has a way, He wants to save everyone,
Though not the way seeming right to man.
Man's way, the Bible says, ends in destruction,
Through God's way alone can we be saved.

Salvation is always God's goal,
Discipline and Love have marked His course.
God's breath made man a living soul,
And through His Word, God calls us to Himself.

From the very beginning God had a plan,
'N goal, for us to repent and be saved.
Jesus, the Sacrificial Lamb, was in God's plan,
When man became a living soul.

Gottes sege dazu winscha
(May God add His blessing)

2

FALLEN MAN ↓ RISEN LORD ↑

It was springtime and the year was 2014. I'd had a call from a potential customer who needed new roofing for their house. There was nothing unusual about getting a call for a new house roof, but this one sounded unusual in that it had a cedar shingle roof that was wearing out after only fifteen years. "Cedar shingles should last twice that long" I thought as I drove there, "at least 30 or even 40 years." The plan was to meet the customer there and see if we could together come to an understanding of the cause for the shortened life-span of the wood shingles that the house had been roofed with when it was built only fifteen years earlier.

The directions I'd been given led me to a home along the lake shore, and as I turned into the driveway I marveled at the beauty all around me. As I walked toward the house my eyes absorbed the natural beauty of the stained-wood siding house with cedar shingles on the steep roof and a majestic stone fireplace chimney on one end. Behind the house the wooded hillside rose, gently at first, and had there a guest house with a full length front porch nestled under the towering trees. With its stained-wood siding and wood shingles it blended into the surrounding woods so well that the thought came to me that "it looks like it grew there."

Upon knocking, the lady of the house came to the front door and responded to my request for her husband by informing me that she expected him home within about ten minutes. I thanked her and turned to walk back to the car, but the beauty of the lake beckoned me to its sandy beach. I took the liberty to cross the front lawn to the lake shore, and in doing so, observed the beautifully blooming flowers planted around trees and shrubs in the well-kept lawn that faded out where the sand began. There was a park bench there so I sat and gazed across the rippling blue of the lake as the sun shone brightly out of a clear blue sky warming the slight breeze coming off the lake. I sat for a long moment enjoying the warm sunshine and the beauty of the lake before reluctantly getting up and strolling back toward the car. It was a beautiful place, a beautiful day, with perfect climate.

"This has to be as close to the garden of Eden as we can get," I thought. And just then … a mosquito bit me. I slapped, and a pesky little reality check barely escaped getting smashed on my bare forearm.

Reality checks. We have them every day. We are continually being confronted by the realities of life.

And death.

For we're not in the garden of Eden anymore and we're not in Paradise yet. So the best we can do is to love the Lord Jesus and look forward to His coming. And that is a glorious Hope. A Hope that anchors the soul and gives courage.

Genesis Chapter 1 gives us the beginning of world history as we know it from God's Holy Word when God on day one created light and separated the light from the darkness. And God called the light day and the darkness He called night. And the evening and the morning were the first day. On the second day God made the firmament and divided the waters under it from the waters above. On the third day God caused the dry land to appear and brought forth the grass, the herbs, and the trees, all with the ability to propagate and reproduce themselves. On the fourth day He made two great lights, the greater to rule the day and the lesser to rule the night when He made light in the firmament of heaven to divide the day from night; and "let them be for signs, and for seasons, and for days, and years." On the fifth day God created all sea creatures and winged fowl. And on the sixth day God caused the earth to bring forth living creatures, cattle and creeping things, and beasts of the earth.

And then on the same day God did something very special. "Let us make man in our image," He said, "after our likeness; and let them have dominion over the fish of the sea and over the fowl of the air, and over every creeping thing that creepeth upon the earth. So God created man in his own image, in the image of God created he him; male and female created he them." Then in Chapter 2, verses 15-18 "the Lord God took the man, and put him into the garden of Eden to dress it and to keep it. And the Lord God commanded the man, saying, Of every tree of the garden thou mayest freely eat: But of the tree of the knowledge of good and evil, thou shalt not eat of it: for in the day that thou eatest thereof thou shalt surely die.

And the LORD God said, It is not good that the man should be alone; I will make him an help meet for him." Verses 21-23 "And the LORD God caused a deep sleep to fall upon Adam, and he slept: and he took one of his ribs, and closed up the flesh instead thereof; And the rib, which the LORD God had taken from man, made he a woman, and brought her unto the man. And Adam said, This is now bone of my bones, and flesh of my flesh: she shall be called Woman, because she was taken out of Man."

Creation was now at the height of its perfection. "God saw every thing that he had made, and, behold, it was very good." (Genesis 1:31) The plants and animals were perfect, the man and woman were perfect, the climate was perfect, and the relationship that Adam and Eve had together and with their Maker was perfect. All nature was in perfect harmony, and death was only heard of as a warning deterrent to not eat of that one tree in the commandment "But of the tree of the knowledge of good and evil, thou shalt not eat of it, for in the day that thou eatest thereof, thou shalt surely die."

Into this garden Paradise came the serpent who must have been different from the repulsive creature he became after the woman gave in to its tempting words and God cursed it, "above all cattle and above every beast of the field; upon thy belly shalt thou go, and dust shalt thou eat all the days of thy life." This serpent must have been a pleasing creature before the fall and able to communicate verbally for Eve is not afraid nor seems startled when the serpent asks the question, "yea hath God said…?" Eve became deceived and gave in to its humanistic arguments which likely sounded reasonable to her ears. She ate of the fruit and also gave it to her husband. Adam, who scripture tells us was not deceived, now has an excruciatingly difficult decision before him. A choice between his wife who was "bone of his bone and flesh of his flesh," and his God who had made him. What all went through his mind in that fleeting moment of time we don't know. What we do know is that Adam chose his wife and the fruit that she gave him. And in that moment of time they both fell from the state of perfection, and perfect relationship with God, to the present state of imperfection. Because of disobedience. Because of disobeying God who is omnipotent, omnipresent, and omniscient. There is no escaping the eyes of Him "with whom we have to do." And God, "who cannot lie" also "cannot deny Himself."

We have much reason to believe from the tenor of Scripture, from personal observation of nature, and from observational science that if God were unfaithful to Himself—which is unthinkable—that all existence, both terrestrial and celestial, would immediately implode upon itself. For all things are upheld "by the word of his power." (Hebrews 1:3) What really happened is that God, who is righteous, true, and holy didn't move from His position. And our first parents left His position, or rather, fell from His position to the degraded state that mankind is in now. God, because of His mercy, did not want them to live forever in such a state, so He expelled them from the Garden of Eden, lest they "take also of the tree of life, and eat, and live forever." (Genesis 3:22)

And mankind has been struggling ever since to return, to reestablish the Garden of Eden here. There seems to be something in each one of us that despite the facts that we know; one of which is that we all die; naturally strives to get as close to the Garden of Eden or at least as close to our own perception of perfection as possible. There is some good in this God-given desire as it causes even the carnal-minded to be concerned about taking care of and preserving the earth, even for coming generations after he or she has passed on.

But there is a reality that needs to be squarely faced up to here. That reality is that the earth is degenerating. Slowly enough perhaps that it can be overlooked by the casual observer living in a free country and an affluent culture. But even the casual observer is forced to admit, when he or she pauses long enough to consider, that "we're not here to stay."

What then encourages and drives this attempt to rebuild the Garden of Eden?

Is it not the outward expression of Eternity in our hearts?

We believe this to be so. And that to continue to grasp after Paradise here is to grasp after an illusion, a mirage in the desert. For having our Garden of Eden here is not in God's plan. And therefore it won't happen. But God has "provided some better thing for us." Restoration to a personal relationship with God through our Lord Jesus Christ. And future perfection. Paradise restored. In heaven.

Fallen man, Risen Lord. God's message to mankind can be said to be abbreviated in those four words. The history of mankind contained in the Bible, and both in historical and contemporary records, can truly be said to be the story of human conflict. Beginning with the conflict with God in the Garden of Eden (Genesis 3) where mankind, contained in one man and one woman, was at the height of his perfection only to fall from it, to the ongoing conflict with each other; this conflict has no sign of ending until time itself comes to an end. From the killing of Abel by Cain, after the expulsion from the Garden, to the butchery of the 20th century and continuing into this 21st century, mankind has been at war with itself.

FALLEN MAN ↓ RISEN LORD ↑

At the signing of Japan's surrender agreement that officially brought an end to World War II on September 2, 1945—on a quiet deck of the USS Missouri—General Douglas MacArthur had this to say to the somber assembly of Japanese and Allied officials, the "Missouri" crew members, and to the world at large. "A new era is upon us. Even the lesson of victory itself brings with it a profound concern both for our future security and the survival of civilization. The destructiveness of the war potential, through progressive advances in scientific discovery, has in fact now reached a point which revises the traditional concept of war ... We have had our last chance. If we do not now devise some greater and more equitable system, Armageddon will be at our door. The problem is basically theological and involves a spiritual recrudescence and improvement of human character..."

The world had just come through its second global conflict in as few as three decades. The coming state of euphoria, vainly heralded by 19th and 20th century intellectuals, had proved as elusive as the proverbial carrot dangled before the hungry donkey. While mankind longs for inner and outer peace, the present and historical reality has a diametrically opposite story to tell. From the offended bitterness rendered impotent in one who has a conviction against it to the deep-seated bitterness once heralded as The Third Reich, mankind has been on a self-destructive quest to create his own reality. But God's reality—like the rising sun—exposes everything, everyone, whether high or low the way the person or thing really is. We may hide things for awhile, we may even hide ourselves for awhile, but reality does, and will, show what really is.

And that is what really matters. Reality. That which is. And when we stop and face reality God has an answer for us. For stopping and facing reality means stopping and facing our sin. And stopping and facing reality means stopping and facing God. And when we face up to our sin while facing up to God, we find ourselves in a truly awful predicament. For we naturally, because of the law of sin which is in our members, love our sin more than God; love darkness more than light, because our deeds are evil. We find ourselves in a truly desperate predicament then, loving the very sin that in turn brings upon us guilt, condemnation, and the wrath of God. But that very desperation turns the heart to God. For when we perceive the desperation of our predicament, that very desperation gives rise to a sincere desire for reconciliation with the God who made us and with whom we have to do.

There was a time when I had so removed myself from reality in pursuit of pleasures in my youth that when the time came to "settle down" I could not be sincere about it. I sensed that my motives were not sincere. Not knowing how to make myself sincere, I began to pray for sincerity. Through contact with Christians and memories of childhood teaching and reading material, I became convinced that I needed to be born again. And to be born again I just needed to believe in Jesus. It sounded so simple and yet it seemed the more I tried to believe, the less I could. So I tried harder and kept praying for sincerity. God in His mercy heard me and answered in a way that I least expected.

He brought me low to the depths of despair. He opened my eyes to my own depravity. He opened my eyes in allowing me to sense the hideously evil, hideously hate-filled presence of the Powers of Darkness. He allowed me to see the carelessness with which I mistreated others, especially my parents. And again and again, He allowed me to sense the other side, the hideously hate-filled spirits of darkness.

And I became sincere. Desperately sincere. Sincerely wanting reality.

Not everyone has to go through exactly what I did, for I think that not all are as stubborn. Yet many hide the real person so as not to become perfectly obnoxious to those around them. And the more he/she hides the real person, the more he/she becomes insincere. And the more insincere the more out of touch with reality. Which is what I was doing. And, really, I don't think I'm some unusual quirk of the human race. I'm a normal human being, though some may argue otherwise. Experience, both my own and with others, leads me to believe that all hide to some extent or another until the heart and life is yielded to God. Those who think they never have are just likely the most deceived.

To one extent or another, everyone before conversion attempts to create their own reality. The way back through that maze can be extremely difficult, but it is pointless to turn back for once the soul has turned towards the Light, there is a pressing need in that soul to press on and a sense that to turn back would be to voluntarily plunge oneself into such depths of despair as to never be able to extricate oneself from it again. So with nothing before him or her in the immediate future except pain, such a one presses on for there is nothing behind him or her except the yawning abyss of eternal destruction and despair. Turning back has become unthinkable, not an option. There is no way but forward. Though forward has pain, to turn back has horror. Though forward looks dark, to turn back is horribly darker. Though forward affords little hope, to turn back is utterly hopeless. And oh, how totally hopeless hopelessness is. The abyss of despair looks deep and hopeless from the perspective of this life, how bottomless then it must be from the perspective of Eternity. The Bible teaches that the lost will be cast into outer darkness. Where there will be weeping and gnashing of teeth. "Where their worm dieth not and the fire is not quenched."

A young lady we knew left her husband and moved in with another man, and from all appearance cast aside all that she'd been taught through Christian influence. When yet in such a state, she died in a hospital from a tragic accident she'd been in. She had been picked up by a friend who then attempted to persuade her to leave the man she was with. Feeling trapped (we think) the young lady exited the van as it slowed down when approaching a red light, leaping into the path of an on-coming truck. She was rushed to the hospital where she lingered in a coma for several days before slipping into eternity. When we received the news, I was gripped by the horror of its hopelessness. But wait! Her brother had called me when she was in a coma, remembering that I had been in a coma for three weeks just a year prior. And could hear and perceive while in a coma, even though to all others in the room, I was totally out of it—except I hadn't died. Oh yes, I assured him, keep reading scripture, praying, and sharing salvation with her as she may be hearing and responding rightly to God as she is face to face with the reality of eternity. He then told me that the doctors think she hears, for when they speak to her, the heart monitor shows that her heart rate picks up. Not much hope, but, oh, what a balm to my soul was that flickering little glimmer of hope, as it was also to many others.

Hope is a wonderful thing. Especially after gazing into the horrible abyss of hopelessness. Hope is a wonderful thing. Hope is a marvelous thing. It is hope that keeps mankind as a whole pressing forward with the desire and virtual expectancy of a better tomorrow. When a people no longer have hope of improving themselves and their circumstances, laboring with hope toward a goal, then incentive becomes lost. As Communism has adequately shown us, when labor becomes reduced to the level of fuel for the insatiable appetite of government machinery, then the loss of incentive will bring the machinery to a grinding halt. Communism in its heyday, and at the outset, was heralded as the delivery of the working class into an equality of community life where everyone had enough and none were lacking. A noble goal perhaps, but why did it fail so miserably?

The answer lies in their vehement denial of God, the laws He put into effect, and conversely, their belief in the inherent goodness of man. This goodness supposedly would lead mankind into the coming state of euphoria where the State was no longer needed.

Divine Response

Proclaiming themselves to be wise, they became fools. For man indeed is fallen.

But Christ is Risen!

And the very acceptance of the reality of our fallen condition opens the mind and heart to the reality of our need in comparison to God's Holiness. For God gives us "the valley of Achor for a door of hope." How could, how does the valley of Achor, that witnessed the stoning of Achan and all that belonged to him, become a door of hope? (Hosea 2:15)

The answer lies in the death, burial, and Resurrection of Jesus Christ. For "if one died for all then were all dead." And since "all" means "all"—as in everyone—and Jesus died for everyone, then everyone was already dead. In the process of dying physically, but nonetheless dead. As God had warned Adam and Eve about not eating of the fruit of the tree in the midst of the garden, the tree of knowledge of good and evil. "For" God said, "in the day that thou eatest thereof thou shalt surely die." (Genesis 2:17) They did not immediately fall down and physically die when they took of the fruit, but their close relationship with God did. The spiritual flow of love, joy, and peace between them and God faltered and then gave way. It severed and then died. And their bodies, made in the perfection and image of God, began from that day to age and eventually became old and died. So death passed upon all men.

And it is these deaths—the physical and the spiritual—that we need to acknowledge, to face up to, and allow the full weight of truth to bear down upon us. For it feels as if the weight of truth would so crush as to disable us beyond the ability to ever recover. We find ourselves pressed into the end of our resources for recovery as we acknowledge the truth about ourselves. For the Valley of Achor is about the discovery and acknowledgment of truth. And truth exposes our sin. It exposes us.

But therein we find the door of hope. For when we are at the end of ourselves, at the end of our resources, then the full, rich, bountiful, and finally glorious resources of Jesus Christ are ours. Not through earning them, for we cannot, but through inheritance as in Colossians 1:11-13. "Strengthened with all might, according to his glorious power, unto all patience and longsuffering with joyfulness; Giving thanks unto the Father, which hath made us meet to be partakers of the inheritance of the saints in light: Who hath delivered us from the power of darkness, and hath translated us into the kingdom of his dear Son: In whom we have redemption through his blood, even the forgiveness of sins." Jesus is the door of Hope in the valley. The door to protection. The door to the sheepfold. (John 10:1 9)

On the one hand we must surrender all our own resources, including, but not limited to, our excuses, our self-justification, our shifting of blame, our subtle attempts to soften God's standard of righteousness to make it more attainable in our own strength which is called self-righteousness.

On the other hand, though we suffer a death-blow to all the above and more, to those attitudes and things we naturally love and go after; yet in that state of brokenness and guilt, Jesus through His Holy Spirit meets us there. He is anointed to preach good tidings unto the meek; He is sent to bind up the brokenhearted, to proclaim liberty to the captives, and the opening of the prison to them that are bound; to proclaim the acceptable year of the Lord, and the day of vengeance of our God; to comfort all that mourn; to appoint unto them that mourn in Zion, to give unto them beauty for ashes, the oil of joy for mourning, the garment of praise for the spirit of heaviness; that they might be called trees of righteousness, the planting of the Lord, that He might be glorified. (Isaiah 61:1-3)

Perhaps we've all heard that the pessimist has a glass half empty while the optimist has a glass half full? While that catchy little one-liner is likely used by many well-meaning people who are trying to promote a positive attitude about life, the pessimist and the optimist both have a problem.

For the pessimist mistrusts positive reality for fear he might miss noticing something negative and therefore dangerous; while the optimist mistrusts negative reality for fear of having his positive psych unsettled. Both are fearful reactions to realism which is at times negative and at times positive. Both are defensive reactions. A disciple of Christ is of necessity a realist for he lives in the real world with its ups and downs. Realism leads the soul to be awake to desperate need, the negative, but then also to the very positive reality of Christ and the Cross. Therefore Truth can guide the realist.

A pessimist lives in fear of the known and of the unknown and sees very little, if any, hope in anything. He or she cannot be a disciple of Christ because he or she has a morbid fear of anything hopeful.

The optimist on the other hand lives in fear of negative reality and is continually refusing to face the negative for fear of becoming discouraged. He or she cannot be a disciple of Christ because he or she cannot face the negative long enough to allow that godly sorrow that leads to repentance flood and overwhelm his or her soul. Ironically, positive spiritual steps forward become difficult, if not impossible.

A disciple of Christ is of necessity a realist, and may be said to have a half glass of whatever is in it, for he lives in the real world with its ups and downs. Realism leads the soul to condemnation, the negative, but also to

Christ and the Cross, the Positive. As a battery needs a positive and a negative post, so the Christian life needs both in order for Power to flow. The Positive, which is Jesus Christ, always has Power available but the negative (us) allows the power to flow.

The realist releases his or her own will to God and has the heart and mind wide open to receive Truth from the Word of God. Both the truth about oneself and then the ultimate Truth, which is Jesus Christ himself. Then comes to pass that which is written in I John 1:9-10 that "if we confess our sins, he is faithful and just to forgive us our sins, and to cleanse us from all unrighteousness. If we say that we have not sinned, we make him a liar, and his word is not in us." Jesus says, speaking to believers in John 8:31-32; "if ye continue in my word, then are ye my disciples indeed; and ye shall know the truth, and the truth shall make you free."

Thus the realist, while he or she may at times only have a half glass of whatever is in it, actually, in the spirit, deep down where courage touches his or her soul, has a cup that "runneth over." (Psalms 23:5)

The pessimist and the optimist are equally fearful of reality, but the realist refuses all such blindness choosing rather to accept the truth and therefore can and does place his or her trust in Jesus Christ our Savior. Our Messiah. Our only mediator between God and man. May we never recover from the over-whelming love of Christ flooding our souls. May we never go back, but keep looking unto Jesus the Author and Finisher of our faith and be continually changed into His image. For it (the heart) has turned to the Lord and the veil (upon our heart) has been taken away. "Now the Lord is that Spirit: and where the Spirit of the Lord is, there is liberty. But we all, with open face beholding as in a glass the glory of the Lord, are changed into the same image from glory to glory, even as by the Spirit of the Lord." (II Corinthians 3:17-18) We tend to become like the person we focus on, so we need to focus on the Lord Jesus Christ. I, for one, have had enough of myself, which is good reason to focus on Jesus Christ and not on myself. Or, for that matter, anyone else except Jesus.

I was finally converted one night in 1983. I was under heavy conviction of sin. I had become desperately sincere. Or so I thought. God wasn't done with me yet. In the stillness of the night, after begging God to hear me, to change me, to save my poor soul, I was finally spent. The heavens were as brass and I became still, hopeless. Was all lost? Had I gone too far? Was there no hope? But then God spoke. Not audibly perhaps. But two words impressed and unmistakably clear upon my heart and mind.

Thou hypocrite.

Two words. Two words that cut deep, for I was proud of not being a hypocrite.

Five or six years earlier when I was a rebellious teenager, my dear mother lovingly tried, as was her way, persuading me to change my ways. And I responded with "Well, at least I'm not a hypocrite." Mom was shocked and asked what I meant so I told her without giving any names about the boys who partied Saturday nights, then went to church like good boys on Sunday morning. Mom had looked so sad, hurt, and withdrawn, so unlike her, that I was sorry and never said that again.

The incident was forgotten. It was buried in the past. Right? Wrong.

God hadn't forgotten. It was still naked and open to the eyes of Him with whom we have to do. Why didn't I run? There was no place to run to. Why didn't I hide? There was no place to hide.

Besides, the heavens, which had been as brass, had cracked open. God had spoken. To me. Finally. I had heard from God. Even though it was condemnation, God had not utterly forsaken me. There was hope! I bowed my head and accepted, then asked the Lord to show me how I was being a hypocrite. And the Lord allowed my memory to serve me well. And besides He showed me that though I was praying for deliverance from sin, deep down in my heart I wasn't letting go as there was still a deep down desire for it.

In that instant, I saw that I didn't even really want what I was asking for. It broke me. Thoroughly broke me. Why would God give me something I didn't even really want? What an impossibility. But with all that, my heart and mind was finally quieted. God had heard me. And God had spoken. And with God all things are possible. There was hope. So I went to bed and slept well.

My life was somehow different after that. I was more at rest, at peace within.

Sometime later, I don't know how many days later, it dawned on me that when I prayed the heavens were no longer as brass. And I no longer had to try to believe Jesus had forgiven my sins because I believed and trusted. No force. A restful trust. And I no longer had to try to like people that I disliked because I loved them. Even one man that I disliked to the point of hatred at times. The love and affection that I now had for him surprised and blessed even me. Without hypocrisy.

And I no longer had to try to not like the former sensual songs I had so loved. They made me sad. It saddened me that these men and women with such rich and beautiful voices were using them to sing about material things, tattered relationships, lust, and rebellion. How powerful it could be if they were converted and sang songs of Zion, of Jesus and eternal riches, with sound doctrine and God-honoring melody.

My risen Lord had arisen in my heart.

And my life has never been the same.

The unbearable burden of sin had been taken away.

Has there been temptation? Yes. But with it a way of escape.

Has there been failure? Yes. But there was a way back, "we have an advocate with the Father, Jesus Christ the righteous." (I John 2:1)

Has there been hardship? Yes. But with the promise of a better tomorrow.

Has there been despair? Yes. But with a ray of hope that enters into that within the veil.

Has there been blessing? Yes. Beyond measure.

Has there been courage? Yes. From the boundless supply of God's grace.

Has there been trust? Yes. In Him who is trustworthy.

Has there been hope? Yes. The living hope flowing from Jesus thy boundless love to me.

"And therefore it was imputed to him [Abraham] for righteousness. Now it was not written for his sake alone, that it was imputed to him; [Abraham] But for us also, to whom it shall be imputed, if we believe in him that raised up Jesus our Lord from the dead; Who was delivered for our offenses, and was raised again for our justification." (Romans 4:22-25)

Galatians 2:20-21 says this: "I am crucified with Christ: nevertheless I live; yet not I, but Christ liveth in me: and the life which I now live in the flesh I live by the faith of the Son of God, who loved me, and gave himself for me. I do not frustrate the grace of God: for if righteousness come by the law, then Christ is dead in vain."

"The foundation of God standeth sure, having this seal, the Lord knoweth them that are his. And, let every one that nameth the name of Christ depart from iniquity." (II Timothy 2:19)

And by the way, we did, by following the advice of a roofer friend from Pennsylvania (whose name is also Emanuel) discover what caused the cedar shingles to wear out prematurely. Wood, even cedar, does not do well on a roof if it can't breathe, and these shingles had no breather, which is a reminder again that good craftsmen work with wood, knowing that if they force it against its nature, it may well cause them grief later.

Which is a reminder again that it is not God's heart to force us against our nature to be good, but it is His heart that we acknowledge our need and for Him to change us from the inside out; by saving our souls, by giving us His word, and by the indwelling of His Holy Spirit.

All scripture revolves around and addresses creation, the fall of man, his subsequent depravity, and then the Promised coming, and fulfillment of the Promise, in Jesus Christ our risen Lord and Savior. Jesus Christ who is the Promised One, Our Messiah, hanging on a criminal's cross in our stead, said, "It is finished," and "he bowed his head, and gave up the ghost." (John 19:30) For His work of teaching and redemption, His work here on earth was done; it was—and is—completed. All that was left was to proclaim that Good News of Redemption. To rise again. Which He did. And now we live in expectation of His second coming.

His rising is proven to us by many witnesses. And it is proven to us by His Life imparted to us. The empty tomb spoke volumes. His resurrection, both bodily and imparted to us, continues to speak. "We have also a more sure word of prophecy; whereunto ye do well that ye take heed, as unto a light that shineth in a dark place, until the day dawn, and the day star arise in your hearts." (II Peter 1:19) "God, who at sundry times and in diverse manners spake in time past unto the fathers by the prophets, hath in these last days spoken unto us by his Son, whom he hath appointed heir of all things, by whom also he made the worlds." (Hebrews 1:1-2)

"All scripture is given by inspiration of God, and is profitable for doctrine, for reproof, for correction, for instruction in righteousness: that the man of God may be perfect, thoroughly furnished unto all good works." (II Timothy 3:16-17)

God, through His Son, has provided the way for us to rise above our fallen condition. For mankind is fallen. And feels inferior. And so often through fighting—or succumbing—to feelings of inferiority, develops an inferiority complex. For either way, by fighting or succumbing, the feelings of inferiority are acknowledged and nurtured. He who has said in His Word that "the fear of man bringeth a snare," is the One that we rightly feel inferior to; but as mankind goes, God in His Word puts us all in the same category. That of having a fallen nature and in need of redemption. Our answer is Jesus. In Him we find peace. Our soul is at rest. Our emotions stabilize. Our complexes dissipate.

AN INFERIORITY COMPLEX

Feelings of inferiority,
Create unpleasant thoughts,
Of gaining seniority,
With undermining rebuffs.

In fearful hearts that fear others,
Resistance gains traction,
And so gossip takes over,
Causing fear-filled reaction.

For it's mortal fear, deep and strong,
Devastating home and church,
Fear of man is always wrong,
And it's inferiority's clutch.

We so rightly feel inferior,
Our pride rightly does fall,
To He whose power is sure,
To our Father, God overall.

Our God's ability is sure,
To give us direction,
He gives us all of fear's cure,
When Heaven's our destination.

In Him we have direction.
In Him we have a cure for our fears.
In Him our destination is Heaven.
Jesus lives!

Gottes sege dazu winscha
(May God add His blessing)

3

TOTAL DEPRAVITY OF MAN

Part 1

OF ALL THE TRAGIC evil that the 20th century gave to the world, Nazi Germany, with all its atrocities and war crimes (judged by the Geneva Accord), stands out. And then, as these hideous atrocities and war crimes were barely coming to an end and the Allied nations were still breathing a collective sigh of relief, one of our own rose in power, perpetrating its own set of atrocities on its own people.

Communist Russia increased its scope of power and its ability to coerce and enslave its own people as it arose from the rubble of the Second World War. Using its loveless fear as the ultimate weapon, it sought to force yet another entire working class of citizens onto and along the narrow path to Utopia. Will mankind ever corporately learn that forced Utopia is an oxymoron? Its very force denies its goal.

The spirit and power of the last hold-out in this second global conflict had been broken by the dropping of atomic bombs on Hiroshima and Nagasaki, with destructive force hitherto unknown to mankind. The incinerating power unleashed by these bombs that split atoms staggered even the inventors and the government officials who authorized its use in the belief that Allied lives saved would be of a far greater count than the Axis lives lost by the bombing. And indeed the Japanese were a formidable foe because of their estimated 500,000 soldiers protecting the Kyushu coastline beaches,

Divine Response

less than 400 miles across the sea from Okinawa Island, now occupied by the Allied military, and from which an invasion was fast becoming the next mission for troops on the ground.

The vast numbers of Japanese soldiers were made all the more formidable in that the Emperor Hirohito was commonly believed to be of divine ancestry and indeed was himself divine, so his command to fight to the death—while he with his family awaited their own fate in the royal palace—was taken seriously. So seriously, in fact, that specially trained suicide pilots, the Kamikaze—influenced by the mysterious psycho power of the Emperor—guided their own planes at and into their targets, blowing up themselves when their bomb-laden planes exploded ... destroying whatever target they had aimed into.

The manipulative power of such rulers stagger the mind. It also raises a very valid question. How is it possible? How is it even possible to convince such masses of people that the mysteriously elusive cause they are fighting for, dying for, is worth all the rigorous hardships of fighting, and is even worth giving their lives for? Surely, if they had known the whole truth—the folly of which is now evident to all—they would have, to a man, laid down their arms and ceased to fight.

But a master manipulator's agenda is never perpetrated by presenting truth, but rather a utopian ideal (however delusional) at which he hopes to arrive despite all the present hardships. And he cannot move the masses by presenting the facts, for if it is presented factually, then all possible outcomes become open to question and exploration. It follows then that manipulation is more emotional than it is factual. For once a people become driven by emotion, the facts fall by the wayside and become less and less relevant to the emotion-driven mind. When therefore emotionally driven opinions become fact in the minds of the people, then the deception is complete and the leading ruler easily usurps totalitarian control. He is successful in that he himself is persuaded, his mind having been manipulated by himself, the devil, or both.

Thus did Adolf Hitler, who presided over the killing of millions of his own "undesirable" countrymen. And Lenin. And Trotsky. Who also killed their millions. Marx and Hirohito, though not personally active in the murders of their own people, nonetheless presided over leadership minds, resulting in the deaths of hundreds of thousands of their own countrymen.

Of these three, Communism, Hirohito's religion, and Nazism, Communism held out the longest, but also failed miserably in keeping the masses convinced, for the emotional center became more and more a center of hopelessness, as the hardship of their circumstances increased their hopelessness, and hopelessness increased the hardship of their circumstances, and the hardship of their circumstances increased their hopelessness and...

When the Communists resorted to physical restraint in order to force their people forward on the narrow path to "Utopia", it was from the ruling classes' perspective a great show of power; but from the sunshine of reality it showed the miserable failure of Communism for what it really is—or was. For while Communism built walls and fences to keep people in, the free world patrolled its borders to keep people out. While the free world's immigration offices were busy, those people under Russian oppression wanted out. Many risking being shot to escape, while many others didn't survive the attempt.

For Communism, whether Russian or Chinese, is an illusion. A tragic illusion brought on by the powerful emotional wave at its beginning that convinced men's minds of better days ahead and overthrew the ruling Czar Nicholas II, gruesomely executing him and his family. When the minds of men are persuaded, their bodies need no force, for the mind will be as a guiding GPS system for the body.

When beliefs are based upon reality, then the more that reality is attacked, so much the more will facts come to the defense of reality. Whereas illusion becomes more and more exposed as a farce the more it is attacked, reality is more and more shown to be grounded upon fact the more it is attacked. While discernment of facts has deep heart-felt emotions, emotions cannot be trusted for discernment. The strong, and especially Christian leaders, are to have the spiritual "senses exercised to discern both good and evil." (Hebrews 5:14)

We do well—with heartfelt emotion—to say of the Holocaust, "Never again." We would also do well to consider how could it even happen? How was it possible to persuade or intimidate upwards of 31 million German citizens into believing or accepting that the forward march of Germany, their beloved "Vaterland," came at the expense of the annihilation of "Undesirables," with Jews supposedly being the major obstruction to the force of evolutionary purification for the "Aryan Race"? How was it even possible to convince or intimidate the majority of German "Christians" to capitulate to Hilter's demands? They were approximately eleven million strong—well over one third of the population of Germany—and had they together formed a coalition to counter the Pogroms, the Holocaust could have been avoided. Why didn't they? Why were men, such as Martin Niemöller, left as those speaking into the wind? By the majority. There were many Christians, God bless them, whose life-stories would well be worthy of a book each, who worked "underground" expending themselves and their resources for the cause of Christ. Enabling many thousands of Jews to evade the Tormentors who plotted against, and hunted them, for the purpose of extermination.

But the same blustery winds of change muting the vehement denunciation of the Third Reich and its policies, also carried along with it—like so many goose feathers—the majority of German Christians. While Niemöller and many like him did what they could, and did it well, they were a pitiful minority compared to the potential that was there, had no Christians and especially not leaders, capitulated.

The name *Adolph Hitler* has become a representation of Evil to all of us. And well it should. But when we say "Never Again," as we do well to, we also do well to stop and consider Hitler's ideology. The ideology that gave rise to Nazism and eventually persuaded the masses. Yes, Adolph Hitler had a powerful voice and a charismatic personality, but it was his ideology that swept the citizens of an otherwise civilized country into its euphoric deception and left destruction in its wake.

Adolph Hitler believed in the superiority of the "Aryan Race," and must have believed that the world would one day recognize and applaud him for his pioneering work in the field of Eugenics. Though we do not have the time nor the space here for a book study on *Mein Kampf*, we do know that Adolph was born at the dawning of a time when the idea of Eugenics was being introduced into national conversation; and that his horrific attempt to perpetrate his ideas for a superior race of people resulted in the Eugenics movement falling into disfavor, being indicted by association. Eugenics—the evolutionary "science" of people selectively mating to propagate desirable hereditary traits—attempts to reduce human suffering by "breeding out" undesirable characteristics from the human population.[1] It was gaining ground in Europe and the Americas, in the late 19th and early 20th centuries, and is one of those dark blots on United States history eclipsed only by the mistreatment of Natives and Blacks.

Between 1909-1979, many thousands of sterilizations occurred in California mental institutions. Thirty-three states eventually allowed involuntary sterilization in whomever lawmakers deemed unworthy to procreate; with "unworthy" and "undesirable" being tragically left open to interpretation. Adolph Hitler may well have been influenced by, and in fact

---

1 https://www.britannica.com/science/eugenics-genetics

TOTAL DEPRAVITY OF MAN

refers to, American Eugenics in his latter 1920s book *Mein Kampf*. Hitler had his own interpretation of "unworthy" and "undesirable" and by 1940 his master-race mania took a terrible turn as hundreds of thousands of people with physical disabilities were "euthanized," the "civilized" word for the uncivilized practice of killing off the handicapped by gas or lethal injection. "Euthanasia" soon also became the Nazi-prescribed destination for the healthy but Nazi-defined "undesirables" and by the end of World War II, in May of 1945, millions of people were dead—among them six million Jews—casualties of the Eugenics Movement. In *Mein Kampf* he gives his early-on view of Eugenics as pertaining to Evolution, giving us at least a glimpse of understanding his depraved ideology leading up to the horrors best described at the Holocaust Museum, 100 Raoul Wallenberg Place SW, Washington, D.C.

Hitler writes: "The stronger must dominate and not mate with the weaker, which would signify the sacrifice of its own higher nature. Only the born weakling can look upon this principle as cruel, and if he does so, it is merely because he is of a feebler nature and narrower mind; for if such a law did not direct the process of evolution then the higher development of organic life would not be conceivable at all."[2]

Again, as was common in the Eugenics Movement, words such as stronger, weaker, sacrifice, higher nature, weakling, feebler nature, and narrow-mind, are left open to interpretation. At the end of the second World War the Nazi interpretations—thanks to their obsession for meticulous record-keeping—were opened up for a horrified world to see. In the aftermath, the Eugenics Movement reeled drunkenly and has never fully recovered. But its ideas are still alive and have again been gaining ground, however slowly, since the landmark Roe v. Wade decision of 1973. The word "undesirable" is again open to interpretation. This time individual interpretation, with the "undesirables" being the weakest and most dependent among us: the unborn. Make no mistake, this present-day Holocaust is taking its toll on the finest of human instincts, the instinct that is most like God's; that of the Strong providing solace for the weak. Protective parental emotions cannot go on being so squashed, shredded, and denied expression without devastating the emotional and moral equilibrium of a society's very foundation, leaving its structure vulnerable to ever-increasing violence. Violence, as in, "survival of the fittest," becomes by default, its first and major tenet.

---

2 In *Mein Kampf* translated to English

Beware. On a globe staying the same size as it has always been, with an ever-increasing population being taught in the Evolutionary principle of survival of the fittest, we have an increasingly vulnerable setup for an increasingly violent struggle for space. As believers in Christ it is our heartfelt desire that on this stay-the- same-size globe, an ever increasing population can believe in God who created us all "in His own image" and be filled with the Holy Spirit. And being filled with the calm strength of caring, we may "increase in the knowledge of God" and increase in the ability to expound that same knowledge and to lead souls to Christ—the Redeemer from destruction to all them that believe. As Believers in Christ we wait patiently for our "Redemption that draweth nigh." For the "new heavens and new earth" wherein dwelleth righteousness.

The point being made above about the evils of Nazism is not merely to show how evil Hitler was, but to consider deeper. Hitler was only one man. One man alone cannot perpetrate the evil of the Holocaust. Left alone, Hitler's charisma had been meaningless. Left alone, his charisma falling flat, his powerful voice fading into nothingness, his ideology unheeded, his maniacal drive for an Aryan master-race would have been impossibly fragmented. It was with his equally persuaded henchmen and to the wild exuberance of Germany's millions chanting "Heil Hitler" that Adolph Hitler—with his demonic goals—came to power. It was because of the consent, or capitulation, of Germany's millions that Hitler's ideology controlled their minds. The depravity expressed by Nazism had been impossible without the depraved consent of the governed.

Adolph Hitler was a gifted man. As a part of his charismatic appeal, his powerful voice expressed his ideology with an extensive vocabulary and a voice that would seem to effortlessly and seamlessly hit every octave on the scale. His speeches could begin in gentle tones that drew his listeners in, then steadily climb to a rasping, screaming crescendo that led the crowd into screaming with the wild passion of thoroughly persuaded carnal minds.

As the ideology of Nazism appealed to mankind's lower nature, it also appealed to mankind's innate desire to succeed in reaching goals. Besides a powerful voice and a charismatic personality, Hitler's organizational skills were nothing short of phenomenal. His skill exacerbated by the newly invented public radio, he organized a weakened Germany—still struggling to recover from its World War I losses—into a world power waging a "blitzkrieg" (lightning war) that had world powers reeling with bewilderment as they awakened to the reality that a transformed Germany needed to be reckoned with if Democracy were to survive.

TOTAL DEPRAVITY OF MAN

The church had its chance to withstand the spread of Nazism, and failing its duty to do so, was soon overwhelmed by the tsunami wave of its pressure.

In persuading the masses, Hitler employed his charisma and organizational skills to win over Germany's young people, organizing local groups with leaders through the public schools in cities and hamlets across the country. Dressed in brown shirts with swastika emblems on sleeves, enthusiastically honoring "Der Fuehrer" (The Leader) with smart salutes and "Heil Hitler," they were given what every young person deep down longs for. Purpose. Goals. Having those goals passionately expounded, together with purposeful direction passionately given and purposefully employed, the youth of Germany gave their hearts to Hitler. And as Hitler created an Antagonist (the Jew) and a Protagonist, (himself and Germany), many an uneasy heart and soul were carried along on the wave of national pride and sense of Providential Direction that brought with it a sense of invincibility. Tapping into the sense of invincibility so natural to the inexperienced young, coupled with Hitler's own sense of invincibility, drew a commitment and emotional exuberance that generally are reserved for gods. A commitment and exuberance that should be reserved for God Himself. Hitler verbally attacked "Der Jude" (the Jew), which in German he could spit out like a curse, and one among the many accusations was for being "Christen Toedter," (Christ-Killers) possibly a calculated attempt to pacify, if not to win over, the Christian church.

But in setting himself up as the Answer to Germany's problems—for they did have problems—Adolph Hitler became a "Christ-Killer" himself, if such a thing were possible; as he took the place of Christ in the hearts and minds of many. That Hitler had a special place in his agenda for the young was evident from his writing in *Mein Kampf* and in his ensuing speeches.

Of Germany's youth he wrote, "I am firmly convinced today that, generally speaking, it is in youth that men lay the essential groundwork of their creative thought, wherever that creative thought exists. I make a distinction between the wisdom of age—which can only arise from the greater profundity and foresight that are based on the experiences of a long life—and the creative genius of youth which blossoms out in thought and ideas with inexhaustible fertility, without being able to put these into practice immediately because of their very superabundance. These furnish the building materials and plans for the future; and it is from them that age takes the stones and builds the edifice, unless the so-called wisdom of the years may have smothered the creative genius of youth."

Here again, we have vital words such as creative thought, wisdom, foresight, creative genius, inexhaustible fertility, etc. left open to interpretation, however carnal they may be.

And so Adolph Hitler drew the citizens of Germany, together with Totalitarian and Democratic powers of the world, into the cauldron of blood, sweat, tears, and confusion that was the second World War.

So what about the Nazis and the Communists of this world? And the many like them over the course of millennia, including the ISIS of today? Have they somehow inhaled the genes of demons? Have they lost their minds? Were they born partly animal?

Or are they something even more terrifying? Are they normal? Are we made of the same stuff? Given the same circumstances and making the same choices, would I become like them? Like that?

The short answer is yes.

But let us briefly consider the enemy of God and man: the devil, and our own natural compatibility with his designs. Isaiah 14 gives his name as being Lucifer, the only time this name is used in the Bible. Otherwise he is referred to as Satan or simply the devil, except in Ezekiel 28 where he is referred to as the Cherub that covereth. Although Isaiah 14 begins as a prophecy against the king of Babylon and Ezekiel 28 begins as a prophecy against the Prince of Tyrus, both these chapters give clear indication of the subject moving on and referring to a being like, and yet distinct from, the King and the Prince. For in Isaiah 14:12 we are given this lament: "How art thou fallen from heaven, O Lucifer, son of the morning" and in Ezekiel 28:13 of the cherub that covereth, we are told: "Thou hast been in Eden the garden of God," so since the prince of Tyrus was never in Eden nor the King of Babylon in heaven, we conclude that the "cherub that covereth" and "Lucifer" are one and the same as the great dragon, that old serpent, called the Devil and Satan, which deceiveth the whole world, that was cast out into the earth, and his angels were cast out with him. (Revelation 12:9)

Isaiah 14:13-14 gives us the reason for this fall from Heaven; "for thou hast said in thine heart, I will ascend into heaven, I will exalt my throne above the stars of God: I will sit also upon the mount of the congregation, in the sides of the north: I will ascend above the heights of the clouds; I will be like the most High."

What pride is this?! That the one created (for he was created) becomes so self-absorbed, so self-focused, so self-exalted, so full of pride that he dares to think that he can handle this himself. That he is even as good or

TOTAL DEPRAVITY OF MAN

better than the One by whom he was created. For he has deceived himself into believing not only that the impossible is possible but also that he himself has become powerful enough to make it happen. Five times in those two short verses he says: "I will…" and then goes on to say in his heart what he will do. He has become thoroughly captivated by thoughts of his own strength as is evident by the expressions of "I will" and his heart was lifted up because of his beauty. (Ezekiel 28:17)

Does this self-absorption sound familiar? For the devil came to Eve in the garden of Eden with that same self-absorption and self-focus in his successful attempt to cause her to ignore and transgress the commandment of God. The commandment was simple enough and easy to understand, but that old Serpent, the devil, successfully planted a seed of doubt about God's trustworthiness and fairness and suggested very effectively that God was keeping her ignorant for the sake of control. The devil's appeal was not through being factual, but rather appealing to her emotions and deceiving her into believing that her emotions were, in fact, fact. And because deception promotes ignorance, Satan was doing exactly what he was accusing God of; gaining control through promoting and keeping her, or them as it turned out, in ignorance. Though Adam was not deceived, (I Timothy 2:14) he did join in with his wife and they both fell from their position of innocence before God to one of humiliation and fear. For when they reached out and partook of the fruit that God had forbidden, they said—perhaps not verbally but surely with their actions—that I will ignore God's will, I will do it my way, I will become wise, I will know as much as God, I will be like the most High.

Satan had successfully manipulated them. He is a master at it. A master manipulator, for manipulation is more emotional than it is factual. He also introduced uncertainty, causing a questioning of the facts, a questioning of God's motives. Stirring up questions about His very character and the purpose of His commandments. Yea, hath God said? Had he begun by obnoxiously accusing God, Eve would have very likely not listened. But he didn't come obviously accusing or boasting. He didn't come obviously arrogant, he didn't come obviously proud, he didn't come obviously sure of himself or of anything else for that matter. At least not at first. He came questioning, seemingly uncertain, perhaps even seemingly humble; and so Eve began to question and actually became uncertain, finally reaching out for the fruit, reaching out for this certainty, that the devil was assuring her was to be found in herself.

In presenting himself as being a bit unsure himself, but still questioning what God was doing, Satan didn't present himself as a know-it-all, but only as one questioning what was really going on here. Only when he had Eve's full attention did he dare to accuse God. By presenting himself as one who was wondering about God's integrity himself, not that he was sure of course, but only wondering; Satan, by his false humility was able to present himself in a pleasing way to Eve who responded to his assumed uncertainty by becoming uncertain herself. But she wanted to be certain so she reached out for the fruit of the tree of knowledge of good and evil, not knowing as she did so, for she was deceived, that she was reaching out for her own, not God's, wisdom. For God's wisdom had told Adam and Eve exactly what would happen.

Even so, as in the post-modern culture that we live in today, when uncertainty successfully masquerades as humility, then any certainty of opinion can easily be labeled as arrogance and pride. For there is a new creed in the land and its name is Tolerance; and for those who embrace it to its thoughtless conclusion, to be tolerant of everyone's beliefs, actions and lusts no matter how unbiblical and against Nature they may be, has now become the new creed to which everyone should attain. And in some cases—as in the baking of same-sex wedding cakes for instance—there is an attempt to force this creed of tolerance on everyone.

So the Tolerant have now become intolerant of the Intolerant. What we seem to see coming is a Tyranny of the Tolerant, what Mark Slade has so aptly suggested we call Toleranny perhaps, as the movement is, so far, nameless. That this movement is an oxymoron should come as no surprise to any Bible-believing Christian, for no one can in reality be totally neutral about everything. We're just not made and programmed that way. For instance, while neutrality has its place when beginning a research project, the deeper one delves into the subject, the less neutral one can be as our opinion becomes formed by what the research reveals. Else there would be no point in research. And on the subject of religion, no one can attempt total tolerance without becoming intolerant of any religion except the "Religion of the Tolerant." At which point they have become the most Intolerant of the Intolerant, for they cannot by force stamp out all religions except their own without becoming tyrants. And besides, in promoting this religion of Tolerance to its natural conclusion is to open the door to, and invite in, Anarchy—a total rebellion against any and all restraints.

If there is anything the devil cannot stand, it is someone who takes a stand on God's side of an issue and knows where he stands.

And where would the "Tolerant" stand? Your guess is as good as mine, for the liberals seem to think they can keep their nose to the grindstone while straddling the fence with both feet firmly planted in mid-air. If this position seems precarious, dangerous, and impossible, it's because it really is. But then again, I hear that given enough time, anything is possible.

If the liberals seem to be attempting to force the fear of man upon everyone in general, and Christians in particular, it's because they really are; for without the fear of God in place, the fear of man rushes in to fill the destabilized void. Woven into mankind's deepest understanding of himself and the world is the need for Law and Order. And when he ceases to depend on God for that Law and Order, he has nowhere to turn for it except to mankind in general and to himself in particular. If he looks to natural law, he must of necessity acknowledge that the universality of natural law everywhere leads one to believe that it all springs from the same Source. And since it all comes from the same Source, that Source should have a name.

From the ages and the sages this name comes rolling consistently to us across the years. Jehovah God. And when God is acknowledged in heart and mind, then natural Law and the Law of His Word must also be acknowledged, clearing up the spiritual vertigo. But Law, while it points out right and wrong, cannot heal the broken condition we all find ourselves in. Try as we might, we have this innate tendency to sin and make a mess out of our lives. Or seemingly have our lives in control and look down our noses in disdain at those who don't. Seemingly, because in reality no one does. Our lives can be interrupted in a moment, in the blink of an eye.

Whether we have much, or little, time left here in this life, it all goes by so fast that most, if not all, older people ask, "where did the time go?"

> When as a child I crawled, time crept.
> As I learned to play 'n work, time walked.
> When I became a teen, time ran.
> As older still I grew, time flew.
> As a Senior I became, time slipped away.
> Soon as time goes on, time gone.
> Then when all is said and done, Jesus Lives!

How shall we respond? The answer God gives us in His Word is for each one in particular—and all equally—to allow the Law of God to settle upon us, revealing our need for forgiveness and the grace of God through Jesus Christ. Of this we are certain, He is for us. "If God be for us, who can be against us?" (Romans 8:31) Uncertainty can be humility, but this much we can be certain of, humility walks in the Light and doesn't hide itself behind Uncertainty, nor Certainty.

THE GREAT DIVIDE

When uncertainty masquerades,
As humility and,
Is successful in doing so,
Along come variegated shades,
Of false beliefs and,
Certainty becomes the new foe.

And of Biblical direction,
We cannot be sure,
To be sure must surely be pride,
Every difficult question,
Just opens the door,
For discussion t' shake up the ride.

Yes, pride can be certain and sure,
'N can just as surely be wrong,
'Cause pride cannot walk in the light;
The Gospel message is pure,
'N self may not be strong,
For the Way, the Truth, and the Life is Christ.

And the things that can be shaken,
Should be let to shake so,
Things that cannot shake may remain,
For God's truth when it's opened,
Brings light and there's no,
Darkness keeping hid what it means.

For the true Light of the Gospel,
Dispels the dark night,
And confusion cannot abide,
Jesus brings light free and full,
Divides wrong from right,
When we draw nigh 'n He in us abides.

Gottes sege dazu winscha
(May God add His blessing)

4

TOTAL DEPRAVITY OF MAN

Part 2

PRIDE TAKES ON MANY forms. The only deliverance is through Jesus Christ. His shed blood, His Resurrection, and His intercession for us.

We live in a fallen world. The fallen brokenness is all around us. And within each one of us. Our spirit is fallen and our self-will is not a safe guide. Our soul is fallen and our emotions are not a safe guide. Our body is fallen and faces corruption.

Into all this fallen brokenness comes the invitation for healing. Healing for the spirit as our will surrenders and flows with the will of God. Healing for the soul as the emotions are righted and sanctified by the yielding of the will and the flowing in of the Holy Spirit. Total healing for the body, though future, in the eternal reality of Heaven. In this experience of inner healing, God's Holy Spirit becomes a very personal and safe Guide as the Inner Word, the Holy Spirit, coincides with the Outer Word, which is God's written Word, the Holy Bible.

The Enemy of our Souls, the devil, has seduced us onto his way. His way has corrupted us and brought about the fallen condition we now live with. And struggle with. A struggle exacerbated by our innate tendency to trust ourselves too far. We tend to trust that our will is a right one, that our feelings are legitimate proof of our rightness, and that the needs of our bodies are all-important. This spirit, soul, and body brokenness has opened so many flood-gates of evil upon this broken world that one wonders: how long, O Lord, how long?

Wherever an honest attempt is made to overcome this fallen brokenness, the devil is there to push it upon us again. Whether overtly or covertly, he has always attacked Bible-believing Christians in his attempt to altogether destroy Christianity. Whenever any good is accomplished, the Destroyer is there to either steal the credit or to destroy the good. The Church of Jesus Christ being his ultimate target.

America has become the most outstanding government on the earth, in modern times, for taking a stand between the devil and the Church, hindering the Destroyer and his minions from the spiritual hatred that would surely be poured out if there were no barriers. These days Satan is leveling his attack at America's most revered and stabilizing institutional document, the Constitution of the United States of America. While the original Constitution with its Bill of Rights, Amendments, and its checks and balances of power makes no claim of perfection, it was nonetheless, an honest attempt by honest men to be honest about the fallen condition of the nature of man and of the world that we live in. An honesty which God has blessed, as His character is honest, and He loves and blesses honesty.

Were the founders of the Constitution always honest in their individual relationships with God? Did they each individually see their need of, and come to the foot of the Cross, unload their burdens and become cleansed from sin and its ravages by the shed blood of Jesus? I like to think they did, but those are questions we cannot answer. They lived in another time and in another place and these are questions we can safely leave with God, who made us all, is all-seeing, all-knowing, honest, and just.

It is a relief to leave Judgment with Him and not with any of us, who are not all-seeing, not all-knowing, not always honest, and not always just. For we have an innate tendency to be partial to those closest to us, and consequently to ourselves. And so to be deceived. Deception is an integral part of the devil. So much so that Jesus calls him "a liar, and the father of it." (John 8:44)

It is this, the devil's deception, that was the original cause, and continues to be the cause, of all the grief in the fallen, broken world that we live in. He deceives into believing that our will is a right one, our feelings are legitimate proof of our rightness, and that our physical needs are ultimate.

Into this cauldron of inner stress and outward strain, he introduces the deceptive idea that we are basically good and are constantly evolving into better people. When in fact, the idea of Evolution should realistically

TOTAL DEPRAVITY OF MAN

be rather called Devolution, as its theory devolves mankind into a shared ancestry with the apes and the monkeys.

And as mankind continues this tragic mental descent from the God who made them in His own image, male and female created He them; many find themselves in such a state of confusion that sexual gender can no longer be biologically recognized, but must rather be determined by emotional orientation.

Must we be so foolish?

Experience tells me that the more I act like a monkey, the more I feel like one. If then, the more I feel like a monkey the more I act like one and the more I act like one the more I feel like one... well, you get where I'm going... Just because I have those days when I feel like a dog chasing my tail, doesn't mean I should act like one. Likewise, there are sinful tendencies we should not succumb to; but rather, we should come to God with those sinful tendencies, surrendering ourselves, spirit, soul, and body, to His Judgment, who then receives us, sins and all, as a precious gift, nails our sins to the Cross, (Colossians 2:14) washes, cleanses, and preserves us blameless unto the coming of our Lord Jesus Christ. (I Thessalonians 5:23) Washed and clean. Because of Jesus. Blameless. Because of Jesus. Thank you Jesus. "Some men's sins are open beforehand, going beforehand to judgment; and some men they follow after." (I Timothy 5:24)

The Theory of Evolution introduces the deceptive idea that we are getting better and better, more able, and more wise; therefore more and more able to determine and control the destiny of this fallen world that we live in. And ourselves?

We are supposedly just a part of the cycle of life and death. In the meantime, the population on this globe continues to grow and population control is being touted by some. And discovery of new worlds in the Cosmos by others. If all we see and know had, in fact, evolved from a common life form and each step upward were, in fact, a result of the struggle for life, then indeed, our life and the future of all evolving life is in our hands.

But if we have been created, which we have, our destiny is in One who is all-powerful, all-knowing, all-seeing, and we look forward to the Promise of a new heaven and a new earth. This is the Hope, though future, of all who trust in Jesus Christ, our Savior and King. He is the Christian's Answer.

There is a question that the devil has never, and will never, dare to address or attempt to answer. That question is the question of all questions. The question of: where does life come from? From where does it originate? What holds it all together? These are questions that unbelieving

Evolutionists grapple with. If indeed they consider them at all. For the Unbeliever these are questions without answers. For the unbelieving Scientist attempting to answer the question with the Theory of Evolution, the answers are elusive, as every answer only begs the question further. Therefore his belief in Evolution is based upon the religious belief that his Theory is correct; a trust in something or other that no one has physically seen nor proven. We may call such a trust religion, but not science.

Mankind is not only fallen and depraved, but is also so uncomfortable with whom he or she is, at the depth of his or her own being, that we are loath to look very deeply and allow who we really are to be uncovered, even to ourselves. It is this covering, which is self-righteousness, that needs to come off before the eyes of "Him with whom we have to do." (Hebrews 4:13) Jehovah God, so that we may be clothed upon with the Pure Righteousness of Jesus Christ, our Messiah and King. We are naturally as uncomfortable with who we are—in the depth of our being—as Adam and Eve were with their nakedness in the Garden of Eden, after they had sinned in partaking of the forbidden fruit. They attempted to cover their nakedness with sewed together fig leaves, (Genesis 3:7) which God saw to be just as insufficient as He sees our self-righteousness to be that we attempt to keep our spiritual nakedness covered with. God then clothed Adam and Eve with coats of skins, (Genesis 3:21) the first record we have of blood being shed. It being after the Fall, and in order to cover the nakedness of the first man and woman, is the first clue God gave in His Word of what it would take to cover the spiritual nakedness of mankind; that of Jesus Christ shedding His blood on the Cross of Calvary to atone for our sins so we might be inwardly clothed with the white garment of His righteousness. He being the sinless, pure, and only begotten Son of God. This word "begotten" is not to be understood that God begat his Divinity; for He testifies to us through the Apostles that Jesus was "God…manifest in the flesh;" (I Timothy 3:16; John 1) but is to be understood that God begat the man, Jesus, which He testifies to in Luke 1:35.

Being therefore begotten of the Holy Ghost, conceived and birthed by a woman, Jesus, having come from God, is fully man while being fully God. He is the fullest expression of God's heart to us, and as such is referred to as the "Word" of God in John 1 and in Revelation 19:13. When we want to understand God's heart, we need to observe the recorded life of Jesus and receive His teachings in heart and mind, as we yield to the Witness of it all, God's Holy Spirit. "Looking unto Jesus," we are instructed in Hebrews 12:2,

TOTAL DEPRAVITY OF MAN

"the author and finisher of our faith; who for the joy that was set before him endured the cross, despising the shame, and is set down at the right hand of the throne of God."

The encouragement here is to not dwell on the present affliction and conflict but to "look unto Jesus," directing us beyond any present conflict or affliction we may be facing to the joy awaiting the faithful. This is God's heart and is the message that Jesus so faithfully conveys to us by the record of His life and His teachings. While giving ourselves, spirit, soul and body to Him is God's heart, it is also His heart that we do so voluntarily without Him forcing us, though He could. God has His own reasons for not using force, which we may not always understand. Especially as we come face to face with evil in this world; but this much we can understand, that God knows what He is doing and is not obligated to explain all His decisions to us. This much we can and do understand from His Word, that His war with the devil is to be won and over, never to happen again. How could it happen in the first place? How could rebellion happen in an otherwise perfect place? How could such conceit and arrogance happen in heaven? How could the devil not see, or at least not accept, his doom upon being the instigator of this war? Though we are not given the answers to all those questions in this time, we can rest, assured by the Word of God, that while God is leaving our freedom to choose intact, He is also giving us as much information as we need to know in order to make the right choices. Which are, at their base, all-inclusive in one choice; that of accepting God's way instead of taking our own. Which is, in reality, the way we love God. "If ye love me," Jesus said, "keep my commandments." (John 14:15)

We naturally love ourselves. We love and care for our bodies, which is good because we are a creation of God. We naturally recoil from a hot stove, from head-on collisions, from falling off house roofs, and a myriad of dangers, both large and small, that are being encountered somewhere every day; and if not avoided, would result in bodily harm or death. It is good to respect God's Creation, and that includes our bodies which he has given for us to temporarily reside in while here on the earth. As we are healthy and able, we naturally feed, sleep, clothe, house, and otherwise take care of ourselves. We rightly accept, or should accept, our bone structure and natural features. While it is good to avoid deformities resulting from close inter-marriage, still, what is done is done, and needs to be accepted. There is a natural love and acceptance of ourselves that is good.

DIVINE RESPONSE

However, the devil, as always, seeks to take of God's good Creation and warp it for his own design, which is bad. Either with an excessive body-awareness resulting in vanity or excessive body-awareness resulting in self-hatred. Neither one is a good expression of accepting ourselves as God created us. It seems all of us struggle, sometimes at least, with the way some part or other of our bodies look or function. How little it would take, we think, to make ourselves look a lot better. And so we tend to look for that little bit that would make all the difference. But because we live in an imperfect world, the excessively body-aware person is never quite good enough; never quite satisfied with his or her looks. And so is led into a body-aware bondage and a constantly dissatisfied unrest—deep in the soul—expressing itself by a near-constant search for some product or clothing to make up the difference.

Excessive awareness of this physical realm can also lead to self-hatred, which is, at its roots, self-destructive. Perhaps all of us have known or know of someone caught up in such extreme self-hatred that he or she has taken their own life. Suicide is a tragic word that we all naturally recoil from. What torments of the mind must one be going through to cause him or her to take such an extreme action against the body that we so naturally protect from danger and pain? What mental anguish must one be going through in the depth of the soul when getting to the point of so desperately wanting to be released from an otherwise healthy body. Or perhaps believing that the spirit and soul will die with the body.

While there are no easy answers, and mind-altering drugs, including medications, may be involved, we can be certain that the devil sees an advantage and takes it. As the ultimate opportunist, he is on constant watch for an opportunity to steal, to kill, and to destroy. (John 10:10) His answer to the problems we face is always death.

The answer that Jesus gives to us is Life. Life in the soul that gives courage for this time and for Eternity. Grace and courage are available to the measure of need. Beware of courage derived or gathered from anything that is temporal, as temporal things are unstable and subject to change, and so will one's courage be. True lasting courage springs from Jesus who inhabits eternity, and flows to us who inhabit time.

One of the devil's tactics is to interrupt this flow of courage and then offer his own paltry dribble squeezed out of things; but things wear out, things rust, moths corrupt, and thieves steal. People let us down. We let people down. And when all lets us down, we need otherworldly courage. God, through his servant John says to us, "love not the world, neither the things that are in the world; if any man love the world, the love of the Father is not in him." (I John 2:15) What we love is also our source of courage. Jesus said it this way, "Where your treasure is, there will your heart be also." (Luke 12:34)

We may find it difficult to accept that our depravity is so total that lasting courage is only to be found outside of ourselves and things, but when we find the ever-flowing courage from Jesus we may well find ourselves saying, "Aah, I didn't know what courage was."

Jesus is a lover of Life, the Giver of Life, the sustainer of Life, is Life itself, and wants us to have a vibrant, abundant, joy-filled life in the depth of our souls where courage is not soon shaken by the difficult circumstances of life here. It is a courage and a life that springs from God, who inhabits eternity, and flows to us, who inhabit time, giving the fortitude to resist the devil. (James 4:7) This is a courage only possible from the in-dwelling Christ through His Holy Spirit. It is the courage of the faithful. It is the courage of the martyrs for the testimony of Jesus. These martyrs who willingly went to their deaths, not because they loved death, but because they loved life. Death to them was merely the difficult river to cross before reaching the eternal fullness of the Life they had learned to love while here in this life. They loved the Life to come. They loved life here, but they loved the Life beyond even more.

When Jesus instructs us to hate our own life, (John 12:25) He does not refer to our bodies, as in physical life, but rather to the fallen nature of sin in our spirit and soul that then govern our bodies in wrong ways. The spirit and soul of man is where the depraved nature of men and women reside. Jesus said, "That which cometh out of the man, that defileth the man. For from within, out of the heart of men, proceed evil thoughts, adulteries, fornications, murders, thefts, covetousness, wickedness, deceit, lasciviousness, an evil eye, blasphemy, pride, foolishness: all these evil things come from within and defile the man." (Mark 7:20-23) This is the life that He refers to when He speaks of loving and hating life. As in Matthew 16:24-25, "If any man will come after me, let him deny himself, and take up his cross, and follow me. For whosoever will save his life shall lose it: and whosoever will lose his life for my sake shall find it." And then He asks those soul-stirring questions in Verse 26: "For what is a man profited, if he shall gain the whole world, and lose his own soul? Or what shall a man give in exchange for his soul?" "He that loveth his life shall lose it," He says "and he that hateth his life in this world shall keep it unto life eternal." (John 12:25) Again, He refers to the life within that governs the body, guiding it into the evil that it does.

It is painfully appropriate to take some time and reflect upon historical examples of depravity. And as we reflect, to also remember that "but for the grace of God, there go I." Yes, given the same circumstances, making the same choices, and reasoning the same way, I/we would become just as cold, just as unreasonable, and just as wicked. From this perspective it is appropriate to reflect, however briefly, upon the Biblical records of evil, and the records of evil even to this day. Records of war, of massacres, of Nazism, of Communism, of ISIS, the records of individual perpetrators of evil. I say briefly for two reasons; one, because we cannot cover them all for lack of time; and two, we tend to become like what or who we focus upon so our primary focus should be upon Jesus our Savior, His life, His purpose and His teachings. "Looking unto Jesus," we are instructed, "the author and finisher of our faith; who for the joy that was set before him endured the cross, despising the shame, and is set down at the right hand of the throne of God." (Hebrews 12:2)

Because of the Fall and depravity of mankind, envy, fear and hatred have and do run rampant in this world that we live in. To the degree that people deny Jehovah God and the in-dwelling Christ, to this degree, to this depth, they sink. And to the degree that people accept Jehovah God and the in-dwelling Christ, to this degree, to this height, they rise. The safest society in which to live is not the society with the most ability to force the nature of man into obedient submission. The safest society in which to live is that society where the people have committed themselves, spirit, soul, and body to the Lord Jesus Christ, our Savior and King. Because, depraved or sanctified, our body is governed by our spirit and by our soul. And to have Jesus Christ take up residence in our spirit and in our soul (in our hearts), is to be sanctified.

TOTAL DEPRAVITY OF MAN

CHOOSE LIFE

Envy went searching around for a mate,
Along came Fear and thought Envy was great.
They united,
Had a baby,
And called its name Hate.

Envy and Fear fed and exercised Hate
Confusion ensued and would not abate.
Dialogue
Didn't happen,
Only tension and fight.

Hate fostered by Envy and nurtured by Fear,
Brought grief upon all yet all would not hear.
God called us,
Gave His Law,
Showing need is right here.

God sent His spirit to earth from above,
He through a virgin His salvation plan wove.
The virgin,
Bore a Son,
Sent from God who is Love.

When to Christ we bow, hearts and lives to Him bond,
Our sins washed away, trusting in His shed blood.
We have peace!
Anticipate!
That glorious beyond!
……..therefore choose Life.

THE TROUBLESOME NOSE

Everybody knows,
That of beauty's woes,
One of the foes,
Is the lowly nose.

God only knows,
How the worst of foes,
Of inner beauty's woes,
Is the haughty nose.

Do we not know,
That our greatest foe,
Causing much woe,
Is our haughty nose?

God help us t' grow,
May we better know,
How 't live for you so,
That Jesus' life shows.

Gottes sege dazu winscha
(May God add His blessing)

5

UNMERITED FAVOR

A FEW YEARS AGO we were having a week of Revival Meetings at our church in the middle of summer. The boys and I work in the building construction trade and it was the busiest time of the year for us. So every evening of the week, it was rush home, rush through supper, rush through showers, rush to church… On Monday and again on Tuesday evening we were five minutes late. But on Wednesday we stayed ahead of schedule. So well, in fact, that on our way to church I saw that we would be at least fifteen minutes early. "Good!" I cheered. "It looks like we'll be fifteen minutes early! So, five minutes can make up for being late on Monday, five minutes for Tuesday, and we'll still have five minutes left for Thursday!"

If we find the thought of moving time humorous, is it not for the reason that time is such a fixed law that the thought of taking some of it from here and placing it there is so ludicrous as to be humorous? Many other laws are just as fixed, but not as noticeable. Such as, but not limited to, the Laws of Chemistry, the Laws of Planetary Motion, the Laws of Physics, the Laws of Logic, the Laws of Mathematics, and the Uniformity of Nature. These laws and more are basic and necessary for the survival of the universe and all living things.

Among the most obvious laws are those such as the law of gravity that even a child subconsciously knows it has to deal with when learning how to walk. Or, as Uncle Abner and his brother Mike know, boys do when learning how to fly. When Uncle Abner reminisces about his boyhood days in the 1940s, his interesting stories (for besides being a good preacher, Uncle Abner is a good story teller) invariably include my father-in-law Mike, who was also

Uncle Abner's brother, only one year older. According to Uncle Abner, he was in awe of his older brother Mike whose inventions in the farm shop were the stuff of little boy legends in the community. So when Mike crafted a set of one-person wings—the workings of which he enthusiastically explained about in detail as he designed and built them—Abner had no doubt but that they would fly. At least not until they were on the farm shop roof and Mike wanted to strap them onto Abner's arms which is how they were designed to work. That's when Abner had some trepidation until Mike explained in his enthused way, that he needed to be able to watch so he could observe if and how improvements could be made. So Abner accepted the wings being strapped to his arms and to being directed to the edge of the roof at the peak of the shop. Mike was excited (more so than Abner) and sure the wings would work. If you just jump off so… and flap the wings just so…

Having received instructions from his "flight instructor", Abner took a deep breath … and jumped … and the wings went straight up and Abner went straight down … and landed on a rock pile. As Abner painfully moved each limb separately to make sure he had no broken bones, Mike came running over, stopped at the rock pile and stared, breathing hard from exertion and stress. He took in the situation of his crumpled brother with his crumpled wings while getting his breath back … and then yelled in a high-pitched, whiny sort of way, "Abnerrr! You broke my wiiiiiiiings!"

In hindsight, the failed flight with its broken wings has become a humorous reminder that we cannot transgress the basic laws of the universe without bearing the consequences. At times humorous, but many times with tragic results, as in a parachute that won't open, a plane run out of fuel, or a deep sea diver coming up too fast. There is no escaping these basic, fixed laws. They are impartial, as basic and necessary for the sustenance of physical life as they can be tragic when not taken into account properly, or when being careless, or when a malfunction happens and is overlooked until too late. These laws are fixed and unchangeable. Until the end of time, when the elements themselves "shall melt with fervent heat."

And just as we cannot move time around to make up for being late, so it doesn't help to put an extra engine into a plane to make up for the plane that has none, or the deep sea diver to come up extra slow today so he can come up extra fast tomorrow to take his wife out for her birthday dinner.

God's moral and ethical laws are just as fixed and His Word is clear that they are just as impartial and immovable as the fixed laws of the universe. While we may think that if we do some good over here it will somehow, though we don't know how, make up for the bad over there, the

Word of God is clear that sin is sin and remains sin even when we do good somewhere else. This is, for the most part, difficult for our finite minds to grasp, as in relation to works, we tend to think in terms of merits and demerits. We tend to think that if we do more good than bad, then God may somehow, though we're never quite sure, overlook the bad because of the good we've done. We tend to picture works as in a balance, and that if our good outweighs our bad, then we're okay.

But the word of God is abundantly clear that God sees our works the way we know time and gravity are. That late is late no matter how often we are early; if we are late, we are still late, and in that particular incident we remain late no matter how often we are or have been early.

We may squirm and call that unfair, but time is time, and if God did change its law for us then it would no longer be trustworthy. And so it is with God's Word. His ethical and moral law. God is trustworthy because His laws are constant and impartial, they do not change for any one of us. The consistent constancy of His laws are how we perceive that He is, in fact, trustworthy. That He is true and righteous altogether, and is, in fact, unchangeable God. Though some may argue that even God changes His mind, citing His removal of judgment upon a people when they repent, as in the case of Nineveh; yet a close examination of the word of God reveals that God is always consistent with His character. Judgment and mercy have met together, He says, righteousness and peace have kissed each other. When we yield to His righteousness, now fulfilled in Jesus Christ, peace comes.

My body did not like gravity when I fell from a roof, but no matter how many roofs I haven't fallen from, or won't fall from, it won't change the effect of that one fall on my body. And so it is in our reckoning with the Word of God. Whether we like it or not doesn't change anything, we either voluntarily reckon with the Word of God here in this life and find mercy and grace, or we reckon with the Word of God against our will in the next. The tragedy of leaving it till the next is that this period of mercy and grace will be over and judgment will be upon the unprepared. We may squirm and not like that, but all our squirming and not liking won't change anything, for we have no choice in the matter. The only choice we have in relation to our destiny is to hear and to yield when God calls us to repentance. Or to not yield and then suffer the devastating consequences. In the first choice we choose the destiny and accept the way; in the second choice we choose the way and must accept the destiny.

Since the pervasive influence of evolutionary thinking has supposedly taken us down from the heights of being made "in the image of God"

(Genesis 1:27) to only being a higher form of the lower animal kingdom; many in the modern and now post-modern culture of our day have in their minds devised ways to prove that this life is all there ever was, is, or ever will be. But this is only a cunningly devised fable, as even a cursory examination does, and will, reveal. Does, because God has put eternity in our hearts, which we prove by our own thoughts and actions every day, for we think and act as those who expect that there is a Higher Being to whom we are accountable and as those who expect to live forever even though the preponderance of evidence shows that 100 percent of us are not here to stay. Even when there are those who seemingly have no conscience left, do something bad enough that it would bring swift retribution upon them if found out, they seek to hide the facts for fear of the consequences. For morality is, and must be, an integral part of a society in order for it to survive. And at what point (we may ask according to the Laws of Logic) did this supposedly physical only existence gain a moral code so necessary for its own survival? Or its love and zest for life?

While there are those who hate life so desperately that they take their own life, it only happens when depression has so removed them from contact with reality that the depressed mind becomes open to devastating inner thoughts of hopelessness and darkness. When the mind is connected with reality, we naturally love life and attempt to take care of it and all it pertains to. If all we are is an advanced form of "primordial soup", why does any of that matter? At what point did this primordial soup develop a conscience, even if only attached to the consequences of its actions? Or an awareness of danger, so necessary for its survival? And the list goes on.

In the "survival of the fittest" idea, history has, the present does, and the future will prove the Biblical model as the fittest, for it alone will survive. And deep down, in the heart of our hearts, in the eternal mind of our brain, we innately know this to be true. If not, then why struggle and fight against it, as the unbelievers do? What does it matter after all, if all we are is advanced primordial soup and there is no eternity? Why even care what people believe? And especially if it even makes them better people to boot? While the atheist may argue that even Christians do horrible things, yet all must admit that the closer one lives to the Biblical standard for life, the more he or she can be trusted, depended on, believed, and the list goes on... In short, such a one is the safest, and the best, neighbor.

So why fight it? The answer is painful, yet necessary for the unbeliever.

That the fight itself proves the existence of God.

Again, if all we are is an advanced form of primordial soup, what does it matter if we believe otherwise?

Why does anything matter? Nay, the very fact that anything matters, and most especially, that believing in God matters to the Evolutionist Unbeliever, the very fact that he fights against the knowledge of God, or even cares, though he may not fight externally, is one of many proofs that God does indeed exist. For the knowledge of God is innate and eternal. And the innate sense of accountability that we have to God, causing us to sense also our responsibility to keep His commandments, is the cause of struggle against Him, is it not?

Today is the day of salvation, "today if ye will hear his voice, harden not your hearts." (Hebrews 3:7-8) "For when the Gentiles, which have not the law, do by nature the things contained in the law, these, having not the law, are a law unto themselves: [that innate knowledge]." (Romans 2:14) Verse 15, which shows the work of the law written in their hearts, their conscience also bearing them witness, and their thoughts the meanwhile accusing or else excusing one another.

That is the word of God and who can refute it? If you, the reader, are an unbeliever, my guess is that your thoughts are even now accusing or else excusing one another. If you are a believer caught in sin, my guess is the same. And my guess has been educated by the word of God, my own experience, and hearing others speak of their own experiences.

Which brings us to the only answer for that deep inner quest all of us are involved in, that quest for inner peace, that search for perfection, that reaching for immortality, that perpetually dissatisfied sense of something better just beyond our grasp, but yet somehow attainable if only…

But we're not in the garden of Eden anymore and we're not in Paradise yet. So the best we can do is to love the Lord Jesus and look forward to His coming. And that is a glorious hope, which hope we have as an anchor of the soul, both sure and steadfast, and which "enters into that within the veil. Whither the forerunner is for us entered, even Jesus, made a high priest forever after the order of Melchizedek." (Hebrews 6:20) And this Melchizedek, priest of the most high God, was a high priest with a continual priesthood, a priesthood that was given directly from God and not after the order of Aaron, for Aaron was not yet. And in being a continual high priest, he was a forerunner of Jesus Christ who is our continual, abiding, eternal High Priest who offered up His own body as the atonement for our sins, once and for all.

DIVINE RESPONSE

When we consider that God sent His only begotten son into the world to give His life that we might live through Him; When we consider that Jesus, who is "God...manifest in the flesh" (1 Timothy 3:16) allowed Himself to be tempted in all points like as we, yet without sin; When we consider that this war between good and evil is being waged by the Powers of Darkness against Heaven itself; and when we consider that Jesus came from the safety of Heaven to the dangers of earth, then by the grace of God, maybe we can get a small insight into the desperation of this war in the spirit. For it is a desperate war.

Before the beginning of time as we know it, when the devil became dissatisfied with his lesser role in heaven, he burned all his bridges behind him. For he thought to "be like the most High," (Isaiah 14:14) to become a god himself.

Though he resided in a marvelous, awe-inspiring place, and though he was a creature of beauty, yet he did not continue in glorifying God in his lesser role. His heart became lifted up with pride, the created thinking to become the creator, and that he himself was worthy and could glorify himself. Thus he thought to bring glory to himself, but was instead cast out of heaven and all his supporters with him, and his tail drew down a third part of the stars of heaven. (Revelation 12:4)

Is this literal history (about the stars) or is it a metaphorical description of the vast number of angels that he deceived and drew away with him? We believe, and many scholars have believed, it to be the latter.

This all happened before the world was founded, before its foundation was "laid". For Jesus is "the Lamb slain from the foundation of the world" (Revelation 13:8) and what He purposed and promised was as good as done at the instant it was spoken; for He is "the Word of God" and what He says, whether it be past, present or future, is to Him reality. And it has, does, or will become reality to us. What has, does, or needs to become reality to us is the completeness of Redemption brought about by the death of Jesus Christ on the cross of Calvary, which completeness He testified to when He bowed His head just before He "gave up the ghost" and said "It is finished." (John 19:30)

When this Redemption has become a personal reality to us in this life, and remains a personal reality to us in this life, then we expect that it will be a personal saving reality to us in the next life. This is the Promise extended to us from the very throne of God, who testified from Heaven, "This is my beloved Son, in whom I am well pleased." (Matthew 3:17) This is the favor given to us without merit. Just as we cannot regain time and become on time once we've been late, so we cannot change an unrighteous act into a righteous one once the unrighteous act has been committed. The being late picture has value only as a metaphor here, for in relation to their seriousness they are light years apart. Unless of course we are late because of being inconsiderate, selfish with our time, or some such wrong attitude at which point it becomes sin to us.

But what we face here is that since we have sinned and "are by nature the children of wrath", the problem is threefold and will end in the personal tragedy of hell unless repentance is wrought and a remedy found. For without repentance and a remedy for the nature of sin with its natural inclinations against God that resides in us, all of us are potential devils. The threefold problem is this: (1) Our very nature is fallen; not that we loved, but He loved. (2) Without repentance we are potential devils. (3) Sin cannot enter Heaven. Our very nature is fallen; we have a natural inclination against restraints, especially when those restraints seem to be restraining us from the pursuit of happiness. I say "seem to be" for the reason that so often what we think will bring the greatest happiness only does so "for a moment," temporarily, or is exposed by time to be an illusion altogether.

When the founding fathers of this country wrote and signed the Constitution of the United States of America, and declared, among other rules of natural law, that all men, having been created equal, are endowed by their Creator with certain unalienable rights—among them are Life, Liberty and the Pursuit of Happiness—they did so in a society, in a culture, that was being restrained by the bounds of its own conscience. The safest society is not the one with the largest, most capable police force that most effectively prevents crime and punishes the evil doer. While these will be needed at times as long as there are wicked people, the safest society in which to live is a society where the inclination for wrong-doing is restrained by the bounds of one's own conscience having been trained by the Word of God or at least by the acknowledgment and acceptance of what the philosophers Aristotle, Plato, and Cicero referred to as "natural law," a universal code of conduct, knowable and universal among all peoples everywhere. A code of conduct which we believe God has woven into the very fabric of nature itself.

This is the only society in which a democracy "of the people, by the people and for the people" can safely govern and is only possible so long as the general populace is governed by the bounds of their own conscience. When each personal life has an inner restraint. Herein is the battle. Because for this type of inner restraint to be effective for any length of time, there must, of necessity, be a proper response to the pricking of conscience. If not, the conscience will become desensitized, hardened, and eventually be unable or unwilling to distinguish right from wrong. Fear of consequences must then govern the life of such a one and be the restraint to keep him or her within the bounds of acceptable behavior. As John Adams so aptly penned about the Constitution of the United States of America, "This constitution", he wrote, "has been written for a moral and religious people; it is wholly inadequate for the government of any other."

For through the restraint of conscience being active individually and corporately (as a whole, that is) it is deemed safe to give liberties, or rather to acknowledge our God-given liberties to such a people.

Now we acknowledge that not all at the time of our country's founding, and possibly fewer than we might think, had a conscience that was rightly taught and trained by the Word of God. Yet there was a common acknowledgment of accountability to Almighty God and His Word, the Bible, which in turn had an active role in restraining the baser passions of this country's citizens overall and encouraging the noble. And, yes, we could and should also acknowledge that there was much evil, among which was the enslavement of Blacks and the repeated breaking of Indian treaties. These are horrendously dark blots in U.S. history. Yet generations have come and gone, having inherited the blessed privilege to live in a country where freedom is the norm.

What have we done to merit our being born here in the land of opportunity? We couldn't earn the right to be born here before we were born, so the answer is: We came without merit. What can we do to merit being born again into the Kingdom of God? We couldn't earn the right to be born again into the Kingdom of God before being born again, so the answer remains the same, we came without merit.

What, after all, would set us apart for such special favor as to be born into a country that needs to patrol its borders for the purpose of keeping illegals out, while countries with totalitarian regimes patrol their borders to keep their citizens in? Certainly we could not merit the favor of being born here.

And neither could we merit the favor of being born again into the Kingdom of God. The best we can do is to repent of our misdeeds, for when we do right, we are only doing what we should have done in the first place. The favor we experience is therefore unmerited. It cannot be earned. For in neither case could we actively earn it. Just as we cannot earn rain for our crops; for "God sends the rain on the just and on the unjust," (Matthew 5:45) so God showers unmerited favor in many other areas of natural life.

Now some may say that while we cannot earn the privilege of being born in the United States, yet we can and must earn the privilege of remaining a citizen. There is truth in this; and yet, when we become born again into the Kingdom of God, we have an ultimate allegiance to it for its dominion has no boundaries, its King, Jesus, reigns supreme everywhere. "Heaven is my throne," God says, "and the earth is my footstool." (Acts 7:49) This ultimate allegiance to the Kingdom of God, with its ultimate rule of conduct being to love God and to love our neighbor, then produces good, desirable, law-abiding citizens for temporal kingdoms. For the law of Christ teaches all to "Do unto others as ye would have them do unto you," among other rules of conduct that train the conscience and so far transcend the laws enforced by officials as to supersede them with their glory. Unless, of course, there appears a law attempting to transcend and cause to become irrelevant a law or rule of conduct that belongs to the Kingdom of God to whom ultimate allegiance rightly belongs. Author Chuck Colson, in writing of ultimate allegiance in *Kingdoms In Conflict*, so effectively makes the point that when governments fail to uphold just laws, it is the church's responsibility to continue to do so despite all pressure to the contrary and to speak out against tyrannical mistreatment of citizens.

He makes the point that if the churches of Germany had banded together against the Third Reich and its Führer whose "final solution to the Jewish problem" meant the extermination of millions of law-abiding citizens, the Holocaust could not have happened. It was with the churches' support that Hitler came to power, and it was at best, in part, the church's silence that allowed him to perpetrate his diabolical plans upon the Jews and other so-called "undesirables." Some churches did—God bless them—stand up and speak out against what was happening, but they were a minority that was weakened by the lack of support.

In all fairness, Hitler's plan only unfolded with time; still, enough was known to arouse the compassion of those who cared deeply, and to arouse vehement denunciation of, or quiet resistance to Nazism from those who dared, and suffered for it. Among whom were: Dietrich Bonhoeffer, Martin Niemoller, The Edelweiss Pirates, Johann Elser, The White Rose group, the Dutch Ten Boom family, and many Christians across many denominations working tirelessly at the dangerous task of hiding and aiding Jews out of the country. But the indictment remains: If all of Germany who named the name of Christ had non-violently resisted Hitler, his power over the minds of men could have been broken. The indictment of history upon the church at large comes partly through the non-Jewish wives of imprisoned Jewish men who protested the arrest of their husbands until Hitler released them in response to this group of a few hundred women taking to the streets in what the world came to know as the Rosenstrasse Protest.

Nazi Germany is now history. Are we now safe? Have we made it through the storm? Have we safely reached the harbor? No. Before and after World War II there was the rise of communism and the ensuing "Cold War" from the close of the second global conflict into the 80's. There was the Korean war, the Cuban missile crisis, the Vietnam war, and now the threat of terrorism. But what about these leaders of nations? What about these leaders into destruction? What about Marx, Lenin, Trotsky, Hitler, Stalin, and the rest? What about the leaders of ISIS? Can we simply dismiss them all as special nut-cases? Were they born devils?

Or, (frightening thought) were they normal? Were they normal babies and children who resisted restraints? And continued to resist until they were resisting God Himself? What about the multitudes who have believed in and followed them? Were they not manipulated by master manipulators? And manipulation is more emotional than it is factual. Then when emotions become strong enough, facts fade into the "back seat" and emotion "drives." And once driven by emotion, deception is complete for emotion has become the new "fact." So in reality it all is a result of resisting facts, is it not? And in resisting facts, God becomes resisted, for it is God that has woven restraining laws or facts into the very fabric of nature. "Doth not even nature itself teach you" the word of God asks, "that if a man have long hair, it is a shame unto him? But if a woman have long hair, it is a glory to her…" (I Corinthians 11:14-15) It behooves us to ask, then, and to seek the answer, of how does nature itself teach us that it is a shame for a man to have long hair. Why is it, at the same time, a shame to the man and a glory to the woman? The writer will leave this question to the reader as this is not a treatise on long or short hair. But the point is that there are laws in nature itself, some obvious such as gravity, and some not so obvious such as long or short hair, that are or should be restraints upon our actions.

In the law of cause and effect in nature there are amoral and moral restraints against which, if we resist, we suffer the consequences. Was it wrong for Mike and Abner to attempt flying? No, it was amoral, but they still suffered the consequences. Is it wrong for a destitute young widow to lead her young sons into stealing to supply the family larder? While our hearts may well go out to her, morally we have to say yes, it was wrong. And the consequences were devastating as both sons became professional thieves and in later years both were incarcerated, wasting many years in prison.

> Adolf Hitler didn't become the Hitler we know about overnight.
> The man on death row didn't just happen. (Assuming he is guilty)
> The murderer wasn't the result of an innocent walk of life.
> The Columbine shootings weren't the result of innocence.
> The Nickel Mines shootings weren't the result of pure thoughts.
> No, there is a downward progression to sin.
> It begins in the emotions. A wrong thought enters.
> The wrong thought is entertained.
> The wrong thought becomes a wrong pattern of thinking.
> Thought becomes action played out in the mind.
> If not curbed, the thoughts become real actions.

All this time, God, through His written and natural law knocking on the door of our hearts and minds, is continuing His attempt to stop this fleeing from Him through what Mose Stoltzfus has so aptly referred to as "Roadblocks to Hell."[1] (Sermon title) The search for happiness, seeming innocent enough at its outset, has become more and more desperate until others are blamed for being a roadblock to that euphoria, that elusive happiness that seems just beyond reach. Until, in the desperate search for happiness, one restraint after the other, one "roadblock" after the other is broken through, leading ever closer to destruction.

What this means is that we all have the potential of being the second of the threefold problem. That without repentance, we are potential devils. Even to the point of having the same destination. For Revelation 14:9-11 tells us this about those who "worship the beast and his image, and receive his mark in his forehead, or in his hand. The same shall drink of the wine of the wrath of God, which is poured out without mixture into the cup of his indignation; and he shall be tormented with fire and brimstone in the presence of the holy angels, and in the presence of the Lamb: And the smoke of their torment ascendeth up for ever and ever: and they have no rest day

---

1 Available at www.ephrataministries.org

Divine Response

nor night, who worship the beast and his image, and whosoever receiveth the mark of his name."

In Matthew 25:41, "Then shall he say also unto them on the left hand, Depart from me, ye cursed, into everlasting fire, prepared for the devil and his angels." In Revelation 20:10 we are given this scene of the future, to be fulfilled just before the "new heaven and a new earth are established" in verse 21. Verse 10: "And the devil that deceived them was cast into the lake of fire and brimstone, where the beast and the false prophet are, and shall be tormented day and night for ever and ever."

Let us emphasize five points in our hearts and minds.

1. Hell was prepared for the devil and his angels. (Matthew 22:41)
2. Hell is an eternal lake of fire. (Revelation 19:20)
3. Hell's torments are eternal. (Revelation 14:11)
4. The unrighteous will go there. (Revelation 20:15, 21:8)
5. Deliverance from being cast into it was committed to by God, and therefore accomplished, from the "foundation of the world." (Revelation 13:8) Because of the merits of Jesus Christ, for we have none of ourselves. "Not by works of righteousness which we have done, but according to his mercy he saved us, by the washing of regeneration, and renewing of The Holy Ghost." (Titus 3:5)

God's unmerited favor shows itself in everyday life, for He sends rain to the unjust as well as the just, to those who curse Him as well as to those who bless Him. (Matthew 5:45) Yet there is a special unmerited favor, special blessings that He bestows upon those who repent, believe, are baptized, and who love His appearing. To these He gives unmerited eternal life. (Hebrews 8:12) Because of Jesus. (1 Peter 1:3) And to these He gives a special courage. A courage that is in no way earthbound, for God gives the ability to soar with the eagles. "They that wait upon the Lord ... shall mount up with wings as eagles..." (Isaiah 40:31)

As Mike and Abner found in later years, this type of flying is much more uplifting than attempting to fly from the farm shop roof with a homemade set of wings. For these are specially fitted wings, empowered by God Himself and lifting the soul above the earthbound downward pressures of this life. And as the soul is lifted above the daily grind on the updraft of God's love, courage flows in. Courage to face the daily grind.

For the daily grind is temporal. But the wings are eternal.

Herein is unfailing courage.
For true courage flows into us from the refreshing wellspring of God's Grace. His Unmerited Favor
Because of Jesus.

LONGING TO BELONG

I was an eager, young wiggly worm,
I thought to see the world,
There must be more in life to learn,
Then getting fat and being bored.

Surely life is more than eating,
One green leaf after the other.
I'll take off and go sight-seeing,
Till I can't "go it" any further.

So I took off in the starlight,
Just as fast as I could wiggle.
It seemed if I would wait for daylight,
I'd stay stuck with all my struggle.

Well up ahead I saw a wall,
The very top I couldn't see.
T'was very long and very tall,
Keeping the "Great Beyond" from me.

The "something better" that I longed for,
Was blocked before my very eyes.
Then I saw what looked like shimmer,
Was really worms climbing up high.

And every worm was struggling,
Trying so hard to get ahead.
And the better step for climbing,
Was boosting from another's head.

That is extremely rude, I thought,
And joined the climbing struggling throng.
I'll be careful and be polite,
And climb this wall, it won't be long.

Divine Response

I soon discovered as I climbed,
It wasn't easy to be polite.
I got stepped on, pushed around,
I had no choice, I joined the fight.

When I get to the very top,
I'll stop and rest, mend all my ways.
This impoliteness has to stop,
I'll mind my manners all my days.

One day with a Herculean shove,
Yes, it was from another's head.
There was nothing but sky above,
I'd made the top, tho I's half dead.

But something now seemed very wrong,
As I gazed from the highest perch.
For all the struggling seething throng,
Were on a struggling upward search.

Every side was struggling upward,
The other side not going down.
What is up here? now I wondered,
Why aren't there any going down?

"What is up here?" I cried aloud,
Some seemed they'd been here quite some time.
"There's nothing up here!" I now cried,
I hoped for an answer from the wise.

The only answer now forthcoming,
Was from a slick fat wiggly worm.
"Don't talk so loud in other's hearing,"
He said, "n I'll tell you why we form."

"I'll tell you what is really up here,
We are where others want to be.
But you're now here so never fear,
We'll be a team 'n always agree.

UNMERITED FAVOR

I'll teach you what you need to do,
To stay where others want to be.
Be nice but in your heart be rude,
'N bump them off the top, you see."

Is it worth it? Now as I thought,
Remembering the ones I'd hurt,
Repentance in my heart was wrought,
I had been very rude and curt.

I'll go back down where I belong,
And make amends as I go down.
Tho the way looks hard and long,
I'll take that way, it must be done.

So I, a sorry wiggly worm,
Headed down, making amends,
Trying not to squash or harm,
Not to hurt, nor to offend.

I came to the very bottom
One day, and wondered what is next?
Have I to eating leaves been destined?
I was uneasy and still vexed.

The uneasiness within me,
Drove me to form a chrysalis.
All else I tried had left me empty,
I'll be safe and secure in this.

Not understanding what was happening,
In that tight confining space.
I had no way of knowing,
Of the change now taking place.

After many days and many nights,
The chrysalis cracked open.
My wings unfurled in the sunlight,
They spread and lift me to the heavens.

Divine Response

Now as we flutter in the breeze,
And drink sweet nectar from the flower,
We don't hunger for the leaves,
Nor seek for "earthy" power.

Why should we be satisfied with piles,
Of worms, that strive to get above?
When we can fly "with wings as eagles,"[1]
On the updraft of God's love.

Unmerited favor! God is willing,
To metamorphosis all of us.
He is seeking, He is calling,
We can be saved, for Jesus lives!

Gottes sege dazu winscha
(May God add His blessing)

---

1 Isaiah 40:31

*Disclaimer: The poem is meant as a depiction of human struggle and as such does not attempt to perfectly portray the life-cycle that includes the caterpillar. EL

Acknowledgment: This poem is based on memories of a picture book that made a lasting impression on me (though not in poetic form) about 1990. I have not been able to locate the book or the author.

6

LOVE MANIFESTED

Part 1

"IN THIS WAS MANIFESTED the love of God toward us, because that God sent his only begotten Son into the world, that we might live through him. Herein is love, not that we loved God, but that he loved us, and sent his Son to be the propitiation for our sins." (I John 4:9-10)

Love. The word has a mystical yet powerful magnetic pull on all of us, for it strikes a harmonious chord, stirs up our deepest desires, even at times drawing out of dormancy a deep innate need to love and to be loved. Who can deny it? From the sensitive to the most cynical and jaded, this need to love and to feel loved is so much a part of our make-up, of who we are, that we can never be fulfilled and content without it.

But with it? Aah, with it we feel fulfilled, content, and happy. Without it we feel unfulfilled, discontent, unhappy and our very life becomes distasteful. For deep within us, love is what we live for. It alone makes life worth living, even if it is merely a dream sustaining us with a hope for it in the future somewhere.

Many books have been written about love. The best of these books (and the most enduring) about love, the Bible, whose author is called Love, for God is love; helps us to understand and to reach out in love to our spouse, our children, our parents, our neighbors, our friends, our acquaintances, to strangers, and even to our enemies. "Herein is love," we are told in 1 John 4:10, "not that we love God, but that he loved us, and sent his Son to be the propitiation for our sins."

Here is love that reaches out to others, a love that does not seek so much to draw from, to receive from others, as it does to seek how best to give, how best to help make this world a better place and how best to help others to a better place when they leave this world.

"Herein is love" God says in Verse 10, and returning to Verse 9, "In this was manifested the love of God toward us," (and here we have the Biblical definition for love), that God sent—God gave— John 3:16; "For God so loved the world [us], that he gave his only begotten Son, that whosoever believeth in him should not perish, but have everlasting life." And Verse 17; "For God sent not his Son into the world to condemn the world; but that the world through him might be saved."

When God sent His Son into the world, He sent of Himself, for God sent His Word to be "found in fashion as a man."(Philippians 2:8) We have God's word in the Gospel of John that Jesus was actually God incarnate, God manifest in the flesh, for "the Word was made flesh, and dwelt among us, and we beheld His glory." (John 1:14) The Word became flesh. The Word that was in God, was a part of God, and was God from eternity past. He is God now, and He will be in eternity future. In this light, God sent of Himself, and in Jesus the Christ taking on flesh as a man—being found in fashion as a man—He became God incarnate, God manifest in the flesh, God's only begotten Son. It is a good spiritual exercise to study Philippians 2:5-11, John 3:16, and John 1:1-14. Verse 14 says, "And the Word was made flesh, and dwelt among us, (and we beheld his glory, the glory as of the only begotten of the Father,) full of grace and truth."

God put His own life on the line, being made in the likeness of sinful man. (Romans 8:3) He was tempted in all points like as we, yet without sin. In that He was tempted, it follows that the unthinkable became a logical possibility, could God have fallen and sinned? God, whose very nature is true and righteous altogether? God, who is pure and holy? It is a useless conjecture, for God didn't. But it is worthy of consideration, that in allowing Himself to be tempted, God voluntarily made Himself vulnerable. For nothing is tempting unless it appeals in some way, shape, or form to our physical makeup, either directly to the body or indirectly through introduction to our thoughts. He was tempted in all points like as we and we can hardly help but have thoughts of what if…? We've been assured that he was "yet without sin," but it is good for us to consider that He allowed Himself to be born into that vulnerable position of being tempted because He loved us and intensely desired our salvation, so much so that He calls the redemption of His children "the joy that was set before him." (Hebrews 12:2)

Again, I John 4:10; "Herein is love, not that we loved God, but that he loved us..." Here is the defining characteristic of Godly love, that God didn't wait till we loved Him, there was no testing of the waters, no attempt to search out what the response might be, just a giving, an offering up of Himself, without reserve, no holding back for "freely ye have received, freely give," we are instructed in Matthew 10:8. The only reserve or holding back was in relation to sin; for in relation to us and our salvation, God, through Jesus Christ, gave our redemption His all. Herein is love.

"In this was manifested the love of God toward us, because that God sent his only begotten Son into the world, that we might live through him." (I John 4:9) The literal definition of the word Gospel is "good news" and the good news is that God loves you personally. God loves us corporately. God, in fact, loves the whole world. "For God so loved the world, that he gave his only begotten Son, that whosoever believeth in him should not perish, but have everlasting life." (John 3:16)

In the fall of 2011, I fell 22 feet from a house roof, of which I have no recollection, but so I am told, and was in a coma for three weeks. I'm also told that a church brother found me lying on the ground in an almost fetal position on my left side. While in a coma I saw myself, or my body, lying in an almost fetal position on my left side with my head at the threshold of an open door. Back in my body, as I lay on my side and gazed through the door, all I could see was blue sky and light. Light brighter than the sun, but though it was so very bright, the light didn't hurt my eyes and I could take in the blue beauty and bright light without any discomfort. Somehow, I knew that beyond this door was eternity and that I was about to go through and into eternity to be with Jesus. The comforting presence of Jesus was so glorious in me and around me that I seemed already to be transported into heaven itself. I was overwhelmed with a sense of safety, of security, a safety and security made all the more overwhelming by the knowledge that it was now always going to be this way, for it was eternal.

The combination of being safe, secure, and that this was the way it was going to be now, never changing, eternal, caused such an overwhelming peace and comfort to rest upon me that my mind has searched the English language for fitting words to describe it and cannot find them. The closest I can come to describing it is this: try to imagine yourself in the most peaceful, safe, secure, and restful place that you can ever remember being in, possibly in childhood, and then add to your imagination that the sense of peace, safety, and security in this restful beautiful place is now an unchanging reality that will always be this way, for it is eternal, it will never change.

That doesn't fully do justice to the experience of it, but it is as close as I've been able to come to its description. The sense of peace, security, and beauty—all in the presence of Jesus—was at the same time so fulfilling and so exhilarating that if this were all that Heaven consists of, one could have an eternity of just lying on one's side and yet be perfectly content and happy. And yet (O glorious thought) Heaven is so much more.

It seems very possible to my finite mind that the confusion of languages caused at the tower of Babel was the result of a perfect universal language being divided into segments which the Bible refers to as tongues and from which all languages spring. If this is so, then possibly, if we could be fluent in this perfect universal language then we could also possibly describe the depth of the mercy and love of God, and the beauty of Heaven. It seems very possible that this universal language will be restructured back together and then be The Language of Heaven. Otherwise, we can only describe all this in bits and pieces. Which reminds me of an experience I had soon after being converted and experiencing the combination of God's acceptance and love for the first time. God's love was such a treasure to me that I wanted more. And more. And more.

One evening, kneeling by my bedside and again asking God for more, a deeper experience of His love, the inner longing of my heart expressed itself by asking for such a fulness of His love that it would be as if I was in Heaven itself experiencing the completeness and fulness of His love. Impressed upon my heart and mind then were these words, which I believe were from God, that "no one can experience such a complete fulness of God's love and live." It cannot be contained by this mortal body. Though we are given the reality of it in part upon being converted, we cannot contain the complete fulness of God's love until our bodies take on immortality.

As God said to Moses when Moses requested to see God's face, "Thou canst not see my face ... and live." (Exodus 33:20) After which He still responded to the request of Moses by allowing him a partial view of God. Moses was not able to stand face to face with God, but God did allow him, because of his request, to see God from behind. And even so, the face of Moses when he came down from the mount shone so brightly, was so radiant, that in order to speak to the people he needed to cover his face with a veil.

And so it is. If any mortal man should be able to see God's face and live, surely Moses, whom God's word refers to as the meekest man in all the earth, would be that man, would have the qualifying credentials. This man, Moses, who was God's instrument to confront Pharaoh, likely the most powerful man on earth at the time, with a request that became a command; to liberate, to let go, a free labor workforce of 600,000 men besides women and children. In one day. Not slowly adjusting and getting used to the idea. No. In one day.

The request, which became a command, must have seemed preposterous to this powerful man, as evidenced by his stubborn refusal and wavering even as the miserable plagues came and went. Until at last the death angel came to Egypt and all the firstborn of man and beast died, except those of the Israelites, which he passed over because of the blood of lambs painted on the doorposts and lintels of each house. After which the Israelites were not only let go, they were thrust out, their departure urged on by the Egyptians. This man, Moses, who was God's instrument at the crossing of the Red Sea and God's instrument in the waters of the Red Sea closing in upon and drowning the entire fleet of horses and charioteers in Pharaoh's army that he had sent after the Israelite slaves to bring them back. This man Moses, whom God verbally communicated with, not even he could see God's face and live.

The fullness of God's glory and love, for He is Love, cannot be experienced by mortal man. But we are given the earnest of the inheritance (down-payment) upon repentance, a down-payment revealed to us by His Spirit. As it is written, "Eye hath not seen, nor ear heard, neither have entered into the heart of man, the things which God hath prepared for them that love him." (I Corinthians 2:9)

But God; (and here is one time that the word "but", in changing the emphasis, progresses on from a reticent thought to one bursting with glory); "But God hath revealed them unto us by his Spirit: for the Spirit searcheth all things, yea, the deep things of God." (I Corinthians 2:10)

For God speaks to us in these last days by His Son, whom God through John calls "the Word." (John 1) "God, who at sundry times and in diverse manners spake in time past unto the fathers by the prophets, Hath in these last days spoken unto us by his Son, whom he hath appointed heir of all things, by whom also he made the worlds; Who being the brightness of his glory, and the express image of his person, and upholding all things by the word of his power, when he had by himself purged our sins, sat down

Divine Response

on the right hand of the Majesty on high; Being made so much better than the angels, as he hath by inheritance obtained a more excellent name than they." (Hebrews 1:1-4) God has spoken by His Son.

Better things than that of Abel, whose blood cried to God from the ground. (Genesis 4:10) God said to Cain after that guilty young man denied knowing anything of his brother's whereabouts even though he had just killed him; "What hast thou done? The voice of thy brother's blood crieth unto me from the ground. And now art thou cursed from the earth, which hath opened her mouth to receive thy brother's blood from thy hand; When thou tillest the ground, it shall not henceforth yield unto thee her strength; a fugitive and a vagabond shalt thou be in the earth." (Genesis 4:10-12)

What was the cry of Abel's blood that assailed the ears of God? God's testimony of Abel's blood wasn't that it whispered, nor even that it merely talked or asked any question; no, it "crieth unto me from the ground." It assailed the ears of a just, righteous, and holy God and did not, could not, miss getting His attention because He is just, righteous, and holy. As the shedding of innocent blood always gets God's attention. As does even the touching of innocence in a wrong way. He says of His forgiven and sanctified children, "For he that toucheth you toucheth the apple of his eye." (Zechariah 2:8) God loves His children.

And He who says "vengeance is mine, I will repay" will respond. Though we may think it is taking too long and respond as if God needs help, we are always best off leaving our personal hurts with Him, committing them to Him, and then leaving them there. With Jesus, who "washed us from our sins in his own blood." (Revelation 1:5) And if the package of personal hurt that we lift up to Him in prayer is a black, oozing mass of bitterness, He receives it as if it were a precious gift; for this, our sins, is what He gave His life for. Because of our sins He died for us in our stead and then rose again for our justification. (Romans 4:25) And He cleanses us from it.

But with that may we also allow the humbling searchlight of God's Word to search out the dimmer, less noticeable nooks and crannies of our hearts and minds to inquire whether our personal hurts may just be a reaction against the Truth of God spoken at what we consider an inopportune time. There is a right and a wrong time for everything, but truth is still truth, and perhaps if we were to more readily accept the truth as it is spoken, there would be more stability and less emotional trauma. And less of being "driven with the wind and tossed." (James 1:6)

LOVE MANIFESTED

While there are legitimate and heart-wrenching cases of actual emotional trauma, it is this writer's finite observation that in an affluent society the expectations from life tend to rise until the desperate attempt, (made all the more desperate by its impossibility) to regain the Garden of Eden is, in itself, traumatizing.

This is not meant to down-play or to minimize the actual presence of emotional trauma, but rather to point us to Christ and the Cross, "who for the joy that was set before him endured the cross, despising the shame, and is set down at the right hand of the throne of God. For consider him that endured such contradiction of sinners against himself, lest ye be wearied and faint in your minds. Ye have not yet resisted unto blood, striving against sin." (Hebrews 12:2-4)

"Lest ye be wearied and faint in your minds" sounds like "emotional trauma," doesn't it? Wearied and faint sounds like it is getting weak and flabby, doesn't it? But a spiritual mind gets stronger with exercise and we are called upon to have our "senses exercised to discern both good and evil." (Hebrews 5:14) And in keeping our senses exercised, God, in His wisdom and His great love does not leave us directionless, but gives us this instruction that is very applicable in everyday life, for He even tells us how to think: "Finally, brethren, whatsoever things are true, whatsoever things are honest, whatsoever things are just, whatsoever things are pure, whatsoever things are lovely, whatsoever things are of good report; if there be any virtue, and if there be any praise, think on these things." (Philippians 4:8)

I've found it to be a very good exercise to think on these things individually, beginning with true, although I confess I've gotten hung up on "true" when what has caused me pain, is still in essence, true. But it is good to work through those unpleasant memories, also committing them to the Lord and laying them down. Then move on, for negative thoughts stagnate the mind when puddled in one spot. Think on those things that are true, honest, just, pure, lovely, of good report, and the virtuous and praiseworthy, with virtue coming from God who is worthy of our praise, our adoration, our reverence, and our fear. The right kind of fear, the kind that in reverence yields to His majesty, not the kind that tries to avoid Him and escape from His presence. For we speak here of reverence and Godly fear that submits and draws nigh, only to be forgiven and received even as the prodigal son was received by his father when he finally gave up and came home. (Luke 15) For God loves. His heart yearns after our salvation. "Like as a father pitieth his children, so the LORD pitieth them that fear Him." (Psalms 103:13)

But the fearful (those who avoid Him), will be lost with all that are ungodly still. "But the fearful and unbelieving, and the abominable, and murderers, and whoremongers, and sorcerers, and idolaters, and all liars, shall have their part in the lake which burneth with fire and brimstone: which is the second death." (Revelation 21:8)

These are the fearful that couldn't find God for the same reason that a thief can't find a policeman. If these fearful would only draw nigh to God (turn themselves in) instead of flee from Him in abject fear, they would discover a God of Love who would draw them into His comforting presence "as a hen gathereth her chickens ... and ye would not," Jesus said. (Matthew 23:37) Will you be one who "would not" or one of those who draw nigh and discover that those who come to Him, He "will in no wise cast out." (John 6:37)

ALWAYS READY

Finally brethren,
Whatsoever things are true,
Whatsoever things are honest,
Whatsoever things are just,
Whatsoever things are pure,
Whatsoever things are lovely,
Whatsoever things are of good report,
If there be any virtue,
And if there be any praise,
Think on these things. (Philippians 4:8)

Press on beloved,
Truth is not always pleasant,
Honest people not always loved
 Still be yet upright and just,
Because we never can know,
Just how close is the searching soul,
To reaching the goal within Heaven's gate,
Where truth will shine unhindered,
The atmosphere always pure,
Always Lovely.

LOVE MANIFESTED

Press on beloved,
Think on things of good report,
Good things also need reported,
To encourage the upright,
Because we never can know,
Just how close the faltering soul,
Though brave, has eyes that waver from the goal,
With virtue wants sights reset,
To praise Jesus afresh, be,
Always Ready.

Finally brethren,
Whatsoever things are true,
Whatsoever things are honest,
Whatsoever things are just,
Whatsoever things are pure,
Whatsoever things are lovely,
Whatsoever things are of good report,
If there be any virtue,
And if there be any praise,
Think on these things. (Philippians 4:8)

7

LOVE MANIFESTED

Part 2

God loves us. He "so loved the world, that he gave his only begotten Son, that whosoever believeth in him should not perish, but have everlasting life." (John 3:16) God shows His love for us in manifold ways. By the affirming Word of His Son, and in many ways through his actions. The following is a list of seven ways that God shows His love to us. There may be more that should or could be added to the list but these are seven (with no claim of being exhaustive), that can be clearly seen in God's word.

1. By sending His Son
2. By touching lives
3. Giving quality time
4. Love "in word" and deed
5. Chastisement
6. The Ultimate gift
7. Forgiveness and release

1. **By sending His Son**. Again, "For God so loved the world, that he gave his only begotten Son, that whosoever believeth in him should not perish, but have everlasting life." (John 3:16) God expressed His love to us by causing a virgin, whose name was Mary, to conceive. "When as

his mother Mary was espoused to Joseph, before they came together, she was found with child of the Holy Ghost." (Matthew 1:18)

In the Gospel according to Luke in Chapter 1, God gives a more detailed account of how it happened that "she was found with child," which is an elegant way of saying that "she is pregnant," (as we would say it less elegantly). Beginning in Luke Chapter 1, verse 26, "And in the sixth month the angel Gabriel was sent from God unto a city of Galilee, named Nazareth, To a virgin espoused to a man whose name was, Joseph of the house of David; and the virgin's name was Mary. And the angel came in unto her, and said, Hail, thou that art highly favored, the Lord is with thee: blessed art thou among women. And when she saw him, she was troubled at his saying, and cast in her mind what manner of salutation this should be. And the angel said unto her, Fear not, Mary: for thou hast found favour with God. And, behold, thou shalt conceive in thy womb, and bring forth a son, and shalt call his name JESUS. He shall be great, and shall be called the Son of the Highest: and the Lord God shall give unto him the throne of his father David: And he shall reign over the house of Jacob for ever; and of his kingdom there shall be no end."

Then said Mary unto the angel, How shall this be, seeing I know not a man? And the angel answered and said unto her, The Holy Ghost shall come upon thee, and the power of the Highest shall overshadow thee: therefore also that holy thing which shall be born of thee shall be called the Son of God. And, behold, thy cousin Elisabeth, she hath also conceived a son in her old age: and this is the sixth month with her, who was called barren. For with God nothing shall be impossible. And Mary said, Behold the handmaid of the Lord; be it unto me according to thy word. And the angel departed from her." (Luke 1:26-38)

Jesus could have come the first time the way God tells us, through John's Revelation, that he will come when He comes again. "And I saw heaven opened, and behold a white horse; and he that sat upon him was called Faithful and True, and in righteousness he doth judge and make war." (Revelation 19:11)

But no, this baby, born and dependent like all other babies, physically vulnerable like the rest of us, was a most adequate and descriptive expression of God's love to mankind. And it has been a very effective expression, as this stable scene of Joseph standing next to Mary sitting next to baby Jesus lying on hay in a manger, and the cow, the donkey and the sheep standing at attention with the shepherds and wise men kneeling and the star of the east shining overhead, has become synonymous with Christianity everywhere.

This scene has become so fixed in the minds of people in places known and unknown, as a visible expression of Christianity, that it has even aroused resistance from the Unbelievers who want this peaceful Christmas scene outlawed from the public square.

And replaced with what? Santa Claus? Reindeer? Of course, because Santa Claus landing on housetops in a sleigh drawn by reindeer is obvious fiction that makes no claims on anyone's life beyond being good enough to receive candy rather than coal chunks.

It is this writer's finite opinion that this is why there are those who desperately use Alexa, Darwin, and whatever other means available to try pinning the label of "fictional" on Jesus Christ, for His claims of divinity make demands on a person's life that infringe upon the so-called freedom to do as we please. Is this also why many ignore Him as if He were, "fictional"?

Santa Claus makes no real demands on anyone's life for he is a jolly old fellow, and if, by some far-off stretch of the imagination, some coal chunks do show up, well, he is a fictional character. At least when he ceases to be jolly.

Not so with Jesus Christ, who was sent from Heaven for the redemption of mankind and in so doing infallibly indicted all of being guilty and in need of redemption. (II Corinthians 5:14) And proved His divinity with many miracles, including multiplying loaves and fishes, healing the sick, even raising the dead; and finally culminating it all by rising from the dead Himself, leaving behind an empty tomb. For He had died for all, even for the wicked who had slain Him. But all need to repent. For all of us are guilty. All of us were the cause of His death. Because all of us need Him. Desperately. Maybe more so than we even know. But upon repentance we gain a measure of insight into the desperation of our situation. And upon believing and repentance we receive a more sure word, than any outward sign, that He lives! For, "we have also a more sure word of prophecy ... as unto a light that shineth in a dark place, until the day dawn, and the day star arise in your hearts." (II Peter 1:19)

For the Holy Spirit of God has come bearing "witness with our spirit, that we are the children of God." (Romans 8:16) As Jesus said to

LOVE MANIFESTED

His disciples just before His departure, when He was yet physically with them. "Until the day in which he was taken up, after that he through the Holy Ghost had given commandments unto the apostles whom he had chosen: To whom also he shewed himself alive after his passion by many infallible proofs, being seen of them forty days, and speaking of the things pertaining to the kingdom of God:

And, being assembled together with them, commanded them that they should not depart from Jerusalem, but wait for the promise of the Father, which, saith he, ye have heard of me. For John truly baptized with water; but ye shall be baptized with the Holy Ghost not many days hence." (Acts 1:2-5)

This "Christ in you, the hope of glory," (Colossians 1:27) is His calling for all of us, as God's word tells us in Romans 8:9-11, "But ye are not in the flesh, but in the Spirit, if so be that the Spirit of God dwell in you. Now if any man have not the Spirit of Christ, he is none of his. And if Christ be in you ... he that raised up Christ from the dead shall also quicken your mortal bodies by his Spirit that dwelleth in you."

This is God manifesting His love by sending His son. He sent His Son physically and then sent His Holy Spirit to dwell in our hearts by faith. "Herein is love, not that we loved God, but that he loved us, and sent his Son ..."(I John 4:10) God manifested His love by sending His son.

2. **By touching lives**. Both physically while He was physically here and now spiritually through His Holy Spirit. Some he "took by the hand" as He did the daughter of Jairus, who had died. Jairus was a ruler of the synagogue who besought Jesus to come to his house, for his twelve year old only daughter was deathly sick. But it took so long to get there because of the many other needs pressing in on every side that even before they arrived at Jairus' house, they received the news that there was no more need to trouble the Master, for she was already dead. She was so dead that when Jesus did arrive at the house the people laughed Him to scorn when He told them she was asleep and not dead. (But He knew that she would rise.) And then He touched her, taking her by the hand, "and called, saying, Maid arise. And her spirit came again, and she arose straightway." (Luke 8:54-55)

Some He touched in other ways, as the blind man, whose eyes he anointed with clay that He had moistened with His spittle and then had him "Go, wash in the pool of Siloam (which is by interpretation, Sent.) He went his way therefore, and washed, and came seeing." (John 9:7)

This was one of the healings that Jesus did on the Sabbath day and the Pharisees of that place stepped across the line into a place they could not readily back out of without losing authority, so they pressed on, demanding an explanation from the healed man for this healing done on the Sabbath, unknowingly attempting to confuse him with their own confusion. But the man stayed on track and came clear of their confusion, when in response to the Jews declaring that they know that God spoke to Moses, but they don't know where this fellow is from. "The man answered and said unto them, Why herein is a marvelous thing, that ye know not from whence he is, and yet he hath opened mine eyes. Now we know that God heareth not sinners: but if any man be a worshipper of God and doeth his will, him he heareth. Since the world began was it not heard that any man opened the eyes of one that was born blind." (John 9:30-32)

And so they cast Him out of the synagogue. And then there were those whom Jesus didn't physically touch, but yet were healed by His virtue when they reached out to Him in faith only to touch the hem of His garment, as the woman whose twelve year long issue of blood dried up "and she felt in her body that she was healed of that plague." (Mark 5:29)

His fame spread and when He came into the land of Gennesaret, it had preceded Him. "And when the men of that place had knowledge of him, they sent out into all that country round about, and brought unto him all that were diseased; And besought him that they might only touch the hem of his garment: and as many as touched were made perfectly whole." (Matthew 14:35-36) A father came to Jesus with his son who had a dumb spirit that caused him to tear, to foam, to gnash with his teeth, and to pine away; and Jesus "rebuked the foul spirit, saying unto him, Thou dumb and deaf spirit, I charge thee, come out of him ... And the spirit cried, and rent him sore, and came out of him: and he was as one dead; insomuch that many said, He is dead. But Jesus took him by the hand, and lifted him up; and he arose." (Mark 9:25-27)

Perhaps we do not always understand why Jesus reached out and took some by the hand, others He anointed eyes with mud, others reached out to Him, having faith in His healing power. But this much is clear; that wherever and whenever that connection was made, the result was life and healing. He was the embodiment of life and healing. So much so that when the hem of His garment was touched, He felt virtue flowing out of Him to the recipient.

And dare we say that even greater miracles than these have been happening these past 2,000 years? I believe we may, because the physical healings were only for a time. Those who were healed, even those who were raised from the dead, have long ago deceased, their bodies have gone back to the dust from whence they came. And we have overwhelming evidence that 100 percent of us are not here to stay. Our bodies also will return to the dust from whence they came. Unless the last day comes first.

But what if Someone held out His hand and took the hand of a spiritually dead loved one we've been grieving over? And the dead loved one arose? Or, what if we, and our loved ones, received the healing touch of His love? Is not this spiritual life and healing, by one whom we can sense but not see, a greater miracle than the physical? Yes, physical healings are miraculous and were given for a sign, but it is the spiritual and emotional healing that has kept the Church of Jesus Christ not only alive, but fairly bursting with revival energy. Even as Old Faithful geyser of Yellowstone National Park cannot be capped and contained, so the flow of love from Jesus Christ through the church cannot be stopped.

And it is this Love that has been the sustaining power of God's people, the keeping power of His Word, and the drawing power for the lost and unbelieving. "In this was manifested the love of God toward us, because that God sent his only begotten Son into the world, that we might live through him." (I John 4:9) God manifests His love by touching lives.

3. **Giving quality time.** On our knees, sitting up, standing, taking a walk, driving, working or playing, when we have time for God, He has time for us. However, some postures and situations are more conducive to prayer and communication than others, to which we need to give heed if we wish to have God hear us and we hear from God. A kneeling or prostrate posture is befitting the sorrowing sinner and the seeking soul. Thankfulness and praise are fittingly expressed in many positions, providing the position is reverent, for reverence is befitting us needy ones before the One who is holy, Omnipotent, Omniscient, and Omnipresent. And in times of extreme distress, any position is

Divine Response

acceptable to Him for He hears the heart-cry of one who is drowning, the coal-miner trapped in the mine, the Marine trapped in a submarine, the accident victim trapped in the wreckage, or the victim of any other tragedy heard or unheard of.

Nowhere in God's word is there any indication that God gets tired of us and our prayers. Provided communication with Him is sincere, honest, upright, and free of hypocrisy. And in times of extreme distress, we are more likely than not to be sincere, honest, upright, and free of hypocrisy.

The story is told of two men fishing from their rowboat as it drifted on the current of the Niagara River. So engrossed were they in catching fish that they drifted too close to the familiar roaring of the falls as the river tumbled off its precipice into the rocky, foaming river hundreds of feet below. By the time they raised their heads in awareness of their danger, the situation was desperate. All their strength was thrown into the oars and their desperate cries ascended to Heaven as the relentless tug of the river pulling toward the falls seemed as if it might well overcome the two men's strength and stamina, plunging them to sure death far below.

They made it to shore.

As they lay on the shore getting their breath and strength back and their wits together, the Christian was thanking God when he thought of something. "I thought you don't believe in God," he said, addressing his atheist companion, "but your cries to God were just as loud as mine out there."

"Aye," quoth the atheist, "atheism is only good for calm waters." It is our hope and belief that this man was nevermore an atheist. In this writer's opinion, and I believe supported by the word of God, there are no true atheists, for deep down in our heart of hearts—perhaps suppressed but nonetheless there—is the sense of a Supreme Being who inhabits eternity. "For the invisible things of him from the creation of the world are clearly seen, being understood by the things that are made, even his eternal power and Godhead." (Romans 1:20) God inhabits eternity and as He inhabits eternity, He has a clear, unhindered perspective of reality. And He continually endeavors to draw us to reality with Him. A reality very possibly initially painful; but as we persevere, we discover that time spent with Him is of the highest quality, for His love provides us with quality time. God manifests His love by giving us quality time.

4. **Love in word and deed**. "God, who at sundry times and in divers manners spake in time past unto the fathers by the prophets, Hath in these last days spoken unto us by his Son, whom he hath appointed heir of all things, by whom also he made the worlds." (Hebrews 1:1-2) For Jesus is God's word, His final word, to us. "How shall we escape, if we neglect so great salvation?" (Hebrews 2:3) For He was in God, was the essence of God, from eternity past. And being in God, being the Word of God, it was He who spoke the world into existence, "and it was so," by the power of Almighty God.

"In the beginning," God says through the Apostle John, "was the Word, and the Word was with God, and the Word was God. The same was in the beginning with God. All things were made by him; and without him was not any thing made that was made. In him was life; and the life was the light of men. And the light shineth in darkness; and the darkness comprehended it not. There was a man sent from God, whose name was John. The same came for a witness, to bear witness of the Light, that all men through him might believe. He was not that Light, but was sent, to bear witness of that Light. That was the true Light which lighteth every man that cometh into the world." (John 1:1-9)

Jesus Christ is God's word, and as such He is the expression of God's love, the expression of God's will, and ultimately, the expression of God's judgment. One's mind naturally recoils at the thought of God's final judgment and we may grapple at times to understand why God created the world only to judge so many to be lost. But we do well to consider that in the presence of God's perfect love and His perfect will there must also be a perfect judgment, and that we can trust His perfect understanding to judge perfectly. He makes no mistakes and he will judge righteous judgment.

God asks that we trust Him. Our understanding is limited.

God's understanding is unlimited.

Why does God limit our understanding when His is unlimited? "For now we see through a glass, darkly; but then face to face: now I know in part; but then shall I know even as also I am known." (I Corinthians 13:12) Might it be so we learn to trust Him and not our own understanding? "Trust in the Lord with all thine heart; and lean not on thine own understanding. In all thy ways acknowledge him, and he shall direct thy paths." (Proverbs 3:5-6) Waiting to trust God until

Divine Response

we understand everything is to live in the vacuum of dichotomy for we cannot have both; we either trust one or the other. To trust one's self is natural, to trust God is a choice. And to trust God is to trust His Word. Both the written and the Living Word of whom the written Word testifies. The Living Word and the written Word always agree.

They are never in conflict, and if ever they seem to be, we need to allow our understanding to be called into question, never God's Word, for it will stand forever. (I Peter 1:25)

To trust God and His Word is a choice, yes, but we are motivated by evidence. There is much evidence that God's Word is supernatural. There is no other explanation, for instance, for prophecies of Christ being fulfilled in such minute detail. Even if the entire Jewish nation had collaborated to bring them to pass, there are so many prophecies that in fulfilling them they brought condemnation upon themselves. One wonders at the ignorance of those trusting in their own understanding and interpretation of the Scriptures.

The disciples themselves floundered in their understanding of the teachings of Jesus until the Living Word, through the Holy Spirit, descended upon them in cloven tongues like as of fire and the prophetic words of Jesus were fulfilled as recorded by John: "But the Comforter, which is the Holy Ghost, whom the Father will send in my name, he will teach you all things, and bring all things to your remembrance, whatsoever I have said unto you." (John 14:26)

As He had said before, "In the last day, that great day of the feast, Jesus stood and cried, saying, If any man thirst, let him come onto me, and drink. He that believeth on me, as the scripture hath said, out of his belly shall flow rivers of living water." (John 7:37-38) And verse 39 "(But this spake he of the Spirit, which they that believe on him should receive: for the Holy Ghost was not yet given; because that Jesus was not yet glorified.)"

If the Jews, who studied the prophets and Old Testament law misunderstood, which they did; and the disciples themselves floundered in their understanding as they did; then it is reasonable to believe that we also need more than our natural understanding. We need the Holy Spirit, the Living Word, to impress the Truth upon our hearts and minds. "But the natural man receiveth not the things of the Spirit of God: for they are foolishness unto him: neither can he know them, because they are spiritually discerned." (I Corinthians 2:14)

LOVE MANIFESTED

While it is true that much of the Word of God is simple enough for a child to understand, yet it is also true that for any in-depth study of the Word, the illumination of the Holy Spirit is a must. As also is the coming to Christ, as He himself said, "No man can come to me, except the Father ... draw Him." (John 6:44) For Jesus Christ is the Living Word. He is God expressing His love to mankind. He is God expressing His redemption to mankind. God expressing His love to us through Jesus coming from the glorious perfection of Heaven to this sin-cursed earth. Ministering to the lost by showing the way, ministering to the groping by showing the Truth, and to the hopeless by showing the Life.

And are we not all lost, groping and hopeless without Christ? But with Him? Aaah, with Him we know the way for He gives direction. With Him we have stability and know the Truth that sets us free. With Him we have Life as fellowship with Him is restored. He is the Way, the Truth, and the Life. No man comes unto the Father but by Him. He expresses His love to us through His Holy Spirit. For not only does He, through the Spirit, warn us of impending doom, but upon repentance, He through His Spirit gives us the witness of His acceptance and love, bringing quietness and reverence. Beginning in the deep recesses of the soul and continuing in accord with surrender to such a degree that the soul becomes full and love spills out onto others. "Out of his belly," Jesus said, "shall flow rivers of living water." (John 7:38) "My cup runneth over," the Psalmist testified in the 23rd Psalm.

This love is reciprocal for as we repent, we are, in reality, loving God more than ourselves. And as we love God more than ourselves, He responds with His love for us, which in reality, was there all along; only His love was convicting, so it didn't feel like love, for God hates sin, and those who love sin more than God will eventually experience the horror of the wrath of Almighty God. But now, upon repentance, God's love flows through us, witnessed to by His Spirit. "In this was manifested the Love of God toward us, because that God sent..." God loves in word and deed.

5. **Chastisement**. Chastisement, by its very definition, does not feel good. The Bible does not uphold the post-modern day idea that "if it's right it will make me feel good."

As a youngster I did get a number of spankings. I knew that if I pulled and tried to get away, it would not go well with me so I endured the pain, resisting the strong urge to escape and run. There was no escaping anyhow, so I squirmed and cried, hoping that each stinging pain to my rear was the last. It never occurred to me to thank my Dad for loving me while I was receiving the spanking; and even if I had, the pain of being spanked would have hindered coherency.

Did I feel loved? No. Was I being loved? In hindsight (no pun intended), yes. How do I know I was being loved? There are two reasons that I know I was being loved: one, because of God's word, "He that spareth his rod hateth his son: but he that loveth him chasteneth him betimes." (Proverbs 13:24) Parents chastening their children with a heart of love for them also receive their instruction from Deuteronomy 6:7, Proverbs 22:6, Ephesians 6:4, I Timothy 3:4, Titus 2:4, Proverbs 13:24, Proverbs 19:18, Proverbs 22:15, and Proverbs 23:13. Love is to be the motivation for disciplining our children which means that we need to discipline ourselves into disciplining our children when it is needed and we don't feel like doing it. If we don't discipline until we feel like it, our motivation has likely degenerated from love to indignation, or even outright anger, and becomes only consistent with our undulating feelings. There is no substitute for Godly instruction, correction, and discipline.

The second reason I know I was being loved is because of the resulting discipline it eventually brought into my life. Like God, my parents had long-range goals in mind. God is not short-sighted, and neither should we be. Rather considering each decision with eternity and our safe arrival there, in mind. And the safe arrival of our children. And our "children's children ... the crown of old men." (Proverbs 17:6)

Being chastened never feels loving, but there may well be those times, when in the midst of chastisement, the eyes of our understanding being enlightened, we see and understand the eternal purposes God has in the hardship He allows. God doesn't create hardships for us, but He allows them to come upon us with an eternal purpose in mind that He Himself best understands; and He will help us to understand to the degree that He sees will be the most benefit to us as we open our hearts and minds to Him. As we open our hearts and minds to Him, He may well help us to understand why He allows those hard times that He allows. Where would I be if it weren't for the hard times? Where would you be?

The exhortation about chastening in Hebrews Chapter 12 is a direct exhortation to me, and indeed, to every one of His children when He says, "My son, despise not thou the chastening of the Lord, nor faint when thou art rebuked of him: For whom the Lord loveth he chasteneth, and scourgeth every son whom he receiveth. If ye endure chastening, God dealeth with you as with sons; for what son is he whom the father chasteneth not?" A question, but then He answers the question: "But if ye be without chastisement, whereof all are partakers, then are ye bastards, and not sons." (Hebrews 12:5-8)

If you are a parent, I hope you have had the experience of having a child relax on your lap after being lovingly disciplined. I have. And have also experienced when my child kept resisting and rejecting discipline when I knew the discipline to be in the child's best interest. We can receive a lesson from God in this, because He never gives up on us, unless we give up on Him. In allowing us the free exercise of our will, God has limited Himself. In His decision not to use force, God has voluntarily taken the position of needing to draw us to Himself by His Love. Love is that gentle whisper of peace in the midst of beautiful flowers; it is the gentle whisper of peace on the mountaintop, in the sunshine of a beautiful day, in the beautiful sights and sounds of nature; Love whispers peace.

Love is also the gentle whisper of peace when the flowers are trampled, when in the valley of the shadow of death, when the day is dreary and cold, when the beauty of nature gives way to blood-thirsty lions, when our lives seem as dartboards; Love whispers peace. And when we are chastened, Love whispers peace. But our ears must be open to His voice. He speaks to us in His Word, the Holy Bible, and illuminates it to us by His Holy Spirit.

When understanding comes concerning something in our life that needs correction, we must needs receive it; this is God's way of chastening His children and resisting only brings more chastening and turmoil. A yielding surrender brings the gentle whisper of peace as the Blood of Jesus heals the need.

As God explains to us through the writer to the Hebrews, "Now no chastening for the present seemeth to be joyous, but grievous: nevertheless afterward it yieldeth the peaceable fruit of righteousness unto them which are exercised thereby." (Hebrews 12:11) God is loving us when He gives instruction. He is also loving us when He corrects and chastens.

6. The Ultimate Gift. What can a man give more than his life? (John 15:13) Many a man has given that ultimate gift, his very life, for the sake of his country. Fighting for the ideals of his country, he faces the rigors and hardships of war for the sake of The Cause. The Cause may or may not have become his own ideal, but in the midst of the battle, The Cause becomes less important than simply survival. Machine guns chatter, tank tracks clatter as shrapnel blasts from the massive barrels, droning aircraft drop bombs that explode upon impact or in the air; but all the explosions, the blasting, and the shooting, pale and fade away in comparison of importance as we consider the flesh and blood of men struggling for survival amidst all the mayhem. And the bloodshed. As blood of the formerly most physically fit and healthiest of the Nation's young men seeps into, and stains, the soil upon which they fall; lives, occupations, skills, and careers drain away with it. Perhaps this one was a young family man who has now left a beautiful young wife and little ones. Perhaps the one over here has left a girlfriend who is now left to deal with the loss of the one she has learned to love. Perhaps another has left behind a family of loving parents and siblings. Multitudes of lives have been wasted as men fall on the battlefield or are shot out of the sky or sink to the ocean floor.

But wait. As these men give the ultimate sacrifice, their lives, do we really call those lives wasted? Or do we praise and give them all due respect and honor as we consider the ultimate sacrifice they have given for … what? Yes, for what? As painful as it is, this is a legitimate and necessary question. For men have given the ultimate sacrifice for the gods of wood and stone, for the cause of Confederacy, Nazism, Communism, and a myriad of other causes besides the cause of Freedom and Democracy.

We Americans, and I believe it to be rightly so, consider the cause of Freedom and Democracy to be the most Biblically correct earthly Government. Yet even this cause is a temporal, and therefore temporary, one. The lives lost all spend eternity somewhere, and in this National struggle, as in all else, final judgment belongs to God. Who we believe does, and will, judge righteous judgment even as He is grieved at His heart over the struggles of mankind as they continue. Despite the Cause of Christ. Whose ultimate cause is not to direct the affairs of men with physical force, but through the Power of Love. The Power of an endless Life. The Power of a Sound Mind.

A sound mind considers life from all angles of Reality and most especially from the Reality of Eternity. Eternity is difficult for our finite minds to comprehend and is best comprehended through a spiritual connection with the One who inhabits Eternity, Jehovah God. Jehovah God, who says, "For what is a man profited, if he gain the whole world, and lose his own soul? or what shall a man give in exchange for his soul?" (Matthew 16:26) We live in a fallen world. Among fallen mankind, of which we are a part. And we long for security. No matter how macho or beautiful and put together we may appear, the longing for security is settled into the deepest recesses of the soul, and seems to ooze out of the very pores of our being.

And we tend to look for security in all the wrong places. We tend to look for it among those things that are highly esteemed among mankind. Houses, lands, cattle, large bank accounts, trucks, conquest, cars, beauty, comfort, luxuries, the admiration of others, popularity, love, lust, greed, and more. But these all let us down, because the only lasting security inhabits Eternity. Time, because it has an end, is insecure. And all that is connected with time has an end and is therefore insecure.

Jesus has given the Ultimate gift. Through His ultimate sacrifice of dying on the cross, He gave His own life for The Cause that He entered this war for. The Cause is not, and was never, to bring death upon His enemies; but to bring life. Eternal Life. The power of an endless Life. He did not come to condemn the world "but that the world through him might be saved." (John 3:17) And in this eternal life is security.

Lasting Security. Eternal Security. The ultimate security, which is the ultimate gift from the Ultimate Gift-giver, God. He gave of Himself, His Word, God Incarnate, Jesus Christ, our Lord and Savior, the Ultimate Gift to fallen mankind. He who died. And arose again! After "he was tempted in all points like as we, yet without sin." He is the King of kings and Lord of lords. He "is made unto us wisdom, and righteousness, and sanctification, and redemption: That, according as it is written, He that glorieth, let him glory in the Lord." (I Corinthians 1:30-31) Jesus Christ gave His life, the ultimate gift. He is God's Love manifested to us.

7. **Forgiveness and release.** When we come to the end of ourselves and bow our knees and our hearts to Him in confessing repentance, when we allow and invite Him into our hearts and minds to go as deep as

He wishes in revealing our sin to ourselves, and repentance finds a deep-seated place in our hearts, then forgiveness—through Jesus' Blood shed for us on the cross at Calvary—also finds a place deep in our hearts and minds. Replacing turmoil with quietness, consternation with peace. Peace that passes all understanding. Peace, that keeps our hearts and minds through Christ Jesus. (Philippians 4:7 paraphrased) Profound in its simplicity, or maybe because of it, this step forward is a simple step, only made difficult by the reluctance to see and come to grips with the nature of sin within. This is the part that is painful, the experience that causes many stumblings and turning back. Back to the self-righteous rags that at least somewhat seem to cover, back to the stumblings in the mire, back to "moving forward" even though downhill, back to the broad, well-traveled road.

But however painful it may be, there is light beyond this dark shadow of repentance. For repentance is not so much a dark valley of despair as it is the dark valley of facing reality as it is. And because Jesus lives in the Reality of Truth, we must also enter reality in order to meet Him. And it is there, in the reality of who we are, that He is to be found. And not only is He found, but He is also seeking us, and is quick to come when we call out to Him for mercy. "Yea, though I walk through the valley of the shadow of death," writes the Psalmist, "I will fear no evil: for thou art with me; thy rod and thy staff they comfort me. Thou preparest a table before me in the presence of mine enemies: thou anointest my head with oil; my cup runneth over. Surely goodness and mercy shall follow me all the days of my life: and I will dwell in the house of the LORD for ever." (Psalms 23: 4-6)

With God's merciful forgiveness comes release. Release from fear. Release from anxiety. Release from the difficulties of a life lived our own way, in our own strength. But be not deceived; there are difficulties still, only now they are different. Now the councils at the very gates of Hell convene and take counsel how they might bring us into the bondage of their gripping slavery again. Whether by large or small steps, the pull of their influence is always in the same direction, onto the broad way leading away from the Bible, away from the teachings of Christ, away from God's Holy Word, away from His Ultimate Authority. And going towards, always going towards being our own boss and becoming one with pride, which is compatible with the devil and his plans. The temptation presented to our first parents in the Garden has taken on many forms, but is still the same. Seemingly pleasant at first and intertwined with a promise of liberty, it leads to increasing destabilization, bondage, and destruction. Promising liberty, they themselves are the servants of bondage. (II Peter 2:19)

"And if any man sin, we have an advocate ... Jesus Christ the righteous." (I John 2:1) Jesus Christ is the One who pleads in our favor and vindicates us by His Blood and Resurrection as He died for us and rose again "for our justification." (Romans 4:25) Justification. Justified. We are made just. As if we had never sinned. Not only are we forgiven in the Valley of Repentance but now we are cleansed, cleansed by the Blood that "speaketh better things than that of Abel." (Hebrews 12:24) When Christ forgives, He also releases. As if we had never sinned. "Justified freely by his grace." (Romans 3:24)

Can we also forgive? And release? Biblical forgiveness has release built into its very context. When the ungrateful steward, in Matthew 18:28, took his fellow servant by the throat and said, "pay me that thou owest," it is expected in the context that if he heeded the voice of his master, who reminded him of all that he, the steward, had been forgiven, and if he promptly forgave his fellow-servant, that he then also promptly released him from the grip on his throat.

Release, in Biblical context, is not something we do apart from forgiveness, but rather, is a proof of forgiveness. How can we say that a wrong done to us in the past is forgiven if we keep on rehearsing that wrong to the ears of the perpetrator?

Or, worse yet, to others.

When God, through Christ Jesus, forgives, He also releases. He sets free. And so should we. While communicative dialogue can be, and is often, needful in working through the issues we face in this broken world of fallen humanity that we live in, still, let us never forget to pass on the torch of God's Love to our fellow-traveler. The Love that is manifested through forgiveness and release.

LOVE MANIFESTED

Crucified by those whom He'd formed,
Beaten by them, mocked and scorned.
Forsaken by those whom He'd taught,
Yet stayed with His purpose steadfast.
    Unchangeable Love

With ridicule heaped upon Him,
Divine Love yet gazed upon them,
Could have called ten thousand angels,
Yet salvation remained His goal.
    Compassionate Love.

A spear pierced the Master's side,
Forthwith came out water and blood.
Alone, by th' world forsaken,
Yet from His purpose unshaken.
    Unshakeable Love.

In Him was Love Manifested,
Love deep and strong when tested.
His spirit as water refreshing,
His blood providing sin's cleansing.
    Divine Love Applied.

Death couldn't keep Him in the grave,
Tho blood was spilt, tho life He gave.
He arose again! The Living Way,
Now in Heaven, He'll come someday.
    Anticipation!

All mansions in the Father's house,
Are provided in abundance.
Jesus will come! The King for His own!
The King! Taking His Redeemed Home!
    Love Consummated!

Gottes sege dazu winscha
(May God add His blessing!)

8

IMMUTABLE COUNSEL OF ALMIGHTY GOD

THE YEAR WAS 1984. As it already had been many a Friday and Saturday night, my pillow was wet with tears as I prayed, tossed, and turned, sleepless until the wee hours of the morning. Not for myself did I pray, toss, and turn. For I had, just the year before, repented and my sins had been washed away in Jesus' blood. My sins were many for I had been swept up in the teenage Rock 'n Roll rebellion of the 70s. Even though the hand of God—I believe through the remonstrating of my Dad, and the prayers and tears of my dear mother—had kept me from the worst of its moral decadence, still, it had been bad enough, and the way back hard.

At first the fear of eternal hell fire had driven me to seek God. I had confessed my sins to the church, received discipline, got married, and settled down to a clean life. Or at least, cleaner. And then we had a baby. A little baby girl. A sweet little bundle of a baby girl. A baby girl who had a hard time settling down and sleeping at night, for she was colicky. Her cries, because of her hurting tummy, tore at her mom's and my heartstrings; and even though her nightly periodic cries disturbed us from slumber, we only loved her the more.

At times, at the request of her dear weary mother, I would drag my own body, still weary from the former day's toil, out of bed and do the only thing we knew how to do at the time with a colic baby—pace the floor while trying to keep her as comfortable as possible in our arms.

At such times when I did the pacing and our dear little one would become overheated from desperately squirming and crying for relief, I opened the front door and stepped out onto the porch where the crisp night air would bring relief and quietness to our precious little one.

Though I didn't dare stay long for fear she would catch a cold, I loved those tender, quiet moments. One moon-lit night as I gazed upon the now relaxed face of our beloved firstborn, the thought entered my mind and rested there that this new life that sprang from our love was now a life that would never cease to exist. As her Dad, I was not only responsible for her physical well-being but also for her spiritual soul that would spend eternity somewhere. And not only hers, but she very likely will have siblings I thought. And these children could someday have children, and their children could have children, and their children… All to spend eternity somewhere.

As the possible enormity of what our love for each other had begun settled upon me, I was filled with a mixture of awe, of desperation, and of great need. "God," I whispered, "I don't know how to do this." And so began a search. A search that eventually led me to the foot of the cross where Jesus met my remorse and repentance with His accepting love. In awakening me to my need, our firstborn had unknowingly led me to Christ.

So, no, it wasn't worried desperation for myself that kept me awake at night. What haunted me, worried me to desperation, was my younger brother. My younger brother, one of the "dearest on earth to me." He was only a year and a half younger than me and we had literally grown up together. We had played together, learned much together, and yes, at times fought together. We walked to and from school together (a one mile trek each way), attended school together, and worked on the farm together. Ever since I could remember, there was Paul. Diligent, fun-loving Paul. Sincere Paul, determined to do what was right.

Until he was 17. I'd never seen anyone change so fast. And the finger of memory pointed at me. I was the cause; I had led the way. He had told Mom (and Mom told me) when he'd turned 16 and became a part of the youth group, that he was afraid of getting into what his older brother Emanuel was into; that he didn't want that kind of life, and was determined not to get involved. And he didn't. For a year he kept himself clean of alcohol and recreational drugs, even though we went to the same parties. When the fun was "clean," he was very involved; but when the booze came out, he was aloof, withdrawn. And it bothered me. I wanted him to have fun. To be popular. To be his fun-loving self at such parties. To loosen up. Though I didn't verbally attempt to persuade him, neither did I give my support.

And then there was that awful evening when one of the guys had jokingly said something about Paul's abstinence and I had responded jokingly, only to see Paul, whom I hadn't known was there, step away from the circle of guys and slowly drift away in the dark. I wanted to run after him. To tell him how sorry I was. To stand with him. Together.

But no. I had messed up. And there was no way to fix it. Or so I thought. So I hardened myself and stayed at a party that something deep within myself cried out against. I was so mixed up inside I felt sick in my stomach.

Not long after, I learned that Paul had become the "life of the party." I was glad and yet I wasn't. But I persuaded myself that it was all a part of growing up, and after all, we were just having fun—while the fun lasted. Was it really that bad, after all? Anyhow, most, if not all, of the youth from this group could be expected to "settle down" eventually, join the church, get married, and never "party" again. And raise their families in the church. So there was nothing really wrong, we were just having some fun while the fun lasted. Or not?

A memory from 1981 still haunted me. It was summertime and the Amish church was to be at our place this Sunday morning. Though there were many Sunday mornings that neither Paul nor I would bother being home for, this was different. When the church was at our house, we were there, helping the men unhitch their horses, leading the horses to water and then tying them in the barn. There was an expectation (unspoken perhaps) from our parents that we would be there and an equally unspoken obligation and desire on our part to not let them down. Though I had moved out and lived 100 miles away to live closer to my girlfriend, I was as yet unmarried so this morning I was home. Home to be "hostler" with the horses as people arrived at our farm for church. Both Paul and I would be hostlers. Together.

I awoke at the breaking of dawn that Sunday morning to the gently pounding rhythm of the milking system diesel. I smiled to myself. I was no longer living at home but I could envision Dad in the barn starting the milking with Paul helping. The sights, sounds, and even smells so familiar through all my growing up years. My southeast upstairs bedroom with its big windows overlooking the garden, the driveway, the shop and barn to the east and pasture to the south with the shady lawn in the foreground all felt so familiar, so comfortable, so restful this morning with the sunlight just beginning to chase the night away. And my familiar old comfortable bed.

I stretched. And yawned. "Emanuel!" Mom called up the stairs with an edge of desperation in her voice. "Dad is alone with the milking. Paul didn't come home last night." I sat bolt upright in bed. Paul not home? Tense, my mind in a whirl, I leaped out of bed. There was only one explanation in my mind for Paul not being home on this particular morning. Something bad had happened. Something really bad. And I was familiar enough with the parties, the revelries, and the fast cars to put my imagination into overdrive, as a feeling of dread hit my gut with nauseous sensation.

I slipped into a shirt and as I fumbled with the buttons, I moved restlessly to the east window, my eyes looking towards the barn just in time to see the nose of a car appear from between the shop and the barn and stop on the driveway. A man appeared from behind the shop, having stepped out of the car, and walked towards the barn. I went rigid. My knees stiffened. My mind reeled. My worst fears had come to pass.

For the man was a police officer. And police officers showed up at law-abiding people's doors for only one reason. A death message. And Paul wasn't home.

And… and… and… I couldn't stay in the bedroom. The familiar coziness of the atmosphere had become charged with tension that engulfed me and felt suffocating.

I had to know…

I didn't want to know…

The tension went with me through the kitchen, past Mom's grim face, out the door onto the front porch and the fresh morning air. If anything, it got worse as I strode out the sidewalk leading to the barn, and as I approached Dad in the cow stable, the dread was fast becoming unbearable. Dad's face was grim and his brown eyes dark and unfathomable as I tensely blurted the question I didn't want to ask, but felt helplessly compelled to. "What did he want?"

Dad had turned to hook up a milker to a cow, and the question hung in the air till he turned to face me. "Paul was in jail for the night and is in for today," he replied gravely. In jail? I had been bracing myself for the worst, but jail meant Paul was alive! And doing ok! The tension oozed out of me and I was so relieved I felt weak. Relieved that my brother was in jail? For a DUI. The irony of it all left me in a daze which continued as I did chores, as people arrived, and as the day returned to a semblance of normalcy.

But the horror of that morning's dread had never quite left me, and once I was converted I yearned after the salvation of my younger brother. The last time we had met was in the graveyard at Grandfather Lapp's burial after the funeral. As I tried to reason with Paul of sin, of righteousness, and of judgment in my immature and fumbling way, he had carelessly lifted one foot onto a gravestone, and leaning onto his elevated knee, said in his decisive Paul way, "I'm not that stupid. I know what it takes to be a Christian and once I'm ready and decide to be one, then I'll be one."

I was stunned into silence, my mind in consternation. Didn't he think about what could happen? Didn't the Bible say something about conviction being from God? What if God quit convicting? Gave up? But I didn't know what to say. So I said nothing.

Now I tossed and turned and pleaded till I thought I would lose my mind. "God," I pleaded in quiet prayer, "I can't go on like this, please give me an answer. I can't go on like this." And God answered. Not audibly but with distinct words impressed on my mind. "I will judge righteous judgment." But how is that an answer, Lord? I was concerned about Paul. About his salvation. "I will judge righteous judgment." And that was all.

Slowly as I contemplated those words, understanding came. God was asking me to trust Him. Completely. God wanted me to entrust my younger brother to Him. To release him. It was a struggle to let go, but as I did so, peace replaced the raging turmoil in my heart and mind. And I marveled. And do still. For I still cared for and loved my brother. Deeply. But the worry was gone. Peace and rest flooded my soul. I was in awe.

And am in awe still. For those five words, impressed on my mind as clearly as if they were heard with my ears, have been as the steadying hand of God on my shoulder many times when my efforts for the kingdom of God have seemed futile and so small in comparison to the enormity of the need. Why, Lord? What about that hitchhiker that I picked up and shared the Gospel with?

"I will judge righteous judgment."

What about the person who died and I don't know...?

"I will judge righteous judgment."

What if the church...?

"I will judge righteous judgment."

What if...?

"I will judge righteous judgment."

God is asking that we trust Him. Fully. Completely. Without reserve. In this frame of heart and mind, we depend upon Him and become enabled to be co-workers with Jesus in His kingdom. For, as Jesus said, the husbandman that laboreth must first be partaker of the fruits. (II Timothy 2:6) We trust Him for the simple reason that He is Trustworthy. Faithful and True.

DIVINE RESPONSE

All wise. Omniscient, all-knowing; Omnipotent, almighty; Omnipresent, everywhere at once. He makes no mistakes. Jesus' recorded response to the question of "what about this one, Lord?" (paraphrased) was "what is that to thee? Follow thou me." (John 21:22) That is still Jesus' answer today. "Follow thou me." He calls us to be faithful in what we know and to trust Him to fulfill His promises, to surrender ourselves to Him, entrusting ourselves and others to Him. In direct opposition to our natural inclination which is to trust in ourselves and to compare ourselves with others, especially with those that we consider inferior.

Because of His promises we have a strong consolation. "For when God made promise to Abraham, because he could swear by no greater, he sware by himself, Saying, Surely blessing I will bless thee, and multiplying I will multiply thee ... For men verily swear by the greater: and an oath for confirmation is to them an end of all strife. Wherein God, willing more abundantly to shew unto the heirs of promise the immutability of his counsel, confirmed it by an oath: That by two immutable things, in which it was impossible for God to lie, we might have a strong consolation, who have fled for refuge to lay hold upon the hope set before us: Which hope we have as an anchor of the soul, both sure and steadfast, and which entereth into that within the veil; Whither the forerunner is for us entered, even Jesus, made an high priest for ever after the order of Melchisedec." (Hebrews 6:13-20)

In verse 13, God sware by Himself for there is none greater. He is Almighty God. No one created God. He always was. He is from eternity past. How can someone just always exist? We may be able to comprehend, at least to a small degree, that God always will be; that in eternity future, as the ages roll on, God is there. Always will be there, for He is God. But it is incomprehensible to our finite minds that God always was. We may say in faith that, oh yes, God always was, but that doesn't mean we comprehend and understand how such a thing could be possible. This is one of those instances where we need to say "God said it, I believe it, and that settles it."

The only alternative presented to us so far is even more incomprehensible, as there is no intelligent design involved, just an explosion out of which all that we see and know—including our emotions and brains—supposedly evolved over millions of years. Just as in God being incomprehensible, so is this, as no one was there, no one saw it happen, the process is no longer continuing and is therefore not observable science. Besides, the rock layers, fossils, coal and oil, etc. are better explained with the Biblical account of a world-wide flood. If in doubt just ask Ken Ham or others at the Creation

IMMUTABLE COUNSEL OF ALMIGHTY GOD

Museum and Answers in Genesis. Or better yet, just pick up a Bible and believe God. Or do both if you need to. God is very convincing to the seeker asking honest questions. Answers in Genesis has uncovered a wealth of remarkable evidence exposing evolution as a myth held to religiously by those who religiously believe it, while at the same time uncovering a vast store of remarkable evidence of a Biblical catastrophic world-wide flood.

Which brings us back to facing God who always was, always will be, upholds all things by the word of His Power and will one day call all of us to judgment. Some to be transported into eternal bliss and others into eternal torment. But God is not willing that any should perish, but that all should come to the knowledge of the truth. "For God so loved the world, that he gave his only begotten Son, that whosoever believeth in him should not perish, but have everlasting life." (John 3:16)

We can be assured and find rest in Him. Because those who come to Him, He will in no wise cast out. He meets our repentance and remorse with His accepting love that we can sense and be assured of. God sware by Himself for He could sware by no greater. That we might have a strong consolation. Not just be consoled—as if we could console ourselves—but a strong consolation, as from the Omnipotent One. Our Almighty God.

For there is at least one thing that our Almighty God cannot do. He cannot lie. (Titus 1:2) His very essence, His very nature is holy. So holy that He cannot lie, so holy that He cannot sin. It isn't that He may not, or that He dare not, nor even that there would be unpleasant repercussions if He did. He cannot. He promised and He cannot lie. Then, to make His point unmistakably clear, He confirmed it by an oath: which He swore by Himself, for there is none greater, that by two immutable things in which it is impossible for God to lie, we might have a strong consolation who have fled for refuge to lay hold upon the hope set before us... whither the forerunner is for us entered, even Jesus. God, from eternity past to eternity future, always was, is, and always will be. He is the One who rent the veil from the top to the bottom, opening up the way into the holy of holies. (Mark 15:38) And then he led the way into that Holy place, even into His very presence, being our forerunner, even Jesus. For Jesus is the Word incarnate. He was in God from eternity past, and in being the Word—what the church leaders at the Council of Nicaea referred to as the Logos,[1] the Word—He was and is the very essence of God. He is the word incarnate and in being the word of God, He is God, the only begotten son of God. He

---

1 *Decoding Nicea* by Paul F. Pavao

took on flesh, was made in the likeness of sinful man. In being conceived of the Holy Ghost, being born of a virgin, living a sinless life, yet dying as a sinner by the hands of wicked men, He became, was, and is willing to take our sins upon Himself. He is the "Lamb slain from the foundation of the world," (Revelation 13:8) having been in God's plan "when the earth was without form, and void." (Genesis 1:2)

Incomprehensible? Yes. All powerful? Yes. All knowing and ever present? Yes. And yes.

And He, in an insecure and ever-changing world, is the essence of security. For not only is He omnipotent, omniscient, and omnipresent, His counsel is also immutable, unchangeable. His judgment is always righteous, just and unchangeable. Some have argued that even God changes His mind, citing His "backing off" from annihilating the children of Israel when Moses prayed for them in the wilderness. But God is always true to His character, His attributes; and one of His attributes, of which there are many, is that mercy rejoices against judgment. He is "longsuffering to us-ward, not willing that any should perish, but that all should come to repentance." (II Peter 3:9) And therefore, in Christ Jesus, "mercy and truth are met together; righteousness and peace have kissed each other," (Psalms 85:10) for this is His ultimate, unchangeable will. His immutable counsel. And being immortal, from eternity past to eternity future, Omnipotent, Omnipresent and Omniscient, His counsel is immutable. "Without controversy great is the mystery of godliness: God was manifest in the flesh, justified in the Spirit, seen of angels ... received up into glory." (I Timothy 3:16)

"God moves in a mysterious way, His wonders to perform ..." (Song #162 *Hymns of the Church*) Judgment and mercy finally met together in brother Paul's heart and life almost ten years after the horror of that Sunday morning had passed. Long years of prayer and long years of God, often through brother Leroy, striving to break through the hardness of materialism that caked itself around Paul's heart, seemingly insulating it from any and all attempts to break through.

From all outward appearances, business prosperity, sports, and social party times seemed to have settled into Paul's heart to stay. Materialism, from all appearances, had captured another victim. Paul had still not "decided to be a Christian," but thankfully God hadn't given up on him. Not all his acquaintances had survived the "wild years," but the inner circle of his friends was as yet unbroken except for those who had married and moved on. Death had, as yet, spared them. God's mercy was yet extended.

IMMUTABLE COUNSEL OF ALMIGHTY GOD

But time was moving on. Buddy and Ruby had gotten married, leaving Paul to live by himself again after having shared the house with Buddy for eight years. The social life with his friends was bound to come to an end sometime before long. At least in the way it had been, for some were getting married, and since he was dating Nelaine, marriage was becoming more and more desirable, until finally nothing else would do. The thought of added responsibilities and the more serious life that went with it felt like a gentle breeze when "Lainey" was seated next to him.

But this evening in February 1992, he was alone, having just left work at the housing project in his work truck. He'd received an invitation again for supper at Leroy's house where he always received a warm welcome, so he was looking forward to that and Naomi's good home-cooked meal. Leroy, it seemed, didn't know what it meant to give up on a guy. After all these years of trying, he had just recently, possibly sensing the seriousness settling on the young couple, offered to study the Bible with them, so they had a small Bible study group going involving Leroy, Paul, Nelaine, Buddy, and Ruby.

So later when he got up from the table after the good, satisfying home-cooked meal it came as no particular surprise when Leroy invited him to his study at the far end of the hallway. Neither did Leroy's earnest seriousness come as any particular surprise. But what came as a surprise to Paul was the almost involuntary yielding of his heart as the neglected inner longing broke through its hard shell and connected with Leroy's pleading question of "what's holding you back?" And then, the almost involuntary falling to his knees at Leroy's gentle question of, "May I pray for you?" As Leroy prayed for God's mercy upon his younger brother, Paul's heart continued to soften, and when Leroy renounced the spirits of darkness, asking God to bind them in Jesus name, the softening kept going deeper.

As he drove home, Paul was so engrossed in thoughts long since dormant that when he arrived at his house, he entered the familiar side door as in a dream and fell to his knees at the couch in the living room. There on his knees, his heart broke. He hadn't cried for thirteen years and when his heart softened and broke a pent up dam of emotions broke free. He wept brokenly, as time went by unnoticed, and he bared his heart to the Lord. "A new heart also will I give you, and a new spirit will I put within you." (Ezekiel 36:26) His life followed as he surrendered what he had loved for so long and committed his life from henceforth to the Lord. The peace of Jesus won. Because those who come to Him, He "will in no wise cast out." (John 6:37)

Divine Response

Paul got up from his knees—and with a resolution borne of conviction—stepped to the refrigerator, opened the door, and pulled all the beer off the shelves, setting them on the counter by the sink. As he opened one after the other and their contents gurgled down the drain, symbolically, his former life drained away with them.

But Paul was beyond caring, for he was trading his lost hopelessness—with its temporary pleasures—for saved hopefulness with its promise of eternal pleasures, which he had just gotten a taste of, and for which nothing temporal was worth the risk.

Life took on new meaning for Paul. His friends didn't always know what to make of him and banteringly tried to "figure him out" in his presence. But Paul was resolute and when the finger of God came down on his idols, including his coveted for and much loved Trans Am, they were done away with, one by painstaking one. It was painful, but a good kind of pain, much like a man painfully burying his dead dog after it had begun to give off an unpleasant odor. The Trans Am got traded for a used brown pick-up truck, with Paul being the financial loser. His moral choices came under the scrutiny and guidance of God's word. But with all that came freedom. Freedom from the bondage of sin and its accompanying guilt. Freedom to not only face the day, but also the future, realistically.

For God calls us to reckon with the reality of His moral law, which was, and is still, our schoolmaster to bring us unto Christ. God's law is our excellent school teacher, showing, teaching us of our desperate need, that we may in turn become as desperate as the need calls for, as God calls us to face the reality of eternity.

So while God's love in sending His Son for the sins of humanity can be said—for this space called time that we live in—unconditional, there is a required condition to receiving and experiencing it. His love is not amoral as some would have us believe. In such a mindset, acceptance of immoral practices is morphed into meaning love, and uncertainty masquerades as humility. To take a stand on morality based on God's Word becomes labeled as a lack of love, even hatred, and to be certain of anything brings forth an outcry against arrogance and pride.

This attitude against taking a stand for morality and/or sound doctrine is the devil's attempt, through people, to silence our schoolmaster, to silence the humbling effect of God's moral law. And the attitude against certainty encourages people to be as the waves of the sea, driven with the wind and tossed, being double-minded, of whom God says, "Let not that man think that he shall receive any thing of the Lord." (James 1:7)

"He that cometh to God must believe that he is, and that he is a rewarder of them that diligently seek him." (Hebrews 11:6) God has a witness of Himself deep in the heart and mind of every man and woman, from the tender-hearted to even the staunchest, most hard-hearted unbeliever. And when the guards against such knowledge come down, then that knowledge comes in, maybe dimly at first, but brighter as the heart and mind are opened to receiving more knowledge. Turning darkness to light, not knowing to knowing God, instability to stability, insecurity to security, and uncertainty to certainty. Especially certainty that God is, and that He is to be found by those who diligently seek Him. Of Jesus it is written that "we have also a more sure word of prophecy; … as unto a light that shineth in a dark place, until the day dawn, and the day star arise in your hearts." (II Peter 1:19) Jesus said of Himself that He is the "Light of the world." (John 8:12, John 9:5 and John 12:46) He is the Light that shineth in a dark place, the daystar arising in our hearts.

The Gospel of John testifies that He is the Word of God "In the beginning was the Word, and the Word was with God, and the Word was God. The same was in the beginning with God. All things were made by him; and without him was not any thing made that was made. In him was life; and the life was the light of men. And the light shineth in darkness; and the darkness comprehended it not." (John 1:1-5)

And going to Verse 10; "He was in the world, and the world was made by him, and the world knew him not … But as many as received him, to them gave he power to become the sons of God, even to them that believe on his name: Which were born, not of blood, nor of the will of the flesh, nor of the will of man, but of God. And the Word was made flesh, and dwelt among us, (and we beheld his glory, the glory as of the only begotten of the Father,) full of grace and truth." (John 1:10-14)

God does have a severe side to Him, but it is not because He likes to punish people. He is severe because He is holy, too holy to allow sin to abide in His presence. Again, it is God's holiness coupled with His impartial severity about sin that makes Him so totally trustworthy. So trustworthy that Job could say—and we should be able to say with him—"Though he [God] slay me, yet will I trust in him." (Job 13:15) Romans 11:22-23 says to us, "Behold therefore the goodness and severity of God: on them which fell, severity; but toward thee, goodness, if thou continue in his goodness: otherwise thou also shalt be cut off. And they also, if they abide not still in unbelief, shall be grafted in: for God is able to graft them in again."

For God is able.

What hope is this! An abiding, eternal hope, for God is eternal!

Almighty God freely offers us a strong consolation!

When we come to Him as we are.

Not, as we try to be.

Not, as we wish we could be.

As we are.

In all honesty and contrition, resulting in sorrow for sin.

Upon such repentance God gives us a strong consolation by the immutability of His counsel. Because of Jesus.

For He is, Almighty God.

THE CALL

The wide road is so easy,
The way is smoothly paved with sin.
Never calling us to reckon,
With the sinner that's within,
The downward slope propels us onward,
Where we're going we cannot tell,
But the slippery slope gets steeper,
It ultimately, and surely, leads to hell.

Sinner, won't you come to Jesus?
And voluntarily bow your knees?
The time is coming when you'll have to,
You'll no more do things as you please.
The rebel spirit that is in us,
Has to go, it has to die,
The self sufficient plan of satan,
Is called, and rightly so, THE LIE.

IMMUTABLE COUNSEL OF ALMIGHTY GOD

THE LIE has had it's way in all,
Since fruit was broken from the tree,
We've all gone down the rebel road,
When we're blind, insist we see,
We don't see those things we ought to,
If we're still clean in our own eyes,
When we see JESUS as we ought to,
Pride gives up, is broken, the rebel dies.

Then JESUS bids us to arise,
As He has promised, all things are new,
He directs us off the broad way,
To walk the narrow with the few,
But it's the narrow that leads to glory,
And to JESUS King of kings,
Nothing of this world compares,
We'll never yearn for, nor miss, these mortal things.

And then the sound of our praises,
From perfected voices shall roll,
As awestruck by His presence,
Our ringing praises rich and full,
Are unshackled from the temporal,
From this mortal set free,
Our bodies metamorphosed,
Death is swallowed up in Vic-to-ry.

Gottes sege dazu winscha
(May God add His blessing.)

9

PROMISES TO PERSEVERING SAINTS

THE PROMISES OF GOD are sure. They are immutable. God is Love. Our All-Powerful God, whose counsels are immutable, whose Promise is sure, also loves us! But we are lost and need to be found. By Him. With our cooperation. He calls and wants us to allow ourselves to be found. Our need to be found of Him is evident because without Him we are lost, without hope, and without God in this world. We live in a fallen world.

Let us consider again our chapter two mosquito. And the Garden of Eden. The pesky mosquito, who seeks and finds our blood through the pores in our skin and leaves behind an itchy welt for us to scratch, surely does not belong in any mental pictures we might have of the perfect garden, the Garden of Eden. The garden we like to, in our minds at least, pattern our own after.

A well-kept garden. A picture perfect garden that beckons the weary to relax beneath the fruit-laden boughs of its trees, or to enjoy of its grapes, its variety of luscious berries, or its lush and wide variety of healthy vegetables, or to breathe in deeply the aroma of its beautiful flowers. A well-kept garden that speaks well for the diligence of its caretaker.

There, especially in the cool of the evening, the time seems right to find a seat away from the day's stressful activity, take a deep breath, and take time to relax the mind and body in the garden's refreshing stillness.

How often, though, instead of peacefully relaxing in dreamy reflection, have we been driven from our own garden by the lowly mosquito? And if it's not mosquitoes, it's gnats. And if it's not gnats, then there are sprinklers to set up. Or there are worm-eaten holes in the cabbage, or mites on the beans, or bugs on the potatoes, or there is a weed over there, or a new crop of weeds sprouting. Or a myriad of other problems, both real and potential may come to mind. Many people just give up and buy from the store, but then there are concerns about the GMOs, the chemical sprays, food-borne harmful bacteria, etc.

And even if there are no mosquitoes, no gnats, no worms, mites, bugs or weeds, chemicals or bacteria, and no sprinklers needed; is our mind at rest, at peace?

Or do we find the perfect setting, the perfect place, the perfect spot, only to discover that our mind cannot rest because of its turmoil? Turmoil caused by the mind being uneasy about the future, either in the short term or in the long term. Or uneasy about the present and its insecurities. For this present life, as we face it realistically, is insecure.

As a teenager I had those days when I was sick and tired of my rebel life, though I barely even admitted it to myself. There were those times when, wanting to be alone, I rode horseback to the Blue Mountain range—up the mountainside in the green of summertime, with a bright sun in a blue sky—and upon coming to an extra beautiful spot overlooking the Cumberland Valley, would stop my horse and dismount. I would stand gazing, or perhaps sit on a boulder, take a deep breath, and absorb the beauty around me with the panoramic view of the beautiful valley with its tidy farms, its woodlands and creeks far below.

But it didn't matter how beautiful or serene the setting, and perhaps because of it, deep thoughts about life, about death, and about eternity soon had my mind in an uneasy turmoil that contrasted and even seemed to darken the serene beauty around me. Eternal insecurity haunted me.

I understand this now to be one of the ways God was calling me out of my hidden fear to allowing myself to be found. When I finally came out of hiding a half a decade later, the Lord Jesus Christ found me. And I found Him. Then I understood. Then I whispered to myself and to Him. I whispered in awe. "I've found what I was looking for up in those mountains." I was looking for Jesus and didn't know it. And I found Him. Or He found me. Kneeling beside our bed in our bedroom in the middle of the night.

Since then I've found Him in the mountains. I've found Him at work. I've found Him at home. I've found Him in sunshine and in the rain. And I've found Him in the hospital. With broken bones, internal injuries, shearing of the brain, my motor skills gone, and my life shattered. He was there. He was peace in the dark night. He was there. He was my Rock of stability when emotions went haywire. He was there. With His comforting assurance that I can trust Him. He was there as I relearned how to brush my teeth, as I relearned eye and hand coordination, as I relearned how to walk. His comfort assured me. His Peace steadied me. His Hope kept me pressing on. And always, His Promise was before me. His Promise of a restored body. He didn't tell me if that restoration would be in this life or in eternity, but the Promise was there. A living, almost palpable reality, the Promise was ever before me infusing me with courage. The Promise of Eternal restoration, safety, and bliss. With Him. In His perfect Kingdom. In the midst of perfect beauty. In the midst of Perfection with perfect peace in heart and mind.

This Promise is for all that believe. "And this is the will of him that sent me," Jesus said, "that every one which seeth the Son, and believeth on him, may have everlasting life: and I will raise him up at the last day." (John 6:40)

This is not a physical seeing to believe. Jesus rebuked Thomas for not believing till he physically saw, and said to him, "Thomas, because thou hast seen me, thou hast believed: blessed are they that have not seen, and yet have believed." (John 20:29) No, this seeing is a spiritual sensing, "the eyes of your understanding being enlightened." (Ephesians 1:18) Real security is found in Jesus Christ. And only in Him.

We talk about job security, but if viewed realistically, any job is only as secure as its customer base, and since the customer base is dependent on a strong economy and a strong economy is dependent on production and production is dependent on its customer base, it is not difficult to understand how quickly a weak link can happen and give way in this circular chain of events that we are all, to some degree, a part of.

We dream of secure homes, but if viewed realistically, we may never let down our guard against Satan's wiles, lest he take advantage of our negligence and finds a way to cause our homes to be insecure. Either through negligent dads, angry mothers, rebellious teenagers, or just simply through drifting away from God. The most subtle catalyst for drifting away from God and His Word, is just simply getting used to things that we should never get used to. Our homes are only as secure as our adherence to God and His Word. Which is the ultimate security; for God is secure; until we view our own place in that equation, and then we realistically see the possibility of failure and our constant need of adherence to God and His Word.

We talk, or maybe long for, financial security, but how large must the pile be before it becomes stable and secure? The observable answer seems to be the same as the response of the proverbial farmer; who bought more land at an auction to add to his already vast holdings. When asked by a friend, "When is enough, enough?" quoth the farmer, "when I own all the land adjoining mine!"

And so it goes. The insecure drive in us for security is never satisfied by things, people, or financial markets, for the more we seek for security in the things that are insecure, the more elusive security becomes.

I say people because all people are themselves only as secure as their faith in God gives them the ability to be. Those poor souls that we lean on for security may well let us down, for they, as well as we, need to find security in the acceptance of our Lord Jesus Christ, our ultimate and only lasting security. (Children need the security found in the love and guidance of parents, but we speak of accountable adults.)

And so, when we seek after security in jobs, possessions, or people, we may as well be grasping the air, for all the securities they give flee when confronted with the reality of eternity.

Our beloved brother, the Apostle Paul, by the inspiration of God, likened the Christian life to a race except that we run for, not a corruptible crown, but an incorruptible. "I therefore so run," he wrote, "not as uncertainly; so fight I, not as one that beateth the air: But I keep under my body, and bring it into subjection: lest by any means, when I have preached to others, I myself should be a castaway." (I Corinthians 9:26-27)

And now, returning our thoughts to the Garden of Eden: From observation it seems fair to say that all of us have a natural inborn desire to return to the Garden of Eden. To return to what we once had. To go home. To have a home. In a peaceful garden.

That natural inborn desire serves us well, as even the carnal mind may be inclined or even motivated to care for and preserve the earth in as pristine a state as possible while still being comfortable. The tragedy is that so many engage in a life-long struggle to create their own little garden of Eden here, to the neglect of the soul that will spend eternity somewhere.

The Garden of Eden has long ago disappeared, if not before, then surely obliterated by the catastrophic world-wide flood of Noah's day.

We can't go back there. Our first parents were driven out by God. And the garden was eventually destroyed.

The only way is forward. Therein, and only therein, are the Promises of God. As Jesus said, "No man, having put his hand to the plough, and looking back, is fit for the kingdom of God." (Luke 9:62.)

"Remember Lot's wife," we are told in Luke 17:32. It is a warning to us to flee Sodom with all its sin and lusts, not looking back, as they were told not to, and when she disobeyed, was immediately turned into a pillar of salt. The prophet Ezekiel, by the inspiration of God, speaking to the Israelites about the sins of Sodom, wrote, "Behold, this was the iniquity of thy sister Sodom, pride, fulness of bread, and abundance of idleness was in her and in her daughters, [cities begun by Sodom] neither did she strengthen the hand of the poor and needy. And they were haughty, and committed abomination before me: therefore I took them away as I saw good." (Ezekiel 16:49-50.)

We cannot stay in the present: time does not stop. For anyone. And we cannot go back, nor bring the past pleasures forward, much as we may like to, and seek after them. The only way, then, is forward. We are moving towards the future, which will one day become the present, while the present becomes the past with a yet unknown future before us.

Until Jesus comes.

Or we pass from this life into eternity.

The best we can do, then, is to look forward. To love the Lord Jesus, have our sins washed away by His blood, and to look forward to His coming. And that is a glorious hope! "Which hope we have as an anchor of the soul, both sure and steadfast, and which entereth into that within the veil; Whither the forerunner is for us entered, even Jesus, made an high priest forever." (Hebrews 6:19-20.)

Herein is security! Security in an insecure world!

Herein is hope! Hope in a hopeless world!

Herein is courage! Courage in a world where much is discouraging.

Herein is promise! The promises of God! The promise of life! Unending life! Eternal life that begins here, giving courage, hope and security.

Courage, hope, and security that is otherworldly, anchored in the Holy of Holies where only the high priest went alone once every year. Not without blood, which he offered for himself and for the errors of the people. "The Holy Ghost this signifying, that the way into the holiest of all was not yet made manifest, while as the first tabernacle was yet standing: Which was a figure for the time then present." (Hebrews 9:8-9)

This holy place of the tabernacle, called the holy of holies, was separated from the inner court by a curtain, called a veil. Behind this veil, in the holy of holies, was the ark of the covenant which we are given a description of in Exodus 37. Considering that a cubit was approximately 18 inches (the approximate length from the tip of a man's middle finger to the outer edge of his elbow), the ark is described as a box approximately 45 inches long, 27 inches high and 27 inches wide, overlaid inside and out with pure gold and a border described as a crown of gold. For the purpose of carrying the ark there were rings of pure gold fastened at each corner through which staves of shittim wood overlaid with gold could be passed, and the ark borne upon the shoulders of four priests. The cover of the box, referred to as the mercy seat, was made of pure gold approximately 27 inches wide and 45 inches long with a cherub at each end, beaten out of pure gold, their wings spread out, "with their faces one to another; even to the mercy seatward were the faces of the cherubims." (Exodus 37:9) Inside this box was placed a golden pot that had manna, Aaron's rod that budded, and the tables of the Covenant (Hebrews 9:4) and thus the box was called the Ark of the Covenant.

This Ark of the Covenant was kept behind the second veil (curtain) in the Holy of Holies where the high priest went alone, once every year, not without blood, which he offered for himself and for the errors of the people. Let us consider the significance of this Ark of the Covenant, for its design, its contents, and its setting have an awesome depth of promise from God our Father, who is awesome in His majesty, dominion and power both now and forever, Amen.

The Ark of the Covenant, everything about it, was either overlaid with gold or made of pure gold signifying: first, the purity of its Designer and His word which contains His truth and His mercy; and second, signifying how we are to come forth as gold tried in the fire when purified in the fiery trials of life.

Within the Ark of the Covenant, under the mercy seat, was a golden pot that had manna, a sample of the manna that God rained from heaven for the Israelites (Exodus 16:4), which they ground into flour for cakes, providing their daily bread. They ate manna for the years of wilderness wanderings before and after being initially denied entrance into Canaan by God. Denied, because they compared their own strength with that of the Canaanites and became fearful, thus proving their trust in themselves rather than God. The second time they approached Canaan their faith in God held firm as the waters of the Jordan River parted when the priests bearing the ark stepped in. They crossed as on dry land and came to Gilgal where they had "old corn of the land" and "the manna ceased." (Joshua 5:12.) This manna signifying the coming of spiritual nourishment and sustenance as Jesus said of Himself in John 6:32-35 "...but my Father giveth you the true bread from heaven. For the bread of God is he which cometh down

Divine Response

from heaven, and giveth life unto the world. Then said they," (those people that had been seeking Him), "unto Him, Lord, evermore give us this bread. And Jesus said unto them, I am the bread of life: he that cometh to me shall never hunger; and he that believeth on me shall never thirst."

Even when they murmured against Him saying, how can this man be bread; He went on teaching them of the everlasting life that He would give to all who believe on Him. Assuring them several times that He is the living bread come down from heaven, and while reminding them that their fathers ate manna in the wilderness and are now dead, said to them, "he that eateth of this bread shall live forever." For this bread that He spoke of is spiritual, its nourishment and sustenance are eternal. For partaking of the bread of Jesus is to have His Spirit, the Holy Ghost, living within us as He promised His disciples in John 14:19-20 "because I live, ye shall live also. At that day ye shall know that I am in my Father, and ye in me, and I in you." And in praying for His disciples, and "for them also [the rest of us who believe] which shall believe on me through their word," (John 17:20) He prayed for this union to happen: "I in them, and thou in me, that they may be made perfect in one." (John 17:23)

Romans 8:10-11 testifies of the indwelling Christ; "And if Christ be in you, the body is dead because of sin; but the spirit is life because of righteousness. But if the Spirit of him that raised up Jesus from the dead dwell in you, he that raised up Christ from the dead shall also quicken your mortal bodies by his Spirit that dwelleth in you." Quickened with spiritual Life!

The manna in the Ark of the Covenant, then, signified the manna which was to come, the bread from heaven, which is Jesus Christ. Who is ready, willing, and able to indwell and so infill the repentant believer as to "quicken your mortal body by His Spirit that dwelleth in you."

He is become the spiritual nourishment, the spiritual sustenance, the spiritual life, and thus the embodiment of God's Promise. Both Old and New Testament. He is the Promised One that should come. The Giver and Sustainer of Eternal Life. Not as the Old Testament manna, which "manna ceased." Wonderful and miraculous as it was, the manna in the wilderness only sustained temporal life. For its time. And then ceased. But it signified, and was a foreshadowing of, an even more wonderful and miraculous event; the giving and sustaining of eternal life! The Old Testament saints looked forward to the coming Messiah and their faith in God's promise was counted to them for righteousness. We have the testimony of God's Promise being fulfilled, and in repenting and believing "receive the promise

PROMISES TO PERSEVERING SAINTS

of the Spirit through faith." (Galatians 3:14) Jesus spoke of Himself as the living bread, which bread was then broken for us, and He spoke of His spirit that then indwells believers as living water. Living water, being taken in and flowing out of the believer. In John 7, at the feast of tabernacles, "In the last day, the great day of the feast, Jesus stood and cried saying, If any man thirst, let him come unto me, and drink. He that believeth on me, as the scripture hath said, out of his belly shall flow rivers of living water." (John 7:37-38)

The promise, then, is for the salvation of our souls. And going forward, the promise of a preserving, and thus refreshing outflow from the wellspring of God's love, which gives hope, courage, and security even in the midst of a troubled world. Thus, allowing that love to spill out on others, without fear. "There is no fear in love; but perfect love casteth out fear: because fear hath torment. He that feareth is not made perfect in love." (I John 4:18.) Jesus Christ, our Promised Messiah, gives love, security, courage, and hope to each vessel that is otherwise broken and hopeless.

The Ark of the Covenant also contained Aaron's rod that budded. The account of it is in Numbers 17 and the setting is the rebellion of Korah, Dathan, Abiram and the children of Israel who stood with them against Moses and Aaron. Against Moses, because they were weary of the journey, which up to now had yielded hardship instead of the promised "land that floweth with milk and honey." And against both Moses and Aaron as they accused them in Numbers 16:3; "ye take too much upon you, seeing all the congregation are holy, every one of them, and the LORD is among them: wherefore then lift ye up yourselves above the congregation of the LORD?"

And when Moses heard it, he fell upon his face. Moses had faced accusations before, but never before had he been accused of making himself their leader. He was so confident that God had called him, and that God had been with him, that when he was accused he knew these men were in trouble. Not in trouble with Moses, but in trouble with God. And Moses fell upon his face. These men were Levites, they should know better. And when Moses spoke he tried to reason with them, but they would not. In the course of reasoning with them, he warned "ye take too much upon you, ye sons of Levi." Moses then called them to a meeting, but they would not come. By the time the day was over, the earth had opened her mouth and swallowed them up. And their houses. And all the men that appertained unto Korah, and all their goods, were swallowed up when the earth clave asunder that was under them and then closed upon them. But the rebellion

Divine Response

was not entirely over, for the very next day "all the congregation of the children of Israel murmured against Moses and against Aaron, saying, Ye have killed the people of the Lord." (Numbers 16:41)

So Moses took twelve rods, one for each tribe, as the Lord commanded him; and each rod had the prince of a tribe's name written on it, one for each tribe; and Aaron's name was written on the rod of the tribe of Levi. "And Moses laid up the rods before the Lord in the tabernacle of witness." There they laid for the night. "And it came to pass, that on the morrow Moses went into the tabernacle of witness; and, behold, the rod of Aaron for the house of Levi was budded, and brought forth buds, and bloomed blossoms, and yielded almonds." (Numbers 17:7-8) This rod that budded was kept for a token against the rebels, "and thou shalt quite take away their murmurings from me, that they die not," (Numbers 17:10) God said to Moses.

In the rod that budded is a promise of life given to that which was cut off from the source of its life and not just a hint of life or a little bit of life, but life so abundant that it was depicted to us by a rod that brought forth buds, blossoms, and almonds! Overnight! This blooming, fruitful rod had a name on it, that of Aaron, the priest, and as such is also a promise of life, miraculous life, abundant life, to all believers who are now referred to as a holy priesthood; (I Peter 2:5) a royal priesthood; (I Peter 2:9) and kings and priests. (Revelation 1:6) Jesus is now our High Priest forever (Hebrews 6:20) and we are kings and priests under Him. Or should be if we are not, for He gives this accepting title to all believers.

And, the rod that budded is also a promise that, as Jesus said in Matthew 7:16 "ye shall know them by their fruits." And in Proverbs 11:28 "the righteous shall flourish as a branch." Scripture gives direction on whose counsel is safe to follow, as the Apostle Paul says, "follow me as I follow Christ." The lives of his followers are part of a leader's fruit, as well as his personal life.

"I am crucified with Christ: nevertheless I live; yet not I, but Christ liveth in me: and the life which I now live in the flesh I live by the faith of the Son of God, who loved me, and gave himself for me. I do not frustrate the grace of God: for if righteousness come by the law, then Christ is dead in vain." (Galatians 2:20-21.)

Last, but certainly not least, in the Ark of the Covenant were the tables of stone upon which the commandments were written, and engraven in stone, by God on Mount Sinai and given to Moses to deliver to the congregation of 600,000 men, besides women and children. This set of two stone tablets, being preserved in the Ark of the Covenant, was the second set given by God to His servant Moses on Mount Sinai. Moses had broken the first set in his wrath upon coming down from the mount and seeing the children of Israel wholly giving themselves to idolatry, dancing, and bowing down to golden calves—the work of their own hands—wrought from the gold they had "borrowed" from Egypt.

These commandments have had a profound and continuing effect upon the whole of mankind ever since. Centered in Israel and spreading out from there, first through the propagation of Judaism and then through the phenomenal spreading out of Christianity. These 10 commandments, however profound, though written and engraven in stone by the finger of God, (Exodus 31:18) were only a foreshadowing of what was to come. While paying all due respect to Old Testament commandments, the Christianity of the first century, as recorded for us in our New Testament Bible, was a call. Not so much a call to have behavior controlled by commandments, but rather, a call to be changed from the inside out—our schoolmaster to bring us unto Christ. Therefore, a change brought about by repentance from dead works and receiving the change of heart and mind made possible by the indwelling of Christ through His Spirit made available to all the repentant. The Holy Ghost initially manifested Himself miraculously to the believers at Pentecost by the sound of a rushing mighty wind, the appearance of cloven tongues like as of fire that sat upon each of them and the speaking with other tongues as the listeners heard what was spoken, each in his or her own language.

The Promise contained in the tables of stone was "keep the commandments and thou shalt live." While the commandment is holy, just, and good, God saw the First Covenant to be weak through the flesh (Romans 3:19-20); that outward pressure does not, for it cannot, regenerate the heart of fallen man (Romans 7), for we have a natural bent towards sin. God always did know that, but He needs us to see and accept it for ourselves. Thus, "the law was our schoolmaster to bring us unto Christ." (Galatians 3:24) "But after that faith is come, we are no longer under a schoolmaster. For ye are all the children of God by faith in Christ Jesus." (Galatians 3:25-26) This means hearing the heart of God in His commandments, and in receiving His commandments, loving Him more than we love ourselves. And loving our neighbor as ourselves.

Upon these two commandments, Jesus said, hang all the Law and the Prophets. (Matthew 22:40) If we hear Moses (the Law) and the Prophets we will also hear Jesus. (Luke 16:16 & 16:29) Jesus is the Promise contained in the Law and the Prophets. They spoke of Him. And if we hear them, if we pay attention to them, our need for Jesus will become a desperation that initially drives us to Him and causes our ongoing adherence to Him for our very life. For to be without Him is fearful, but to be with Him is peace and rest. Peace and rest so profound it has remained attractive to rulers and slaves alike, despite the chopping of heads, the tearing of wild beasts, the burnings alive, the burning of human torches to light the arena, and whatever inhuman torture that man, with the help of demons, have been able to devise. And the very gates (counsels) of hell shall not (promise) prevail against the Church. (Matthew 16:18)

This promise of Jesus opening up the way for us to be personal with God, to personally draw close to God—to have the boldness (in a good way) to enter into the holy of holies on a personal basis, and no longer needing the Levitical priesthood—was profoundly exemplified for us at His crucifixion when the veil before the holy of holy place (now located in the temple) was rent. From the top to the bottom. (Mark 15:38 & Luke 23:45) God Himself (for who else could tear it from the top to the bottom?) opening up the way for the common man into His very presence. Reconciled to God by the death of His Son. And much more, being reconciled we shall be saved by His life.

Because He lives!

And He is coming again!

To receive His own unto Himself!

But there is a condition to God's Promise of Everlasting life. We must hear Moses (the law), our schoolmaster that teaches us of God's heart for our love and obedience. And we must hear the Prophets who prophesied the coming of the Just One, Jesus.

And we must hear our Lord Jesus. And receive and experience Him changing us from the inside out, indwelling us.

That the righteousness of the law might be fulfilled in us who walk not after the flesh but after the Spirit.

And one day every eye shall see Him. "Every knee shall bow to me, and every tongue shall confess to God." (Romans 14:11)

To the unbelieving it will be a fearful reality.

To the persevering saint (believer) it will be the glorious and ultimate fulfillment of Promise.

"For ye are not come unto the mount that might be touched, and that burned with fire, nor unto blackness, and darkness, and tempest ... But ye

PROMISES TO PERSEVERING SAINTS

are come unto mount Sion, and unto the city of the living God, the heavenly Jerusalem, and to an innumerable company of angels, To the general assembly and church of the firstborn, which are written in heaven, and to God the Judge of all, and to the spirits of just men made perfect, And to Jesus the mediator of the new covenant, and to the blood of sprinkling, that speaketh better things than that of Abel." (Hebrews 12:18, 22-24) Abel's blood called for judgment. Jesus' blood calls for mercy. And, Hebrews 9:28; "So Christ was once offered to bear the sins of many; and unto them that look for him shall he appear the second time without sin unto salvation."

No longer do we need to fear truth, for when we face the truth, we not only discover the truth about ourselves, but we also discover the cleansing power of the blood of Jesus and His mercy for another guilty sinner.

There is much that we don't know of what Heaven will be like, but it is depicted very much like a beautiful garden as in Revelation 22:1-2. A crystal clear river is described for us with the tree of life on either side. Jesus said, "In my Father's house are many mansions: if it were not so, I would have told you. I go to prepare a place for you … that where I am, there ye may be also." (John 14:2-3)

And for the present time, we have the Promise of His Spirit, as Jesus said, "… how much more shall your heavenly Father give the Holy Spirit to them that ask him?" (Luke 11:13)

"Ask and it shall be given you; seek, and ye shall find; knock, and it shall be opened unto you: For every one that asketh receiveth; and he that seeketh findeth; and to him that knocketh it shall be opened." (Matthew 7:7-8)

The reward is to those that persevere. For those hardy souls who have their attention so much on the celestial goal ahead of them that nothing deters them from it, nothing can turn them aside. Though they may falter and even fall at times, they rise again and are refreshed at the fountain of Life. "For a just man falleth seven times, and riseth up again." (Proverbs 24:16) For "we have an advocate … Jesus Christ the righteous." (I John 2:1) "In my Father's house," Jesus said, "are many mansions: if it were not so, I would have told you. I go to prepare a place for you. And if I go … I will come again, and receive you unto myself; that where I am, there ye may be also." (John 14:2-3) This, Beloved, is Eternal Security.

Ye Children of God, Persevere! Together.

DIVINE RESPONSE

FOREWORD TO: THE BLIND MEN AND THE ELEPHANT

First Corinthians twelve tells us,
How giftings vary in the body,
We need each other for discernment,
For balance, and to walk uprightly,
We need each other, brothers,
We need to hear each other out,
For we don't see so good alone,
But together, there's much less doubt.

So oft in theologic wars,
The disputants are wrong,
As we don't stop to recognize,
We're being way too strong,
As each one sees a partial picture,
And no one sees the whole
When we listen we get a bigger picture
And knowledge becomes more full.

God has formed us with two ears,
And only a single mouth,
Which means two places for sound to go in,
And one for sound to go out.
Maybe God meant, to tell us a thing,
Or two about relating well,
When He formed us one mouth for telling a thing,
But two ears for listening well.

PROMISES TO PERSEVERING SAINTS

THE BLIND MEN AND THE ELEPHANT

John Godfrey Saxe's (1816-1887) version of the famous Indian legend

It was six men, of Indostan,
To learning, much inclined,
Who went to see, the elephant,
(Though all of them, were blind)
That each, by observation,
Might satisfy his mind.

The first, approached the elephant,
And happening, to fall,
Against, his broad and sturdy side,
At once began to bawl,
"Excuse me, but the elephant,
Is very like a wall."

The second, feeling of the tusk,
Cried, "Ho, what have we here?
So very round, and smooth, and sharp?
To me, 'tis mighty clear,
This wonder of an elephant,
Is very like a spear."

Divine Response

The third, approached the animal,
And happening to take,
The squirming trunk, within his hands,
Thus boldly, up and spake:
"I see," quoth he, "the elephant,
Is very like a snake."

The fourth, reached out his eager hand,
And felt about the knee.
"What this, most wondrous beast is like,
Is mighty plain," quoth he,
"'Tis clear enough, the elephant,
Is very like a tree."

The fifth, who chanced to touch the ear,
Said, "E'en the blindest man,
Can tell, what this resembles most,
Deny the fact, who can,
This marvel, of an elephant,
Is very like a fan."

The sixth, no sooner had begun,
About the beast, to grope,
When seizing on, the swinging tail,
That fell, within his scope,
"I see," quoth he, "the elephant,
Is very like a rope."

And so these men, from Indostan,
Disputed, loud and long,
Each, in his own opinion,
Exceeding stiff, and strong,
Though each was partly in the right,
And all were in the wrong.

PROMISES TO PERSEVERING SAINTS

THE MORAL OF THE STORY

When arguing in our minds,
Or disputing loud and long,
Seeing darkly through a glass,
We are weak 'n often wrong.
When we are weak in our own eyes,
Jesus for us will be strong.

When we're sitting in a circle,
Deciding wrong from right,
We need each others' input to,
Turn our feelings into sight,
As we discover the big picture,
Walk together in the light.

Jesus Savior would have us,
Together be his eyes,
Confronting each mortal problem,
Resisting Satan's lies,
Understanding the big picture,
As fools, but being wise.

Without Jesus we're very wrong,
He is forever right.
He calls to follow all the way,
Jesus is shining light,
He helps us "sense the elephant,"
Jesus has perfect sight

Gottes sege dazu winscha
(May God add His blessing)

10

SABBATH REST MESSIAH

When God created the world He rested the 7th day. The work He'd set out to do was finished and He rested. God, who is omnipotent—meaning all-powerful—rested.

History as we know it began in Genesis Chapter 1. The earth was created in the beginning with the heaven (sky). The earth was dark, without form, and void. And the Spirit of God moved upon the face of the waters.

And there was a Lamb that was slain "from the foundation of the world." (Revelation 13:8) God, who is not limited to time, lives in the reality of eternity, so when He gave His word to be and to send the Lamb that was slain, the deed was as good as done. In that respect it was done.

Jesus, who is the Lamb that was slain, gave His life for the sins of the whole world. "For God sent not his Son into the world to condemn the world; but that the world through him might be saved." (John 3:17) Jesus being the "Lamb slain from the foundation of the world" (Revelation 13:8) gives us a strong indication that the Creation Week was a response to the war being fought in Heaven. The devil becoming full of pride and thinking to be "like the most High" (Isaiah 14:14) was, and finally will be, defeated by the crucifixion death, burial, resurrection, ascension, and finally, the second coming of Jesus Christ. (Revelation 19)

Jesus will come.

And will cast the devil, the beast, and the false prophet—with all those whose names are not written in the Book of Life—into the lake of fire. (Revelation 20:10 & 15)

"And these shall go away into everlasting punishment." (Matthew 25:46) A place "prepared for the devil and his angels." (Matthew 25:41)

The everlasting punishment also awaiting the self-righteous and unrepentant. (Matthew 25)

"There shall be weeping and gnashing of teeth." (Luke 13:28)

"Where their worm dieth not, and the fire is not quenched." (Mark 9:44-48)

"I am a worm, and no man," the Psalmist declared, (Psalm 22:6) in his distress.

But distress can be turned into joy because of "the Lamb slain from the foundation of the world." (Revelation 13:8)

So from the first day of Creation Week—from the foundation of the world—there was a plan.

For God always, always has a plan.

And in His plan Light wins over darkness.

On day one of creation, Sunday, God said, "Let there be light, and there was light. And God saw the light, that it was good: and God divided the light from the darkness." (Genesis 1:3-4)

On day two, Monday, God made the firmament and divided the waters under the firmament from the waters above the firmament.

On Tuesday He caused the dry land to appear and the gathering of the waters He called Seas; then He caused the earth to bring forth grass, also the herbs and fruit trees all with the means of reproduction.

On Wednesday God created the sun, moon, stars, and all planets, except the earth, which was already here, and caused them to be for signs, for seasons, and for days and years.

On Thursday God created the creatures of the sea and of the air, from the great whales to the smallest fish, from the hummingbirds to the soaring eagles.

On Friday God caused the earth to bring forth the living creature after his kind, cattle and creeping thing and beast of the earth.

And then God turned His attention to the purpose for all this, to the crowning glory of His creation. "Let us make man in our image," He said, "after our likeness: and let them have dominion over the fish of the sea, and over the fowl of the air, and over the cattle, and over all the earth, and over every creeping thing that creepeth upon the earth. So God created man in his own image ... male and female created he them." (Genesis 1:26-27) He

Divine Response

gave them dominion over all His creation, and the fruit of the herb and tree for food.

And then on Saturday, the seventh day of Creation Week, God rested from all His work which He had made.

Why did God—who is all-powerful—rest? The Bible doesn't tell us why He rested, just that He rested on the seventh day and was refreshed. What the Bible does tell us is that the day was later set aside as a day of rest for His people, and not just a day of rest, but a day to be hallowed. A day set aside as being so special that God gave many laws to His people as concerning the observance of it. But before He gave the laws to His people on how to observe the Sabbath, there, of necessity, was a law given concerning the special status of the seventh day.

That law was the fourth of ten commandments, first spoken then later written on tables of stone by God and given to His servant Moses on Mount Sinai, which Moses then delivered to the people. The three preceding commandments tell us how we should relate to God, the fourth tells us how we should relate to His day of rest, and the following six are on how we should relate to our fellowman. Jesus—when asked by one of the scribes which is the greatest commandment—made reference to at least the first three and the last six when He answered, "The first of all the commandments is, Hear, O Israel, the Lord our God is one Lord: And thou shalt love the Lord thy God with all thy heart, with all thy soul, with all thy mind, and with all thy strength: this is the first commandment. And the second is like, namely this, Thou shalt love thy neighbor as thyself. There is none other commandment greater than these." (Mark 12:29-31)

Why did Jesus not say anything in response to this question—not even in passing mention—of the Sabbath? He knew how important a day the Sabbath was to the Jewish people, whom He was seeking to reach with the truth of His word which He embodied. Why then was He so conspicuously silent on that one, the fourth commandment?

I wish to consider, with the reader, three possibilities:

> **Possibility 1.** Jesus considered the 4th commandment as abstract, having little to do with our love for God or our neighbor, and therefore of minor importance.
>
> **Possibility 2.** Jesus considered the 4th commandment as incorporated into, and inseparable from, loving our neighbor as ourselves.

Possibility 3. Jesus considered the 4th commandment as incorporated into and inseparable from, loving the Lord our God above all else.

Possibility 1. This fourth commandment, as given to Moses by God Himself on Mt. Sinai, is recorded for us in Exodus and reads thus: "Remember the sabbath day, to keep it holy. Six days shalt thou labour, and do all thy work: But the seventh day is the sabbath of the LORD thy God: in it thou shalt not do any work, thou, nor thy son, nor thy daughter, thy manservant, nor thy maidservant, nor thy cattle, nor thy stranger that is within thy gates: For in six days the LORD made heaven and earth, the sea, and all that in them is, and rested the seventh day: wherefore the LORD blessed the sabbath day, and hallowed it." (Exodus 20:8-11.)

Considering number one in our list of possibilities; this fourth commandment sounds to be very important to God that we keep it, not at all like some abstract lesser important commandment that we can take or leave. And neither do the commandments concerning the Sabbath that God gave at a later date to the children of Israel in the wilderness. In Exodus 31:12-17 God gave this even more detailed commandment concerning His day of rest, the Sabbath; "And the LORD spake unto Moses, saying, Speak thou also unto the children of Israel, saying, Verily my sabbaths ye shall keep: for it is a sign between me and you throughout your generations; that ye may know that I am the LORD that doth sanctify you. Ye shall keep the sabbath therefore; for it is holy unto you: every one that defileth it shall surely be put to death: for whosoever doeth any work therein, that soul shall be cut off from among his people. Six days may work be done; but in the seventh is the sabbath of rest, holy to the LORD: whosoever doeth any work in the sabbath day, he shall surely be put to death. Wherefore the children of Israel shall keep the sabbath, to observe the sabbath throughout their generations, for a perpetual covenant. It is a sign between me and the children of Israel for ever: for in six days the LORD made heaven and earth, and on the seventh day he rested, and was refreshed."

There are at least four key words that appear in the above text at least twice and thereby emphasizing the importance of what they convey to us. The word *sabbath* appears five times. Clearly God wanted no mistake as to which day he was referring to. The word *work* appears three times, and the word *death* twice, emphasizing to us that any work done on the sabbath was to be punished severely. By death. Far from being an abstract

Divine Response

commandment of minor importance, the transgression of this one commandment required the Israelites to correct the transgression by administering capital punishment to the offender. By putting him to death. There are other commandments in the Old Testament that, upon transgression, called for the death penalty, but why this one? Why tell someone that if he or she doesn't voluntarily rest on the sabbath, but works instead, then he or she will be involuntarily laid to rest in a grave? Let us lay this question to rest for now and come back to it later.

Possibility 2. Jesus considered the fourth commandment as incorporated into, and inseparable from, loving our neighbor as ourselves. This is hardly even a possibility. How could it be possible to love our neighbor as ourselves while stoning him or her to death? While church discipline, even to the extent of excommunication, can be said to have the recipients eternal welfare in mind and therefore it being an act of love for him or her; not so with the death penalty. Although it is our hope, and seems possible, that the condemned repented before the eyes were closed in death; to call the act of stoning someone an act of loving him or her as oneself seems a stretch of the imagination at best and ludicrous at worst. The example Jesus gave was to give and give, even the clothes off our back. Also the good Samaritan who took up, on his donkey, the man who had been left for dead by thieves; took him to an Inn and paid for his needs.

Possibility 3. Jesus considered the fourth commandment as incorporated into and inseparable from, loving the Lord our God above all else. This does seem more possible as the Bible nowhere separates loving God from keeping God's commandments but rather links the two together in such close harmony that they become truly inseparable. In Matthew 5:17-20 Jesus has this to say about the law: "Think not that I am come to destroy the law, or the prophets: I am not come to destroy, but to fulfil. For verily I say unto you, Till heaven and earth pass, one jot or one tittle shall in no wise pass from the law, till all be fulfilled. Whosoever therefore shall break one of these least commandments, and shall teach men so, he shall be called the least in the kingdom of heaven: but whosoever shall do and teach them, the same shall be called great in the kingdom of heaven.

For I say unto you, That except your righteousness shall exceed the righteousness of the scribes and Pharisees, ye shall in no case enter into the kingdom of heaven." Jesus then continued with what we today refer to as the Sermon on the Mount, having begun with what we today refer to as the Beatitudes. The Sermon on the Mount has the list of "Blesseds" as well as many "jots and tittles" brought forward as truth and justice with mercy added to them, as was prophesied in Psalms 85:10. "Mercy and truth are met together; righteousness and peace have kissed each other." These commandments, brought forward with mercy added, all have to do with loving God and our fellowman. And not only loving our fellowman who is lovable, but also the unlovable, even reaching out with compassion to our enemies.

In all of the Sermon on the Mount, however, Jesus gives no commandment concerning the Sabbath. Nor does He teach the keeping of it in any of His teachings, as recorded for us in the four gospels. Why the omission? we may ask, and rightfully so. For in Old Testament law the keeping or breaking of the Sabbath was not taken lightly. The keeping of it was taken so seriously by the Pharisees (at least the keeping of their own interpretation of it) at the time Jesus walked and taught among the hills of Judea and Galilee, that when He was perceived to have broken Sabbath keeping laws, they justified themselves in seeking to kill Him because He had broken the Sabbath.

Is it not thought provoking that the only time Jesus is recorded in the Gospels as even mentioning the Sabbath is on those occasions when He, in His wisdom, considered it necessary and worth His time to explain a justification for His breaking its laws, again, as interpreted by the Pharisees?

His teaching on keeping the Sabbath holy is conspicuously missing. In all of the Gospels. In the Acts of the Apostles. In the epistles to the churches. In the Revelation of Jesus Christ as recorded by John. We could well rest the case there and conclude that keeping the Sabbath in accordance with Old Testament law is no longer in effect. But let us go on, for we cannot conclude that our righteous and holy God has made a law so important to Him that the breaking of it brings the penalty of death upon the law-breaker, only to simply back away from it at a later date with no explanation.

Unless He has fulfilled it.

Which He then considers explanation enough. So the question is not only "shall we keep the Sabbath?" For there is a larger question that encompasses and so engulfs the above question as to render it even greater relevance in everyday Christianity. That question is: Is Jesus Christ the fulfillment of the Sabbath? Could this be why Jesus could teach that one jot or one tittle shall not pass from the law till all be fulfilled and then be silent on Sabbath-keeping? We could well say "yes" and rest our case there, but let us go on and consider how it is that Jesus Christ is the fulfillment of the Sabbath, its function, its purpose, and all the commandments surrounding it.

First, its function. Genesis 2:2-3 says, "And on the seventh day God ended his work which he had made; and he rested on the seventh day from all his work which he had made. And God blessed the seventh day, and sanctified it: because that in it he had rested from all his work which God created and made."

This day was a day set apart and distinct from the other six days of the week. For God rested from all His work on this day. The word function may be separated from the word purpose, in that the word function always implies purposeful action, while purpose is an object or an end to be attained. So while God's purpose in giving the Sabbath to man has a specific goal, that goal is not reached without us willingly entering into God's purposeful Holy Spirit-given direction.

So when God set apart the seventh day and sanctified it, He set apart a function that is not subject to us reaching the goal that He purposed. We may respond rightly or wrongly to His purpose, but what He set up as a function remains, despite our response. What this function consists of may be listed from the above passage of scripture in Exodus 31 and is also reiterated numerous times throughout the Old Testament:

Rest; God appointed this day as a day of rest for His people, having rested on the 7th day from His own work of creation. (Genesis 2:2)

Sign; "for it is a sign between me and you." (Exodus 31:13) And again; "It is a sign between me and the children of Israel." (Exodus 31:17)

A sign with purpose; "that ye may know that I am the Lord that doth sanctify." (Exodus 31:13)

Perpetual Covenant; "wherefore the children of Israel shall keep the sabbath … throughout their generations, for a perpetual covenant." (Exodus 31:16.)

Forever; "It is a sign between me and the children of Israel forever." (Exodus 31:17)

So this day of rest is to function as a sign of perpetual covenant between God and His people forever.

Is our Lord Jesus Christ the fulfillment of the Sabbath? Hebrews 4 has much to say to us concerning rest.

> Verse 1 is a warning lest we come short of entering into "his rest".

> Verse 2 is a reference to those who fell in the wilderness, that, "the Word preached did not profit them, not being mixed with faith in them that heard it."

Verse 3 refers to the believer entering into rest.

Verse 4 is a reminder that, "God did rest the seventh day from all His works." Verse 5 "If they shall enter into my rest."

Verse 6 refers again to those who "entered not in because of unbelief."

Verse 7 We are exhorted not to harden our hearts.

Verse 8 "For if Jesus had" (referring to the Old Testament) "given them rest then would He not afterward have spoken of another day."

Verse 9 "There remaineth therefore a rest to the people of God."

Verse 10 "For he that is entered into His rest, he also hath ceased from his own works as God did from His."

God created the world—and everything in it—in six days, then rested on the seventh day and was refreshed. Hebrews 4:10 cannot mean that we are to follow God's example and create a world and everything in it in six days and then rest on the seventh day and be refreshed. That is an obvious impossibility. We cannot look upon our work, as God did upon His, and behold that it is "very good."

It follows then that the only part of the creation week that we can copy is the part where God ceased from His own works. This corresponds with the Gospel message of our inability to save ourselves and then the saving redemption of Jesus Christ our Lord, our Messiah. The Apostle Paul, through the inspiration of the Holy Spirit wrote, "I am crucified with Christ: nevertheless I live; yet not I, but Christ liveth in me: and the life which I now live in the flesh I live by the faith of the Son of God, who loved me, and gave himself for me." (Galatians 2:20)

Hebrews 7:19 tells us that "the law made nothing perfect, but the bringing in of a better hope did." And in Matthew 11:29-30, Jesus gives us clear instruction to "take my yoke upon you, and learn of me; for I am meek and lowly in heart: and ye shall find rest unto your souls. For my yoke is easy, and my burden is light." And in Galatians 2:21, "if righteousness come by the law, then Christ is dead in vain."

What does it mean to be "crucified with Christ?" What does a wooden cross used for capital punishment by the Roman government of ancient times have to do with us? Jesus tells us, in Luke 14:27, that if we refuse to take up our cross we <u>cannot</u> be His disciple. But how can we, as God's word says, be "crucified with Christ" and yet live? No one questions whether we are all supposed to nail our physical bodies on a wooden cross and die there, as that would violate the entire tenor of Scripture. What then does it mean to take up our cross and follow Jesus? Let us consider that Jesus died on the last day of God's work week, his body lay in the grave during the Sabbath day and then He rose on the first day of God's work week. Incidentally, it was also the day God created light, separating the light from the darkness.

Friday, the last day of God's work week, is also when the work Jesus came to do was finished, as He said "It is finished", and gave up the ghost and died. (John 19:30)

We are also to cease from our own works as God did from His. (Hebrews 4:10) Why? Because we can say "mission accomplished?" Because we can look upon our own work, as God did upon His, and see that it is good? No, the fall of man and our consequent inability to satisfy God's just demands for holiness is the subject that permeates all of Scripture, always being co-mingled with God's redemptive purpose. "For all have sinned, and come short of the glory of God." (Romans 3:23)

It follows then, that something in us needs to die in order to "be crucified with Christ." Something that we are born with. Something inherent and natural to us all. This something has to do with the innermost part of our being. It is where we live. This something has to do with who we love.

The most.

We naturally love ourselves more than God, and are in opposition to the Ten Commandments. We naturally trust ourselves. We trust that given the right circumstances, the right environment, if we surround ourselves with people who make us feel good—allowing and even helping us get what we want, while saying nice, flattering things to us—that then we could and would be good. For we naturally believe in our own inherent goodness.

And therefore we are in opposition to God and His Word.

We seek happiness in things, comfort, fullness of bread, idleness, and other people. These become our idols. But we find our happiness is dependent on what happens. And as so much of life happens contrary to our will, happiness becomes a chased-after illusion. A mirage in the desert. And the more that we rush headlong after happiness along this course, the more we become mired in the miry pit of sin. And there, stuck in the miry clay, we cling to our last idol; Ourselves. Until … we give up and look up, crying out to Jesus for deliverance.

But what takes us to such depths of misery is the confidence we have in ourselves and our ability to find happiness, which becomes elusive, seemingly in equal capacity to the extent we grasp after it. It is this inherent confidence in ourselves that needs to die so that we cease "from our own works, as God did from his." (Hebrews 4:10) "For we are the circumcision, which worship God in the spirit, and rejoice in Christ Jesus, and have no confidence in the flesh." (Philippians 3:3) Crucified with Christ. Buried with Him. And arise to newness of life. "Yet not I, but Christ liveth in me." (Galatians 2:20) And so the weary find rest. And we find JOY. Jesus first. Yourself last. And Others in between. And the Rest that we find in Jesus enables us then to get—and be—involved in the work of the Lord. The work that we had no heart for and could not do until we found that Rest. That inner peace that only Jesus can give, and that He gives through out-pouring of comfort, peace, and empowering from the Holy Ghost. Which is given unto us, and has been given to true believers since first evidenced by cloven tongues of fire and the miraculous translation of foreign languages at the day of Pentecost out-pouring.

God did his work and then rested. We cease from our own works as God did from His, not because we're done with the work and see that it is good, but because we become done with ourselves and see that it is not good, thus confidence in ourselves dies. And when our trust and confidence turn to Jesus Christ, we find rest. Deep, heartfelt, peaceful rest. "Come unto me," Jesus says, "all ye that labour and are heavy laden, and I will give you rest." Then, and only then, are we empowered to work in His kingdom. As Jesus goes on to instruct us, "Take my yoke upon you, and learn of me; for I am meek and lowly in heart: and ye shall find rest unto your souls. For my yoke is easy, and my burden is light." (Matthew 11:28-30)

Back to Exodus 31. The Sabbath was given for a sign between God and His people. A sign in this context meant to signify some future event. Jesus in Matthew 12:39-40 told the scribes and Pharisees that "an evil and adulterous generation seeketh after a sign; and there shall no sign be given it, but the sign of the prophet Jonas: For as Jonas was three days and three nights in the whale's belly; so shall the Son of man be three days and three nights in the heart of the earth." They had rejected other signs, now this was their last one.

As a side note; if Jesus died on Friday, which He did, for the Jews wanted His body removed on the same day He died lest He hang there on the Sabbath; and if He rose again on Sunday, which He did, "on the first day of the week", then how could He be "three days and three nights in the heart of the earth?" This is a good question and worthy of consideration, for Friday night was one night, Saturday night was two nights, so where is the third night? The answer is in the expression of what we refer to as "a day." Whereas we would refer to it as three days if we were to go somewhere for three days, even if the first and last days were only partial days, the expression of the same time period also included the night, making each twenty-four hour period a day and night even if the first and last "day and night" were only partial. A "day and night" simply meant what we refer to as "a day".

But back to "the sign of the prophet Jonas." The sign was fulfilled in the time period encompassing the death, burial, and resurrection of Jesus. And the sign is also a very personal one to us. Had we been there when the whale swallowed Jonah, we likely would have shaken our collective heads and sadly muttered, "only a miracle can save him now." And we can safely presume that Jonah was also thinking those thoughts. And, that he was praying for a miracle.

We also need a miracle.

It was Jonah's confidence in his ability to do things his own way, in this time, that had to be destroyed. And when Jesus died on the cross, our hope to do what we want, our hope to have what we want in this world, in our own strength, in our way, in this time, died with him. Until then the disciples were still wondering when He would "restore the Kingdom again to Israel." Their self-confidence died at the cross. The same self-confidence that causes us to think we can serve God our own way, on our own time, becomes destroyed there. At the cross. Not only did Christ die on the cross, but our confidence in the flesh dies with him, as we take up our cross and our life is spiritually nailed to the cross in sacrifice to Him. As He said, "If any man will come after me, let him deny himself, and take up his cross, and follow me." (Matthew 16:24)

And then the relief that must have flooded Jonah is a sign of the "rest" we find in Jesus. Then, "we have also a more sure word of prophecy; whereunto ye do well that ye take heed, as unto a light that shineth in a dark place, until the day dawn, and the day star arise in your hearts." (II Peter 1:19) Jesus said to His disciples, "It is expedient for you that I go away: for if I go not away, the Comforter will not come unto you; but if I depart, I will send him unto you." (John 16:7) And in verse 13, "Howbeit when he, the Spirit of truth, is come, he will guide you into all truth: for he shall not speak of himself; but whatsoever he shall hear, that shall he speak: and he will shew you things to come." In Revelation 22:16, Jesus identifies Himself as "the root and offspring of David, the bright and morning star." Jesus said of Himself in John 12:46, "I am come a light into the world, that whosoever believeth on me should not abide in darkness."

Jesus gives rest. Jesus gives light, spiritual rest, and spiritual light. Jesus is the sign of the prophet Jonah. In his death, burial, and resurrection. In three days. Further, Jesus is the sign with purpose in the fourth commandment; "that ye may know that I [God] am the LORD that doth sanctify you." (Exodus 31:13) This God, concerned that we know Him, is concerned for our sanctification. Sanctification becomes very personal, though God never intrudes, but knocks on the door of our hearts until we open up to Him.

Thus, Jesus is the fulfillment of the rest, the sign, and the purpose of the sign in the fourth commandment.

Jesus fulfills the fourth commandment in being a perpetual covenant.

Webster's Dictionary (Collegiate) gives this definition of *perpetual*, ":continue forever; everlasting; valid for all time; holding (as an office) for life or for an unlimited time." Webster's dictionary (1828) gives the same, ":never ceasing; continuing forever in future time; destined to be eternal; as a perpetual covenant; a perpetual statute." (Literally true with respect to the decrees of the Supreme Being).

This perpetual covenant, then, is a forever covenant (Exodus 31:17), an everlasting covenant that extends from this life into eternity. The first covenant (do this and thou shalt live) was weak through the flesh and because of that weakness, crumbled under the scrutiny and test of time. How much less will that first covenant be able to stand under the scrutiny and test of eternity.

It cannot.

There is a better covenant—a superseding covenant—established in and through Jesus as expressed for us in Hebrews 8:6-7, "But now hath he [Jesus] obtained a more excellent ministry, by how much also he is the mediator of a better covenant, which was established upon better promises. For if that first covenant had been faultless [not weak through the flesh], then should no place have been sought for the second."

Jesus is the Word of God to us, as in John 1:14. "And the Word was made flesh, and dwelt among us ... full of grace and truth." He is "the way, the truth, and the life," (John 14:6) no man comes to the Father but by Him. He is now the fulfillment of the perpetual covenant of the fourth commandment and the mediator of it. Thus, Jesus fulfills the fourth commandment in its entirety. For He is our Rest, our Sign, our Sign with purpose and our perpetual covenant—forever. And if we abide in Christ, we live, for He is life. And our work is accepted and recognized by Him.

If we abide not in Christ we die, for the death penalty of the fourth commandment applies to us spiritually if we do not find rest in Him who is our Sabbath day rest. Thus, Jesus is also the answer to the question of "why the death penalty" upon those who did any work on the Sabbath.

The answer is that apart from finding rest in Jesus, there is no spiritual life, only death.

God, who is Almighty, did His work first and then rested. We cannot, for we are fallen man. But God provided a way for us to first rest in Jesus, the Word incarnate, so we can have His enabling grace, enabling us to work. God did His work first and then rested; we need to enter into His rest first so we can do His spiritual work.

Of the three possibilities we began with: 1) of the fourth commandment being of lesser or little importance to God; 2) of it somehow being incorporated into the commandment to love our neighbor as ourselves; or 3) of it being incorporated into the commandment to love the Lord our God with all our heart, soul, mind, and strength, this latter blends in and flows with the fourth commandment; Remember the Sabbath day to keep it holy.

Let us remember though that God knows our frame, and in His all-knowing wisdom saw our need for a day of rest, once a week. As Jesus said, "The sabbath was made for man, and not man for the sabbath." (Mark 2:27) What better day for us Christians to lay aside our work for the day and gather for worship, for prayer, and for teaching than on the day our Lord rose from the dead, The Lord's Day, the first day of the week, Sunday.

This first day of the week is the day that God created light. And is the day the Holy Ghost fell upon the Christians at Pentecost.

The early Christians, both before and after the Council of Nicea, as a general rule, met and worshiped on Sunday.

We have much reason to do likewise, for Jesus fulfills the demands of the fourth commandment.

As the songwriter wrote: verse 2 of "Oh Day of Rest and Gladness;"

> On thee, at the creation, the light first had it's birth,
> On thee, for our salvation, Christ rose from depths of earth,
> On thee our Lord, victorious, the Spirit sent from heav'n,
> And thus on thee most glorious, A triple light was giv'n
> (Number 44 in *Hymns of the Church*)

The writer, for one, is with the songwriter who promoted the belief, in song, that it was more than coincidence that these three, the creation of Light; Jesus, the Light that shineth in a dark place, rising from the dead; and the Spirit of God being sent from heaven giving spiritual light and understanding at Pentecost; all happened on the first day of the week, Sunday. So since He designed us in such a way that we do much better, actually need, one day of rest per week, does it matter which day we choose? After all, "one man esteemeth one day above another: another esteemeth every day alike. Let every man be fully persuaded in his own mind." (Romans 14:5) And, after all, "neither circumcision availeth any thing, nor uncircumcision," right? (Galatians 6:15)

True enough, except that in the letter to the Galatians they are told "Behold, I Paul say unto you, that if ye be circumcised, Christ shall profit you nothing." (Galatians 5:2) So while God no longer judges His children on whether they are uncircumcised or not, yet we have this warning about Christ profiting us nothing if we are circumcised.

It follows then that it matters why we do it. Whether we are doing it to keep the law from an Old Testament perspective—which denotes "confidence in the flesh", as the Galatians were doing—or not. And it follows also that it matters why we keep which day. Whether we are keeping the law from an Old Testament perspective or not, for "the law was our schoolmaster to bring us unto Christ, that we might be justified by faith." (Galatians 3:24) Though Sabbath-keeping and circumcision are in appearance very different, yet they are both rooted in the law that was our schoolmaster to bring us unto Christ.

In verse 12 of Chapter 3: "And the law is not of faith: but, The man that doeth them shall live in them." And the preceding, verse, 11, "But that no man is justified by the law ... it is evident: for, The just shall live by faith."

Romans 6:1-2 has this warning for us though; "What shall we say then? Shall we continue in sin, that grace may abound? God forbid. How shall we, that are dead to sin, live any longer therein?"

Man is fallen, therefore unable to rise to the demands of the law.

Christ is risen, and is become the light that shineth in a dark place. And by pouring the Light and Life of Himself into us, He enables us to live right. (Romans 8)

Fallen man ↓ Risen Lord ↑ Whom shall we trust?

"Trust in the Lord with all thine heart; and lean not unto thine own understanding." (Proverbs 3:5) One who labors in Christ's kingdom must first repent and be a partaker of rest in the finished work of Jesus Christ on the cross of Calvary. "If a man also strive for the masteries, yet he is not crowned, except he strive lawfully. The husbandman that laboreth must be first partaker of the fruits. Consider what I say; and the Lord give thee understanding in all things." (II Timothy 2:5-7)

The response of Jesus to the Pharisees, in answer to their question on why His disciples do on the Sabbath day that which is not lawful, is yet relevant to us today. For He ended His answer with these words, "The sabbath was made for man, and not man for the sabbath: Therefore the Son of man [Himself] is Lord also of the sabbath." (Mark 2:27-28) Only in finding rest in the finished work of Jesus Christ on the cross and in His resurrection, both bodily and in us, do we find rest from our own works, "as God did from His." (Hebrews 4:10) As in I Corinthians 1:30-31 "But of him are ye in Christ Jesus, who of God is made unto us wisdom, and righteousness, and sanctification, and redemption: That, according as it is written, He that glorieth, let him glory in the Lord."

In Christ Jesus we keep the fourth commandment, for in Him—and only in Him—we find rest from our spiritual and emotional labors, as we look forward to the redemption of our body.

Where "there shall be no more curse." (Revelation 22:3)

And to the call to "glory in the Lord," there has been—down through the ages—a clear resounding response from the faithful, saying, "AMEN!"

SABBATH REST MESSIAH

Jesus said, come unto me all ye,
That labor and are heavy laden,
And I will give you rest.
Take my yoke upon you, And learn of me,
For I am meek, And lowly in heart.
And ye shall find rest, Unto your souls,
For my yoke is easy
And my burden is light. (Matthew 11:28-30)

SABBATH REST MESSIAH

God chose to rest on the seventh day,
From all the vast work which He had done,
He called it Sabbath Day,
And of it gave commands.
This special Day,
A day of rest,
To be strictly kept.
Those who didn't rest,
Should be condemned,
Taken and stoned to death,
God's laws were very strict.

Do Sabbath Laws to Christians apply?
Or can we rightfully ignore them?
Did God really mean it?
Does His patience overlook?
Will He someday
Lose all patience?
Is the handwriting
Coming on the wall?
Must we yet see,
That we're in transgression,
Of God's holy commands?

Or did Jesus fulfill the Sabbath?
Do those keep God's law who rest in Him?
As a thief who finds police,
Turns himself in to them?
'N ceases to try,
Ways of escape.
Acquitted of guilt,
One taking His place,
He now finds rest,
And now is enabled,
To do the work of God.

Divine Response

We cannot like God call our work good,
And then rest from our labors as He.
All our righteousnesses,
Are as the filthy rags,
Used to clean up,
Our dirty spills.
God did His work first,
We have to find rest,
To rightly work.
The vine dresser knows fruit,
Has tasted of the grapes.

Jesus the Christ is our Sabbath,
In Him Sabbath commands are fulfilled.
The first day of the week,
He arose from the dead.
The day God said,
"Let there be light."
The Holy Ghost came,
Down on Pentecost.
These all took place,
The first day of the week,
This day we celebrate.

Jesus said, come unto me all ye,
That labor and are heavy laden,
And I will give you rest.
Take my yoke upon you,
And learn of me,
For I am meek, And lowly in heart.
And ye shall find rest, Unto your souls,
For my yoke is easy, And my burden is light.

Gottes sege dazu winscha
(May God add His blessing)

11

IT IS FINISHED

"Eloi, Eloi, lama sabachtani." (My God, my God, why hast thou forsaken me).

THE WORDS TORE FROM the lips of the man on the central of three crosses whose emaciated body had shown no resistance to the sure death awaiting it. The cry was, and is yet, a startling response to imminent death, as it came from this man with an otherworldly spirit. Who was now being mocked by His tormentors as He surrendered and succumbed to the inevitable fate of one nailed to a wooden cross, spikes through out-stretched hands, a single spike driven through over-lapped feet, the muscles of His arms and upper body stretched thin from the surrendered hanging of His own weight.

His surrendered body, hanging from His out-stretched arms, hung in stark contrast to the bodies of the two men being crucified on either side of Him. And indeed, hung in stark contrast to the struggle for life considered normal at other such scenes of crucifixion, as the natural instinct for survival caused men to push themselves up on the spike driven through the feet, despite excruciating pain, for the despairing privilege of drawing another breath.

Crucifixion was perhaps the cruelest form of capital punishment ever devised by the Roman government of ancient times. Certainly it was the most shameful. Reserved for the worst criminals, unless they were Roman citizens, the condemned would hang outside in the open air for all to see. The length of time before succumbing to death depended on the strength of constitution coupled with the strength of survival instinct, as the internal organs strove to keep functioning despite the external strain upon the ghastly body. The weight hanging from out-stretched arms and hands stretched and tightened the muscles across the chest. Making it difficult, and eventually impossible, to draw another breath, as the wearied body became unable to raise itself to relieve its compressed lungs. Or, as in this unprecedented case, the body simply hung without the struggle for survival, surrendered to its inevitable fate.

For Jesus knew that He was fulfilling the commitment—committed to from the foundation of the world—to be the Lamb that was slain. (Revelation 5:6) As depicted by the slaying of the Passover lamb once every year and even now being slain in preparation for the Passover celebration the next day. (Matthew 26:17) In full knowledge of this commitment and in full knowledge of the prophecies prophesying of this event, and having bowed his heart to it afresh in the garden of Gethsemane just the night before, He now committed himself to God the Father with these words, "Father, into thy hands I commend my spirit." (Luke 23:46) And then He said those words ringing down through the ages and giving hope to the hopeless who are hopelessly ensnared to the bondage of sin. "IT IS FINISHED!"

And creation shook, the rocks were rent apart, the temple veil covering the front of the holy of holies tore from top to bottom, many graves were opened and many bodies of the saints which slept arose and went into the holy city after His resurrection and appeared to many. Even the sun was darkened for three hours. (Matthew 27:50-54; Luke 23:44-45)

Creation may well shake at the death of this man. It should shake. It must shake.

Thankfully it only shook momentarily, as momentarily God the Father forsook His Son, who bore the penalty for our sins.

Forsook Him so He could die.

Forsook Him as He took our sins upon Himself and became sin for us. For God cannot abide in the presence of sin.

Until it is paid for. And, in our case, repented of. Then sin, and the condemnation going with it, cannot abide in the presence of God. "Come now, and let us reason together," He said "though your sins be as scarlet, they shall be as white as snow; though they be red like crimson, they shall be as wool." (Isaiah 1:18)

So Creation shook momentarily, for Jesus was momentarily forsaken as He took upon Himself the sins of the whole world. His body died and His spirit transitioned from the realm of time into the realm of timelessness, the realm of eternity. Creation rightfully shook during that momentary transition, for He, being the Word that was in and of the essence of God from eternity past, is the Word of God that spoke creation into existence. As God has spoken through the apostle John, "In the beginning was the Word, and the Word was with God, and the Word was God. The same was in the beginning with God. All things were made by him; and without him was not any thing made that was made. In him was life; and the life was the light of men. And the light shineth in darkness; and the darkness comprehended it not.

There was a man sent from God, whose name was John. The same came for a witness, to bear witness of the Light, that all men through him might believe. He was not that Light, but was sent to bear witness of that Light.

That was the true Light, which lighteth every man that cometh into the world. He was in the world, and the world was made by him, and the world knew him not. He came unto his own, and his own received him not. But as many as received him, to them gave he power to become the sons of God, even to them that believe on his name. Which were born, not of blood, nor of the will of the flesh, nor of the will of man, but of God.

And the Word was made flesh, and dwelt among us, (and we beheld his glory, the glory as of the only begotten of the Father,) full of grace and truth. " (John 1: 1-14)

Yes, creation rightfully shook, as the Word, who had spoken it into existence, "gave up the ghost." It is significant for us that none of the Gospels say that He died, but only that He "gave up the ghost." From eternity past to eternity future He was, is, and will be alive. Death has no part in Him. He is Life!

But He also became the son of man when He was born of a woman. His body was conceived in Mary's womb when the Holy Ghost came upon and overshadowed her after the angel Gabriel informed her "therefore also that holy thing which shall be born of thee shall be called the Son of God." (Luke 1:35) Thus, He became God's only begotten Son. His body was born of a woman as the Word became flesh to dwell among us. Therefore, His body could, and did, die. He died for us, taking upon Himself our sins. To give us Life! Eternal Life! His Life! And then He Arose, for He is Life. Of His body the Roman soldiers testified of His death. For the Jewish rulers, not being sure that Jesus was dead and possibly believing that all three crucifixion victims were still alive, were religiously concerned that the bodies not hang on the crosses the next day, on the sabbath (that sabbath was also a high day). They went to Pilate asking that the men's legs be broken, "and that they might be taken away." (John 19:31) Broken legs were

Divine Response

to hinder the crucifixion victim's ability to push up to gain another breath and would therefore hasten their death.

"Then came the soldiers, and brake the legs of the first, and of the other which was crucified with him. But when they came to Jesus, and saw that he was dead already, they broke not his legs. But one of the soldiers with a spear pierced his side, and forthwith came there out blood and water." (John 19:32-34)

The events surrounding the death of Jesus were fulfilling prophecy in minute detail. Prophecy as prophesied by the Prophets, and as foreshadowed by the Law of Moses and before. Even to the garden of Eden where, after the fall into sin of the first man and first woman, God gave this sentence to the deceiving serpent, "And I will put enmity between thee and the woman, and between thy seed and her seed; it shall bruise thy head, and thou shalt bruise his heel." (Genesis 3:15)

Hidden in this sentence being pronounced upon the devil is a Promise. A Promise of One coming who would tread on the reasoning powers of the devil and ultimately destroy him. That his reasoning powers were bruised was evidenced when he brought about his own destruction, while darkly believing that he was destroying the Son of God—in spirit, soul, and body—on a wooden cross that was unspeakably flimsy in comparison to the power of the One he was attempting to destroy. Jesus had already overcome the devil by resisting his temptations in the wilderness and by living a sinless life. The bruising had already begun before the cross. Now, by the body of Christ and His Resurrection, Satan's ultimate destruction of being cast into the lake of fire is sealed. Where the smoke of their torment ascends forever and ever. (Revelation 14)

The devil is doomed. The war in heaven has been won. It is over.

But the battle still rages here. For the devil goes about "like a roaring lion, seeking whom he may devour," while the heavens rejoice, the earth groans under his oppression. "Therefore rejoice, ye heavens, and ye that dwell in them. Woe to the inhabiters of the earth and of the sea! for the devil is come down unto you, having great wrath, because he knoweth that he hath but a short time." (Revelation 12:12)

God, through the Apostle Paul, writes of a mystery being hidden from generations, now being made manifest to His saints, including Jew and Gentile, "which is Christ in you, the hope of glory." (Colossians 1:27) Were the birth, life, death, and resurrection of Christ tucked into the prophecies and foreshadowings in such a way as to thwart the understanding of the rulers of darkness so that they bring about their own destruction? We have reason to believe this to be so. (I Corinthians 2:8)

We also have reason to believe that there were those, as evidenced by Simeon, (Luke 2:25-32) who understood and trusted in Messiah who was to come. Scripture also indicates that there were those repentants who died without the full knowledge of Christ, but to whom grace is extended, because of Christ, in response to their repentance and belief in the Promise of God by faith for deliverance. (I Peter 3:18-20; Hebrews 11) As children who—though born in sin and under the curse—are yet saved through the sacrifice of Christ on the cross when they die in their innocence, so these also when they died in their repentance.

There is no other mediator. "For there is one God, and one mediator between God and men, the man Christ Jesus; Who gave himself a ransom for all, to be testified in due time." (I Timothy 2:5-6) He is the Mediator of a new and a better covenant. (Hebrews 8:6, 9:15, 12:24) A covenant that Jesus the Christ sealed with His own blood by His death on the cross. "And for this cause he is the mediator of the new testament, that by means of death, for the redemption of the transgressions that were under the first testament, they which are called might receive the promise of eternal inheritance. For where a testament is, there must also of necessity be the death of the testator." (Hebrews 9:15-16)

When we go to a lawyer to have him type a will (testament) for us, that will takes effect after we die, not before. Someone must die before a will goes into effect. What we had before Jesus died on the cross was a Promise. "For a testament is of force after men are dead: otherwise it is of no strength at all while the testator liveth." (Hebrews 9:17) The Promise was secure but the present reality of Jesus fulfilling the Promise is even more so, and the culmination, ours by Promise but yet in the future, exponentially so. Security. O, to be secure. Is not this the cry of the human heart?

In tradition, women leave the home of their parents and become married to men whom they look to for security. But it hardly matters how well cared for and loved she is by her man, at heart she is still a little girl desiring the security she knew as a child under the protection of an earthly father.

Grown men, even strong men, even the macho type, successful business men, young and ambitious or old and seasoned, have a measure of insecurity, a measure of doubt about their abilities to keep up with the everyday demands of life. Do we not?

Divine Response

Insecurity is a part of life as it pertains to this world. True, lasting, solid, unshakeable security must then, of necessity, be otherworldly. A security not kept within the close, stifling confines of this world. Though this reality is initially and at times hard to accept, the unavoidable reality is that we cannot avoid the demise of our bodies. They are mortal and will only take on immortality if we have truly repented of our sins and have truly believed in Jesus Christ our Savior and Lord. Though the Bible indicates that the lost also eternally exist (O, horrible thought); it very clearly refers to separation from God as death and being redeemed here and with Him in heaven as Eternal life or immortality. Though our hearts and minds naturally recoil at thoughts of hell, those same thoughts should, and need to, cause us to be earnest in securing the reality of being right with God. This God, through the comfort of the Holy Ghost and because of Jesus, gives the one and only true security, for it alone never ends and it alone will stand the test of time and circumstances here in this life. It is otherworldly, lasting, and the only true security.

When we consider the horrible condition of the lost, our minds may grapple with thoughts and even mistrust about the final Judgment. How is it that some have so much privilege and others so little? And yet, both the privileged and under-privileged are to be judged by the same standard, found lost, and sentenced to the same fate? How can an innocent baby be born to godless parents, live a godless life as an adult, die a godless death, and be justly judged and condemned by a standard little known and untaught? How can the heathen be born in the jungle, live in the jungle, and die in the jungle, having no or very little contact with the outside world or the Gospel all through their lives, and yet be justly judged by a Gospel unheard of?

Our minds can somewhat understand, if not fully accept, the concept of guilt in one born into privilege, having Godly parents, a Godly church, and a clean neighborhood, being rightly judged upon turning their back in contempt against such privilege and Godly teaching. What about God's judgment? What about that "great and dreadful day of the Lord? (Malachi 4:5) That day that our physical body, even our very soul, recoils from? That day when the "dead shall hear the voice of the Son of God, and they that hear, shall live?" That day when all, both small and great, both rich and poor, no matter our station in life, will all be gathered together before the Judgment throne of Almighty God? That day when those buried in the ground, those buried at sea, those cremated whose ashes were stored in

IT IS FINISHED

urns or scattered; will be gathered with those which are alive and remain? All together before our God. Who created the earth and everything in it, including our first two ancestors, man and woman, in six days? He who knows and sees everything. He who understands us better than we understand ourselves. Can we trust Him to judge righteous judgment? Do we trust Him to judge righteous judgment? Or does His Judgment need to make sense to our finite minds?

The question, in reality, is do we trust Him to rightly judge our actions and our very thoughts even now? Or do we even now justify ourselves, our thoughts, and our actions? Our response either opens or closes the flow of grace.

Job, when he thought life had dealt him a harder blow than he deserved, fell to complaining about his lot in life. And his lot in life was extremely hard, harder than most will ever face. He lost his livelihood, all his children died, horrible boils covered his body, his wife turned against him, and last of all his friends tried convincing him that all these calamities befell him because he had somehow sinned. Even though they didn't know for sure how he had sinned, they had some guessing suggestions. And besides, the calamities themselves were all the proof needed to prove that he had somewhere, somehow sinned. Were they not? So Job fell to justifying himself. For 29 chapters, (Job Chapters 3 through 31) And the more his three friends accused him, the more Job justified himself.

A fourth man speaks up. And this man, Elihu, proves to be a true friend. One who turns Job's attention, away from himself and his hard circumstances in life, to God. To God and His Majesty, His Power, His Glory, and His unmistakable righteousness in judgment that is beyond our ability to change and useless to refute. Elihu pointed Job to God, endeavoring to show him how useless it was to continue justifying himself to his accusers, and even complaining of God being unjust, as he compared the good he had done with the evil that he didn't do.

It is unfair, Job is saying, life is not treating me fairly. But Elihu rightly understood that as Job justified himself and complained about life being unfair, he was actually, in a round-about way, accusing God. And because Elihu understood, he was able to help Job turn his attention back to God. Elihu succeeded, Job became quiet before God and his heart and mind cracked open to hearing what God had to say.

And God spoke.

DIVINE RESPONSE

God spoke to Job, helping him to clearly see how in the wrong he was to justify himself. He spoke to Job, helping him to see how fruitless and vain it was of him to complain. How his complaints availed him nothing and besides he was actually complaining against God, to whom he should be turning for help instead of turning away with complaints of being treated unfairly. Perhaps we think God was unfair with Job? Or perhaps we think God is unfair to us? Or perhaps we think life has been unfair to us? Or perhaps we think people have been unfair to us? While we should be concerned about fair play, and most especially that we treat others fairly, to insist upon being treated fairly ourselves only brings us into emotional misery, often seeming in direct proportion to our insistence.

Job had reason to be truly miserable. If anyone had a right to complain, Job did. His children… gone; his wealth… gone; his health… gone; his wife's respect… gone; the respect of his friends… gone. And with all that he had lost, Job still had his emotions to deal with. These were as alive and functional as ever and he felt the pain of it all. Deeply.

Yet, we hear God, through the Book of Job, not catering to Job's complaints in an effort to help Job feel better about himself; but rather, He is silent. Until one "stands in the gap" and speaks up for God. Elihu successfully draws Job's attention back to a right and just view of God. That of God being Omniscient, Omnipresent, and Omnipotent. "Nay but, O man," God says in Romans 9:20-21, "who art thou that repliest against God? … Hath not the potter power over the clay … to make one vessel unto honour, and another unto dishonor?" God has Eternal Purpose in doing, or allowing, the things that He does or allows. God is the Creator of all that is good, but He allows the bad. He is the Creator of all things beautiful, but He allows the ugly. He is the Source of Joy, but He allows sadness. He binds up broken hearts, but He allows broken hearts. He sets the captives free, but he allows captivity. His Will is perfect, yet He allows the free will of a fallen humanity. Do we understand it all? Not always. And it is in the "not always" that our trust at times stretches to, and beyond, the breaking point. Does it not?

This was the breaking point Job had reached. His trust was stretched. Well nigh to breaking. But it held. It healed. Trust returned fully while Elihu, and then God, spoke. And Job said to God, "I have heard of thee by the hearing of the ear: but now mine eye seeth thee. Wherefore I abhor myself, and repent in dust and ashes." (Job 42:5-6) This is a rightful state of heart and mind to have when confronted by the One who made us. He understands. His Purpose is Eternal. His Grace is enabling. His Goal for us does not end

IT IS FINISHED

in a pile of dust and ashes. His goal is to "revive the spirit of the humble," (Isaiah 57:15) to "appoint unto them that mourn in Zion, to give unto them beauty for ashes, the oil of joy for mourning, the garment of praise for the spirit of heaviness." (Isaiah 61:3) "I can do all things," wrote God-inspired Paul, "through Christ which strengtheneth me." (Philippians 4:13)

It is finished. Those words flowed from the heart and lips of One who knows. One who knows ugliness, knows sadness, knows broken hearts, knows captivity, and knows fallen humanity. He knows all and is touched with the feeling of our infirmities for He dwelt among us, "was in all points tempted like as we ... yet without sin." (Hebrews 4:15)

It is finished. Those words flowed from the heart and lips of One who also knows Beauty, knows Joy, knows Whole and Free hearts, knows Liberty, and knows the Perfection of God's will.

It is finished. He Redeemed us from Eternal Destruction.

It is finished. He Redeemed us from our self-willed spirit.

It is finished. He Redeemed us from the emotional complaints of the soul.

It is finished. We look forward to the Redemption of our bodies, of which Job is a type when poverty was turned on its head, and his latter wealth out-stripped the former.

Why did God let Job go through all this? Why did God allow the devil to bring so much misery into Job's life when He could as well have disallowed it as He disallowed the taking of Job's life? Why does God allow bad things to happen to upright people? Why does God allow bad things to happen at all?

He gives us the answer in His word, that we may come forth as gold, tried in the fire. (I Peter 1:7) I have, regrettably, never encountered the need to purify gold, so I don't have experience in the process, but it is my understanding that gold is separated from rock fragments, gravel, and dirt through an extreme heat process, the gold becoming liquid and separating itself from the dross. We are made in the image of God, and even as our purpose is not to destroy the gold but to purify it, so it is God's desire not to destroy us through the fiery trials we go through, but to purify us.

Can God ever relax into His throne and cease to purify any one of us while we are yet in the realm of time? No, because the devil "as a roaring lion, walketh about, seeking whom he may devour." (I Peter 5:8) Or, he approaches as a harmless one, a sheep even, humble, unsure, watchful, on nimble feet, one of the flock. But he is a ravening wolf. When once the flock is unaware, he lets go of his sheeply attire and tears into the flock, destroying the faith of the weaker ones. He is subtle, deceptive. We are not "ignorant of his [Satan's] devices." (II Corinthians 2:11) And all things being open and known to God, He knows and sees the danger we are in. Having limited His intervention, by allowing us to choose our own way or His, He therefore is ever calling us to higher ground.

As the young parents of four little girls ages 6, 4, 2, and a baby, my wife and I were determined to do this raising of children right the first time, driven by the obvious, that we had one chance at it. There would be no do-overs. There could be repentance, yes, but once these little ones are grown and we see our mistakes, we can't make them little again and do this child-rearing thing over again. So we were very diligent to train, correct, and discipline. Whatever it took, that's what we did. But about the time all was well and we were becoming one of those smooth, put-together families, there would be a rude awakening. One of the little ones would do something crazy like refuse to put toys away at bedtime. Another, refuse to settle down for the night. Another, fuss and fidget the next day in church. Or... you name it; and if you are a parent, you probably can. So we would diligently work at it again till we peaked... and then... downhill we would go. I remember where I was sitting one evening when it dawned on me that rather than stay consistent we tend to be diligent till we "arrive." Then we relax... and then "downhill we go." Where was I sitting when I received this revelation? In my easy chair.

In this sense our loving Heavenly Father never relaxes. He is ever diligent, ever consistent, and ever loving. Though it does not always feel like love (who feels loved while being chastened?), the more that we bask in His Love in communication with Him in His Word and prayer through the Holy Spirit, the more aware we become of the good outcomes of the hard things we go through; in short, the more that we sense the Father heart of God, the more we trust Him and the deeper and more steady our faith becomes. In Him.

The shaking of things temporal is simply for the purpose "that those things which cannot be shaken may remain." (Hebrews 12:27) We begin as spiritual babes, "as newborn babes, desire the sincere milk of the word, that ye may grow thereby." (I Peter 2:2) Growing, being a sign of physical life to us, is also a sign of spiritual life as we grow spiritually, but our spiritual growth needs to be measured by the Scriptural measure that God has provided. Caution is in order here, because we have this innate tendency to be partial to ourselves. Or to those we love. We need the impartial illumination of God's Word, through His Holy Spirit, to our hearts and minds. Growing is a part of life. And because we tend to forget, to slip back, to revert, to become dull, we need the continual loving correction, direction, and comfort of our loving Heavenly Father.

When our oldest children were yet small, my wife and I still young, our debts paid, our needs met, though not extravagantly so, there came a time of life when I wished time could just stop now and all remain as it is. But changes came; those oldest children are now married with families of their own, we live in a different state and are getting older. When celebrating the 10th birthday of our youngest, I told her that I love her exactly the way she is and that I want her to stop growing and just stay the way she is from now on. But then I was quick to correct myself because, after all, it wouldn't take long for us to get concerned if she quit growing. And besides, we did it to our parents too; we also grew up. Now it's our children. And grandchildren.

Grandpa leaned into his easy chair, pulling the little lever that released the spring-loaded footrest elevating his feet. The sound caught the attention of granddaughters, four year old Mikayla and her two year old sister Kassya, who'd been playing nearby. To both of them the sound was an invitation to choose a small stack of children's books and carry them to Grandpa for him to read aloud. The oldest one clambered on by herself and the youngest one with a little help from Grandpa. They settled back on each side, each in a crook of Grandpa's arms as he held the book between. After the usual reading of several "Little House" picture books was a number book, meant to teach counting. "One, two, free…" goes Mikayla counting flawlessly to ten. Her little sister "mimic" tried following along, but soon her loud "counting" not at all in sequence, had us both just watching, Grandpa amused but Mikayla drowned out and a bit miffed. "She doesn't know her numbers yet," says she. "No, but she's trying and that's good," says Grandpa. "But," said Mikayla pensively, "she doesn't even say them right. She says "shee" for "free."

My Grandpa heart found them both too cute and amusing to correct. So I didn't, but went on with the book. Does the Father heart of God at times feel the same way? He likely does. When he sees no danger. But when He sees soul-danger, He is alert, wanting to help us overcome, to avert the danger. He goes on with The Book, wanting us to reckon with it. Would I get concerned if my granddaughters never grew past saying "shee" and "free?" Of course I would, even though neither mispronunciation would be a problem in and of itself. But it could be a small sign of a deeper developmental problem, and herein lies the concern.

And herein lies the concern when a Christian's growth seems stymied, not that every little thing is necessarily bad in and of itself, but that it may be; and especially so when there is an accumulation of "little things;" a sign of a deeper problem, that of resistance to God in small ways that add up in a big way. God is ever concerned for our growth in sanctification. But first we must be born. Born of the Spirit. Lest we be of those who are "ever learning, and never able to come to the knowledge of the truth." (II Timothy 3:7) The Truth about ourselves. And Jesus, who is the embodiment of Truth.

The more deeply and fully that we comprehend the truth about ourselves, the more we can also comprehend the depth and the fullness of meaning in the words coming from the tortured lips of the emaciated figure, Jesus, on the cross of Calvary when He said, "It is finished." The Apostle Paul, though he initially believed himself blameless, "touching the righteousness which is in the Law," (Philippians 3:6) also referred to himself as the chief of sinners. (I Timothy 1:15) Paul seems to have seen in himself the depth of human depravity, and that it was only Jesus making the difference that protected him from himself and the potential of his lower nature.

The work is indeed finished. Jesus Christ "is made unto us wisdom, and righteousness, and sanctification, and redemption." (I Corinthians 1:30) Every wise saying, every inspiring and wise Proverb, every wise law, every wise deed, every wise thought, the order in the universe, and all else well put together and wise, have their origin in God.

Every good and right thought, every good and right word, every righteous deed, every righteous law, and all else righteous, have their origin in God.

Every sanctified thought, every sanctified action, every sanctified word, and all else sanctified, have their origin in God.

All that is redeemable and redeemed has its origin in God.

In Christ Jesus all has been made available to all of us. As we avail ourselves by being available. Available for His in-filling. Available to be a vessel unto honor. (Romans 9:21) "That, according as it is written, He that glorieth, let him glory in the Lord." (I Corinthians 1:31)

Paul, by the inspiration of God, wrote to the Church at Galatia, "I am crucified with Christ: nevertheless I live; yet not I, but Christ liveth in me: and the life which I now live in the flesh I live by the faith of the Son of God, who loved me, and gave himself for me. I do not frustrate the grace of God:

for if righteousness come by the law, then Christ is dead in vain." (Galatians 2:20-21)

We have this privilege.

A privilege to be crucified?

Crucifixion doesn't feel good. It means self-denial. But it is a necessary precursor to the glorious grace of God in Jesus Christ. And this is a privilege. A glorious privilege. The wisdom of the choice of the Disciples of Christ was not understood till Pentecost, when, in reflecting upon the birth, life, teaching, crucifixion, burial, resurrection, and ascension of Jesus, it all came together in their hearts and minds and made sense.

The wisdom of Bible-Christianity will not be understood until we have a personal Pentecost and only fully understood at the second coming of Jesus Christ, when He will divide the sheep from the goats. (Matthew 25:32) The sheep being those dependent and surrendered to Jesus Christ, and the goats being those who depend upon themselves. We have every reason to give our hearts and lives to Jesus, who says to each of us personally, and to the world at large, "It is Finished."

THE FINISHED WORK

It is finished! the Master cried,
Then he bowed His head and died.
His body limp and beaten,
Slumping forward, stretched out thin.
What meaneth now this spectacle?
Where is now our lofty goal?
Why hangs He from this cruel cross,
O cruel grave! O cruel loss!

The Master's gone, disciples cried,
Soaring hope was crushed and died,
Rocks were rent, the sun went dark,
Earthquakes shook, things fell apart,
All matching the disciples' mood,
Hopeless they could see no good.
How did our hope for Israel soar?
In this hope our lives out-poured?!

Divine Response

On Sunday Jesus rose again!
He then appeared to women,
Two men walking, to Emmaus,
"He speaks to us, then disappears."
He appeared behind closed doors,
Once earnestly spoke to Thomas,
Told him nail prints and scars to feel,
Tried to persuade, that He is Real.

Trembling faith, hovering above,
Hardly daring to believe,
That the Master has flesh and bone,
At times appears, but then is gone.
The Spirit had not yet descended,
To open the eyes, of the mind,
Not understanding, yet the puzzle,
Why is life so out of control?

"I go a-fishing," Peter said,
Went to do what he once did,
Back before this life he tried,
Before hope soared,
was crushed 'n died.
Returning to their livelihood,
To the sea these men returned
Their boat into the water shoved.
Nets into the waters heaved.

They fished all night, but caught no fish,
Seas not yielding what they wished.
Struggling hope again was crushed,
All seemed lost, all Heaven hushed.
Why did the Master have to die?
In his presence hope could rise.
Why was He scourged and crucified?
Mercy and respect denied?

IT IS FINISHED

Hark! Whose voice? lilting from the shore,
Wafting on crisp morning air?
Rising, falling, in soft breeze,
As rippling of the gentle waves?
About our lack of fish concerned,
Bidding cast on the other side?
On other side the net was cast,
Now it filled, it well nigh burst.

Peter, convinced it is the Lord,
'N casting himself overboard,
In a rush, waded ashore,
For he'd been heartsick and sore.
Overcome by fear, denied his Lord,
Wilted by a woman's word.
Now to Jesus, he came again,
For assurance he still yearned.

Again as Christ, appeared to them,
In awe they gazed upon Him.
While He stooped, prepared them food,
On the coals were fish 'n bread.
A spirit does not stoop and serve,
Fish and bread He to them gave,
They must have reasoned in their mind,
Knew for sure, this is the Lord.

Life didn't end there on the cross!
Hope now soared above the loss.
Here was Jesus, the one they loved,
Fish and bread He to them served.
They gazed upon Him, and believed
God's Spirit giving, sowing seed.
Salvation full, salvation free,
Christ has won the vic-to-ry.

Divine Response

When He appeared, though doors were closed,
They trembled on, Life's threshold,
But still gave food, when He asked,
Broiled fish, and a honeycomb.
When He'd eaten, gave more teaching
Opening, their understanding
He led them out, to Bethany,
Taught them how, to be truly free.

And there He lifted up His hands,
He blessed them, 'n while He them blessed,
Rose to the clouds, disappeared again,
Wonder affixed, their gaze to heaven,
Two men in white, by them appeared,
Told how Jesus, though disappeared,
Shall come again, in the clouds appear,
Shall come again, as He had gone.

All our wayward ways are doomed,
But Finished the work of God.
Christ has overcome sin's pain,
Soaring hope alive again.
The work was finished! on the cross,
Full understood at Pentecost.
That Life for us is in His blood,
'N by His Spirit, Life sustained.

Arise in Him, O Church of Christ!
The victory's won, in Him is Life!
The finished work, Christ on the cross,
Saved us from eternal loss!
He arose! Is alive! Gives us Life!
And Saves us from sin and strife!
Victorious! He is God's Word!
King of kings! And Lord of lords!

Gottes sege dazu winscha
(May God add His blessing.)

12

THE EMPTY TOMB

The crowd that had gathered on the lonely hill of Calvary were all gathered for the same reason, but the expression on their faces showed clearly that they were not all of one heart, nor all here for the same purpose. For while some thought their mission accomplished, the victorious elation reflected on their faces was in stark contrast to the defeated dejection reflected on the faces of others. The dejection of the defeated was exacerbated ever deeper by the mocking taunts even now being hurled at the beaten, emaciated figure nailed through his hands and feet to the central of three crosses planted firmly on Mount Calvary; on this day that was depressing despite the sunshine.

But the mocking of the victors was short-lived. For even their mocking carried an element of uneasiness with it. What was it about this man? The unshakeable serenity surrounding him—as an impenetrable barrier to their taunts—caused even their pious hatred for him to seem impious.

What was it about this man?

Even now, all eyes turned, riveted towards him as He cried out, "My God, my God, why hast thou forsaken me?" One ran for the sponge close by, soaked up vinegar with it, put it on a reed, and lifted it to him for a drink. After which He said, "It is finished," bowed His head, and died. As His last breath faded away, so did the last faint hope of His followers. For as long as a body continues to draw breath there is hope, however slim it may be, that somehow, someway, strength may be regained, the body may yet fight off whatever affliction or infliction it is suffering and recover. But with the last breath drawn, all hope flees. Even though this man had raised others from the dead, now He Himself was gone. And there was no one left with such powers, no one to raise Him up. Death is so final.

And to His devoted followers, even His amazing powers over sickness and death had died with Him. For when something we do not wish to be final actually happens, or is perceived to have happened, to a loved one, we discover that the deeper our love, the more deeply we hurt. Which has caused many a well-meaning person to draw away when relationships get too close, for being once hurt, or perhaps many times, creates a natural innate fear of being hurt again. For the deeper we love, the deeper we hurt. And so it was with the disciples. They loved deeply, they hurt deeply, and in the midst of their deep hurt and grief all seemed lost.

The victors were not so; they would seem to have much reason to rejoice. But victory brought with it an unnameable fear that this man's claims were not all groundless. And even as their impious piety shook within them, the very ground they stood on trembled and shook. Trembled and shook, as the area was gripped in the throes of an earthquake so violent that even rocks were rent apart and graves were opened. The veil in the temple was rent—as by unseen Almighty hands—from the top to the bottom! The sun was darkened and there was darkness over all the earth for the space of three hours. Three hours of darkness! Caused by a darkened sun!

And the victors were no longer victors. Their groveling desperation likely showed itself first in the overcoming fear on their desperate faces; and later after the burial they desired of Pilate that the tomb be sealed where the body was laid with a band of watchmen stationed there to guard the dead body, lest, they said, his disciples steal his body and declare Him to be risen from the dead as He Himself claimed He would. For though they had rejected Him, now, despite themselves, they understood and feared His claims.

Joseph of Arimathaea sought for and received permission from Pilate to take away the body of Jesus. With the help of Nicodemus—who had come to Jesus by night and to whom Jesus had said those words yet reverberating down through the ages, "Ye must be born again"—they removed the body of Jesus from the cross, wound it in linen with spices and laid it in the tomb hewn into rock that Joseph had prepared for himself (and presumably for his household) and rolled the prepared stone before the opening.

This body—bruised almost beyond recognition by the scourging he'd received from the bone fragments woven into the multiple thongs of Roman whips, its spear-pierced side out of which had flowed blood and water, though not a bone was broken—was fulfillment of prophecy. (Psalms 22:16-17; Zechariah 12:10; Psalms 34:20)

As was the parting of His garments. (Psalms 22:18)

As was His burial. (Isaiah 53:9)

As was His resurrection. (Psalms 16:10)

And it was His resurrection, this claim of Divinity, that His enemies now feared. They feared what a false report that He had risen from the dead would do for the furtherance of such "false doctrine" that set men free from the keeping of ceremonial law.

For ceremony was the cohesive strength left to the nation of Israel. Many had fought for, and died for, the right to keep their own place and nation in the midst of this foreign government now centered at Rome. An uneasy co-existence continued since the Maccabean war of just over 200 years ago between the ruling government and the nation of Israel; and despite its uneasiness, many had become comfortable with political maneuverings to maintain the uneasy truce.

But even as political maneuverings maintained their place and nation, ceremony maintained their identity as a nation.

Despite a Ruler's attempt to eradicate their ceremonial laws.

When Antiochus Epiphanes became ruler of the Empire in 175 B.C., he burned and banned the Hebrew Bible, making its possession punishable by death.

He also banned many of the Jewish ceremonial practices, including the circumcision of males, observing the Sabbath and feast days, and offering sacrifices according to the law of Moses.

But Antiochus underestimated the devotion of the Jews to their God and His laws. For he demanded that they cease to worship the God of Israel and instead worship the foreign gods that he wished to bring in. If they refused to change, they were to be put to death.

But the Jews took seriously and held firmly to the commandment in Exodus 20:3-5 "Thou shalt have no other gods before me ... thou shalt not bow down thyself to them, nor serve them: for I the LORD thy God am a jealous God ..."

The breaking point of no return came when Antiochus sent troops demanding that the Jews sacrifice a pig to the Greek gods. A Jewish leader named Mattathias fled to the hills where many of the devout joined him and there formed a guerrilla army led by a son of Mattathias, named Judah, who was nicknamed Maccabee (The Hammer). Led by "The

Divine Response

Hammer" this guerrilla army, known as the Maccabees, revolted against Antiochus. They preferred to die as martyrs rather than forsake their God and His laws as recorded in their Bible.

The Maccabees fought from the hills, many losing their lives in the desperate struggle to retain their worship of the one true God. The battle was hard but the "Hammers" kept "bringing the hammer down." Victory was sweet as they finally overcame; and despite the odds against them, re-entered Jerusalem in triumph and re-dedicated the temple. To this day the Jews celebrate this exhilarating religious event every year with the festival of Hanukah (meaning to dedicate).

Deeply engrained in the Jewish psyche was this continued need to be a nation set apart from other nations. A nation set apart in its worship of the one true God. A nation whose ceremonial laws set them apart in their worship of the one true God. And as the years went by, ceremony, instead of the God of the ceremonies, became their identity.

Then along came this young Jew, preaching the kingdom of God. At first His message was exciting as the mood was ripe for a powerful revolutionary, one who would "restore the Kingdom again to Israel." This young man had the credentials, the youthful energy, and the power to make things happen if only he could be channeled against Rome and for Israel.

But as he consistently refused to align himself with the national pride of Israel and consistently spoke of His kingdom not being of this world, it became more and more apparent that the two concepts of kingdom rule and authority would not mesh. Step by excruciating step, the majority of Jewish Rulers turned against this young man who seemed too independent to be pressed into their mold. And as His teaching continued, He became more and more pointed in His rebukes against their attitudes about others, themselves, and life in general. As their hatred for Him grew, so did their resistance to His teaching. Or perhaps it was vice versa. Whatever it was, it reached a crescendo when He called them a generation of vipers, and reached the fever-pitch of a mob by the time they corralled Him at night in a place apart from the adoring crowds and drew Him to the Judgment Hall. They were surprised at His lack of resistance, even going so far as to tell the only disciple willing to resist, to "put up his sword again in its sheath." And then healing the servant's lopped off ear so quickly that they would seem to be left wondering, "Did I just see that or didn't I?"

But this man's miracles, even His healings, His raising people from the dead, His casting out of devils, were overshadowed in their minds by His

THE EMPTY TOMB

disdain for the ceremonies and His lack of interest in national pride. And so they hated Him. And were afraid of Him. For while hatred is not always the outflow of fear, one cannot hate without being afraid. Whatever He was doing, even good, could not be of God they reasoned, and so they accused Him of casting out devils by the prince of the devils. (Matthew 9:34)

His response had been typically unnerving as he asked the question, "If I by Beelzebub cast out devils, by whom do your children cast them out?" And he had also asked them, "If Satan cast out Satan … how then shall his kingdom stand?" (Matthew 12:26-27)

Questions they had no answer for, and now while creation itself shook the very ground they stood on, the memory of this man's life, teaching, and questions was likewise shaking their trust in national pride and ceremony, even while it also shook the Roman centurion who cried out, "Truly this man was the Son of God." (Mark 15:39) For some it went deeper than others, shaking their trust in themselves that they were righteous, their hearts creaking and cracking open to receive the words of eternal life offered to them by this man whom they had crucified.

Many were possibly not even aware that their hearts and minds were being changed until the shaking of their confidence came to fruition at Pentecost causing them to cry out "men and brethren, what shall we do?" upon the revelation that this Jesus, whom they had crucified, was "both Lord and Christ." (Acts 2:36-37)

But for now, they had more to fear than a false report of Jesus rising from the dead. What if he actually did arise? What then? While some hearts and minds were yielding and being prepared to believe, other hearts were hardening into a deep and pervasive unbelief, determined that national pride and ceremony was the ultimate of Jewish experience and actually remained exclusively theirs.

And such was the rift already happening in the Jewish nation as Sunday morning dawned and the fresh morning sun showed itself on the horizon of Roman occupied Israel. Very early on that Sunday morning, as it began to dawn toward the first day of the week, a small group of women who on Friday already had prepared spices and ointments to prepare the body of Jesus for proper burial, made their hushed way along the garden path toward the sepulchre. They didn't know what they would do to be able to get next to the body, for they had seen and knew there was a heavy stone rolled before the entrance to the sepulchre.

There was another earthquake. They were frightened, and especially so when they found the stone rolled away, and upon entering the sepulchre, saw a young man sitting on the right side, clothed in a long white garment. And suddenly there were two men standing by them in shining garments; and as the women were afraid and bowed down their faces to the earth, the two men in shining garments said to them, "Why seek ye the living among the dead? He is not here, but is risen: remember how he spake unto you when he was yet in Galilee, Saying, The Son of man must be delivered into the hands of sinful men, and be crucified, and the third day rise again. And they remembered his words." (Luke 24:5-8)

And saw the empty tomb. The body that they'd come to anoint was gone. And the soldiers guarding the tomb were stunned and silent. For when the earth quaked and the first angel appeared, the keepers shook and became as dead men. There was nothing more to do or to say so the women turned away from the empty tomb with, we can well imagine, wonder on their faces and hesitation in their steps.

The soldiers also turned away from the empty tomb, but went to give their report to the Jewish Chief Priests. Reporting to their Roman superior officers would surely have brought forth a reprimand, if not worse, so it was natural for them to seek consolation from the priests who had shown clearly by their vehement outcry against this man, that they wanted him dead and wanted him to stay dead. If avoiding reprimand—which was surely the case—is what they were seeking, they received even more than they sought for from the Jewish rulers. For the Chief Priests had a meeting with the elders and when they had taken counsel, they gave a large sum of money to the soldiers with instructions on what to say. With the bribe came instructions to say that His disciples came by night and stole him away while we slept. Slept!? That must have made the soldiers' ears to tingle. If a Roman watchman slept on the job, it could well cost him his life! What good was money to a dead man? But then, with the offer came the assurance from the Jewish rulers that "if this come to the governor's ears, we will persuade him, and secure you." So the soldiers "took the money, and did as they were taught: and this saying is commonly reported among the Jews until this day." (Matthew 28:14-15)

Mary Magdalene turned away from the empty sepulchre. She knew what emptiness was like, for Jesus had emptied her of seven already empty devils. He had not left her empty, but had immediately filled her with the spiritual love that was so much a part of Him that it emanated from Him wherever He went. And Mary returned that spiritual love with all of her heart and soul. The seven devils had caused her to be continuously drained, empty of love, unable to give or to receive love. But this Jesus! From the day when He had cast out the devils, she was so filled with spiritual love for Him and others that life had become full and rich. A fullness and richness that she could formerly only dream of.

Now she ran to the house, not far distant, where she knew Peter and John were staying. Likely breathing hard from exertion and stress when she found them, she said, "They have taken away the Lord out of the sepulchre, and we know not where they have laid him." Peter and John wasted no time and left, running for the sepulchre. John outran Peter and arrived first at the sepulchre. Stopping at the entrance, he stooped and looked in, seeing the linen clothes lying there. When Peter caught up, he didn't stop at the entrance, but charged on into the sepulchre and stood gazing wonderingly at the now empty linen clothes lying there. And the napkin that was about his head, not lying with the linen clothes, but wrapped together in a place by itself. John followed Peter into the sepulchre, and saw, and believed. What did he believe besides that Jesus was no longer there? For as yet they knew not the scripture, that He must rise again from the dead. So they wondered as they both turned away from the empty sepulchre and returned again to their own home.

But Mary stayed, weeping. As she turned away from the empty sepulchre again, her eyes blinded by her own weeping, her only thought was, as she responded to the angel who asked why she was weeping; "Because they have taken away my Lord, and I know not where they have laid him." Surely if she could find Him, even though His body was now dead, she would be able to sense once again the spiritual love that had never failed her, emanating from Him once again. Beyond that, she didn't know—and really didn't want to think that far. The present was painful enough. So painful that her eyes were again blinded by her tears. As she turned, she saw through her tears the form of a man standing by her. She supposed he was the gardener, so when he asked, "Woman, why weepest thou, whom seekest thou?" she responded with the one question uppermost in her mind. "Sir, if thou have borne him hence, tell me where thou hast laid him, and I will take him away." Jesus saith unto her, "Mary." Only one Person said her name like that! What thrill and wonder must have gripped Mary and coursed through her at the sound of that voice that she had just been longing to hear once again! Saying her name! As only He could! And here He stood! She, who had been longing to find His lying down dead body suddenly was in the reality of His presence standing by her! Standing! Yes, standing! Not lying down as a dead corpse, but standing!

Mary turned towards Him and said, "Rabboni" (Master), and her hands must have simultaneously reached out to Him because Jesus saith unto her, "Touch me not; for I am not yet ascended to my Father: but go to my brethren, and say unto them, I ascend unto my Father, and your Father; and to my God, and your God." (John 20)

Mary was stunned. As the other women joined her, Jesus greeted them with, "All hail" and they all fell at His feet together, held Him by the feet and worshiped Him. Then said Jesus unto them, "Be not afraid: go tell my brethren that they go into Galilee, and there shall they see me." (Matthew 23:10) So the women fled; they ran with renewed vigor and hope to find the apostles. When they found the apostles, their excited regaling of events seemed to the downcast apostles to be idle tales, and they believed them not. This was too good to be true! For men, as well as women, when hope is severely crushed, can become so wary that it seems too risky to allow the inner surging of hope to burst into joy, for fear of the renewed disappointment that could follow.

Their hope had soared high that this was He that would deliver Israel and with each miracle, their hope and belief in Him strengthened. Such hope, dashed as theirs had now been, seemed impossible to revive again. For such hope, once dashed, fears being dashed again.

That same day two of them traveled to Emmaus, about three score furlongs from Jerusalem. (Luke 24:13) Walking was a common mode of transportation in those days and as the two walked they talked. Their talk was earnest as they reasoned about the trust they'd had that Jesus of Nazareth, a prophet mighty in deed and word before God and all the people, should be the one to deliver Israel and make of her a great nation again. This time forever? But then, how the chief priests and their rulers had turned against Him and delivered Him to the foreign government now occupying Israel to be condemned to death and crucified. How could they do such a thing? How could they deliver one of their own, one mighty in good deeds, one mighty in good teaching, one with claims on a kingdom, though not of this world, yea, and even claims of divinity itself. That claim by itself would make Him God, wouldn't it? And wasn't it illegal for their rulers to turn to this foreign, idol-worshiping government for help to judge and overcome an enemy, even one of their own? They indeed lived in a perplexing world that didn't make sense.

THE EMPTY TOMB

But what astonished them now was the news of His rising! From the dead! They had heard from the women. About the empty tomb. Empty except for the angels. Real angels or visions? Did it matter if they were visions or real? Visions or real, the angels said He was alive. Peter and John had run to the sepulchre and found it empty as the women had said. The tomb was, sure enough, empty. But did they dare believe? Was it possible to hallucinate from all the tension of the past few days? But even if it was possible, was it possible for a group of women, even a small group, to all hallucinate at the same time?

As they communed together and reasoned, a man drew near and walked with them. Having noted their sadness, he wished to hear what they were talking about. What was it about this man? Something familiar caused their hearts to open as they poured out their hearts and minds with all the perplexing questions they had been mulling over and couldn't figure out. But then the man had a rebuke for them. "O fools," he said, "and slow of heart to believe all that the prophets have spoken: Ought not Christ to have suffered these things, and to enter into his glory?

And beginning at Moses and all the prophets, he expounded unto them in all the scriptures the things concerning himself." (Luke 24:25-27) For the man walking with them was Jesus. "But their eyes were holden that they should not know him." (Luke 24:16) As He expounded the scripture to them about Himself, they drew near to Emmaus where the two men expected to stay the night. But what about this stranger? Their hearts were open to Him and what He was saying was beginning to make sense to their confused minds. Their jumbled thoughts were coming together as the scriptures He spoke of slowly came together, becoming more and more solidified into a sensible understanding of the Fall and Redemption of mankind as depicted through Moses and the Prophets. A light was shining in the darkness, the day was dawning, and the day star arising in their hearts. (II Peter 1:19 paraphrased)

As the three drew near to Emmaus, still engrossed in the depth of their communications, the stranger made as though he would have gone further. But the two constrained him, for the day was well past and it was toward evening. So he turned and went in to stay with them. Were they at an inn that also served food? Whether there or at someone's house, they sat down to a prepared meal that they were undoubtedly hungry and eager for. The three of them settled into chairs at the table, no doubt a welcome respite for their travel weary feet, and the stranger took bread, and blessed it, and brake it, and gave it to them. There was something so familiar about this stranger. The way he walked, the way he talked, the depth of his teaching, his sure yet compassionate manner, his judgment and yet his mercy, the righteousness and yet the peace, the blessing and breaking of bread, the giving it to them ... suddenly they knew ... their eyes were opened, and they knew Him. This was Jesus! The one their broken hearts longed for! The Deliverer the Prophets spoke of! The One Moses spoke of! He was alive! He talked with them! And they with Him! "And their eyes were opened, and they knew him; and he vanished out of their sight. And they said to one another, Did not our heart burn within us, while he talked with us by the way, and while he opened to us the scriptures?"(Luke 24:31-32)

Fast forward almost 2,000 years later. We have the opportunity and the privilege of these two men, to have our hearts burn within us while He talks with us by the way, while He opens to us the scriptures. We do not naturally understand the Word of God given to us by His Spirit. "The natural man receiveth not the things of the Spirit of God: for they are foolishness unto him: neither can he know them, because they are spiritually discerned." (I Corinthians 2:14)

After the Resurrection, when with the disciples, Jesus spoke to them of the Gift He would send after His departure. Of His going away to the Father. And that it was best for them that He does go. Because He would send the Comforter, the Holy Spirit. If He stays with them, the Comforter wouldn't come, but if He goes He would send Him to them. This promise—fulfilled for them at Pentecost, when many of them were assembled together, by the Spirit descending upon each in cloven tongues like as of fire with a sound from heaven as of a rushing mighty wind—had a profound effect upon the disciples and continues to this day having a profound effect upon individuals, churches, societies, cultures, governments, and the world at large.

For the Holy Spirit reproves men of sin, of righteousness, and of judgment. (John 16:8) In accord with the Bible the Holy Spirit convinces us of sin, its nature, its deep roots, and its far-reaching effects; then in contrast shows us the nature, the deep roots, and the far-reaching effects of righteousness, calling us to judgment and repentance while yet in this realm called Time. And then offers to us the imputed righteousness of Christ. And then gives to us the imparted righteousness of the indwelling Christ through His Holy Spirit.

THE EMPTY TOMB

All will come to judgment. Either voluntarily in repentance while yet in this realm of time, or involuntarily and past the ability to repent in the realm of Eternity. We have no choice in this matter of life and death, as the overwhelming evidence clearly shows that 100% of us are not here to stay. And since we are not here to stay, the question is, where are we going? Where am I going? Where are you going? Herein we do have a choice; to repent and choose the destiny, accepting the way; or to not repent, choose our own way, and unequivocally accept the destiny.

We have one life to live. One choice. One destiny.

"God, who at sundry times and in divers manners spake in time past unto the fathers by the prophets, Hath in these last days spoken unto us by his Son, whom he hath appointed heir of all things, by whom also he made the worlds." (Hebrews 1:1) Yes, Jesus Christ speaks to us today; His speaking burns in our hearts; His speaking opens unto us the Scriptures. The Author of Scripture is the only always reliable Interpreter of Scripture. Either directly or through others He brings into our life. (Galatians 1:9) And even that calls for discernment. (I Corinthians 2:14) The discernment given by the Spirit of God. All Scripture revolves around twelve profound realities:

- Creation
- The defeat and Fall of Man.
- World-wide flood
- Giving of the Law
- The Prophecy
- The birth of Jesus
- Christ and His Doctrine
- The Crucifixion of Christ
- The Resurrection of Christ
- Pentecost
- The Church of Christ
- Consummation and final security

The devils didn't know they were bringing defeat upon themselves by crucifying Christ. Is this why the prophecies of the Old Testament were so hidden? So the devil wouldn't know?

We believe this to be so.

And that the Old Testament faithful are redeemed through the blood of Jesus Christ. As well as we. For we have "one mediator between God and men, the man Christ Jesus." (I Timothy 2:5) The Old Testament faithful received the Promise of God by faith. We receive the reality of Christ, our risen Savior, by faith.

The day of Pentecost has had a profound and far reaching effect on our world, on that day and ever since. God only knows, and only eternity will reveal to us, how far-reaching the effect has been or will be. On that day and ever since, God has opened the mouth of the dumb, and the dumb spake. Consider Peter, who had vehemently declared that he would stand by Jesus even if no one else did, and then denied even knowing the man; now preaching his Risen Lord with such conviction and Holy Ghost power that three thousand souls were saved. And that saving has never stopped. Men and women are still, as even I was and am, being saved through the conviction and power of our Lord Jesus Christ by His Spirit.

For the tomb is empty!

He was born of a virgin.

He was wise from His youth. He never sinned.

He healed the sick. He raised the dead.

He died for us. For our sins.

He rose again. Our justification. He ascended to the Father.

He is seated on the right hand of the throne of God.

He is interceding for us.

He waits while His bride is made ready. (Revelation 21:2)

That Bride is the Church. (John 3:29-36)

He is coming again! To receive His own!

And so shall we ever be with the Lord. (I Thessalonians 4:17)

THE EMPTY TOMB

WE LIVE BECAUSE HE LIVES

Jesus Christ our Lord is risen,
He is risen from the dead.
Where He preached to souls in prison,
For He'd suffered in their stead.

Jesus Christ our Lord is risen,
His death for sin has paid.
Was in the Law and Prophets hidden, '
N in a garden tomb was laid.

Christ arose the hope of Glory,
Left behind an empty tomb.
Saving us from Satan's fury,
Calling us to be His own.

Jesus Christ our Lord is risen,
He is risen from the dead.
He redeemed us out of prison,
For He suffered in our stead.

Christ in us the hope of Glory,
Left behind an empty tomb.
He is searching for the needy,
Fills each heart where there is room.

Jesus Christ our Lord is risen,
New Life to us He gives.
Giving up to Him as bidden,
We live because He Lives.

Gottes sege dazu winscha
(May God add His blessing.)

13

LEGALISM, ITS FRUITS, AND THE TRUE GRACE OF GOD

Part 1

LEGALISM. THE WORD BEGS defining as it is being cast this way and that these days, seemingly to label, and hence to silence, the critics of one's actions. Certainly it is not the only label thus abused; if indeed what the writer is noticing is true; but it has been, for a number of decades, ungraciously used against churches and individuals that wish to retain the Biblical values adhered to by former generations. The word is not found in the Bible, nor in Webster's 1828 Dictionary, so it is a word not in common use until more recent times, possibly in response to "Mr. Legality" of Pilgrim's Progress fame; the word and its definition being found in today's dictionaries, giving its meaning as a strict, literal or excessive conformity to law; and since being a law-abiding citizen is a good thing, we could possibly think of legalism as a good thing.

Why then, this negative connotation on the word legalism? Is it not good to conform to law? Possibly not excessive, but is it not good to be strict and literal about conforming to law? When we think of a people in Bible history that were strict and literal about conforming to law, do we not think of the Pharisees? And even they, in accusing our Lord of lawlessness, could not say that Jesus taught unrighteousness. He told His listeners they

LEGALISM, ITS FRUITS, AND THE TRUE GRACE OF GOD

should do as the Pharisees say, only not what they do. The Pharisees, we can then assume, were being faithful in teaching the Word of God. Where they failed was in application. Taken up with ceremony, they wrongly thought that if they kept up a form of law, to fit the comfort zone of their lives, rather than adjusting their lives to the law that they were then pleasing God. Form and ceremony had become their personal and national identity, an identity that they expected this influential young Jew to bless and uphold; and when He did not, they slowly but surely turned against Him even as His rebukes became ever more candid and blunt in His "tough love" attempt to show them the error of their self-justifying ways.

Many of them did yield, as evidenced at Pentecost and from then on, but as an organization they not only did not yield, they also spread the false report that His disciples had stolen His body, for they were not willing to accept the evidence and testimony of His rising. They wanted this young Teacher who had corrected and rebuked them time and time again to be dead and to stay dead. He had not accepted their form and ceremony, even rebuking them for saying and not doing, instructing the gathered crowd to do as they say, but not as they do, "for they say, and do not." (Matthew 23:3)

In the following pages I will at times use the word legalism in lieu of self-righteousness, as that is the way the word is commonly used, the Pharisees being stereotyped as the epitome of legalism or self-righteousness. In our culture at large, the legalist has been stereotyped as a conservative kind of guy who is always concerned and looking down his nose at others, he being the modern-day Pharisee. He may live an outwardly pious life, but the suspicion is, that all is not as it appears.

The liberal, however, we are influenced to think, has no such inhibitions, and is a benevolent kind of guy who, fortunately or unfortunately depending on which camp one belongs to, has been endowed with an overabundance of "grace," not being infected by the judgmental attitude of the conservative. However, the liberal is generally quick to judge the actions of the conservative, ever holding him to a standard higher, or at least more narrow, than his own and has a readily judgmental attitude about the judgmental attitude of the conservative. But whatever his faults may be, we are influenced to think that the liberal has clean escaped the error of legalism. Has he really? We want to explore the answer to that question and other questions as well.

Divine Response

We may all have heard the word picture given of two road ditches—with one ditch being legalism, the other ditch liberalism—and the need for us not to fall into either one, but to stay on the road between the two.

Quite frankly, that word picture bothers me. For several reasons.

One: It is a serious shift of focus; for the word of God in its perspective of fallen mankind, has only two roads. The broad way that leads to destruction; and the straight and narrow way to glory and eternal bliss. While the narrow may arguably have a road ditch on either side, when the blind lead the blind (Matthew 15:14), there are a myriad of ditches one may fall into, including the lust of the flesh, the lust of the eyes, and the pride of life. (1 John 2:16)

Two: When tempted, those who trust in themselves—as our first parents Adam and Eve initially did—Bibically speaking, are on the broad way; and those who trust in God as a "great cloud of witnesses" have, (Hebrews 12:1) are on the narrow way that leads to life. Whom we trust affects our decisions, our choices, and our way of life; and there is no indication in the Scripture that the liberal trusts in himself any less than the conservative. And when the liberal trusts in himself instead of in God, whether that be a Pharisaical "fudging" of Heaven's Laws or a Romish discarding of them, all the while by his life, words, and conduct, claiming the right to do so, is he not trusting in himself that he is righteous? And when he trusts in himself that he is righteous, is he not a legalist? So we have a liberal legalist.

Perhaps the two ditches would be best named "conservative legalism" and "liberal legalism," as both have been deceptively formed by the belief and claim of one's own rightness or righteousness, in opposition or neglect of the righteousness of Christ. "For they ... going about to establish their own righteousness, have not submitted themselves unto the righteousness of God." (Romans 10:3) Biblically speaking, their own righteousness is not righteousness at all, but an illusion. An illusion brought about by spiritual blindness. "And if the blind lead the blind," Jesus said, "both shall fall into the ditch." (Matthew 15:14)

But there is hope here. For the blind. And only for the blind. That the blind may see. The blind are given sight. While the seeing are made blind. (John 9: 39)

Because we are all born with a natural spiritual blindness, that is both difficult to see and difficult to accept. Jesus gave this warning to those of yesteryear, and to those of today, who trust in natural feelings and inclinations, "Now ye say, We see; therefore your sin remaineth." (John 9:41)

Jesus gave this parable to certain who trusted in themselves that they were righteous, and despised others:

"Two men went up into the temple to pray; the one a Pharisee, and the other a publican. The Pharisee stood and prayed thus with himself, God, I thank thee, that I am not as other men are, extortioners, unjust, adulterers, or even as this publican. I fast twice in the week, I give tithes of all that I possess. And the publican, standing afar off, would not lift up so much as his eyes unto heaven, but smote upon his breast, saying, God be merciful to me a sinner. I tell you, [Jesus continued] this man went down to his house justified rather than the other: for everyone that exalteth himself shall be abased; and he that humbleth himself shall be exalted." (Luke 18:10-14)

Those people to whom Jesus gave this parable, and all others even to this day, have the blessed privilege of this undone Publican, to be smitten with our own sense of undoneness, to pray to God for mercy, and to be given mercy. But as long as they claimed to see what wasn't there, they remained blinded to their own deception.

Even as we do, as long as we claim to see what isn't there, our own righteousness, which is spiritual nakedness. (Revelation 3:17)

Hans Christian Andersen, in writing the tale *The Emperor's New Clothes*, may not have meant it as a parable about self-righteousness, but whatever his intent, the principle is drawn from the story, is it not? And as such, it is a graphic depiction of the swindling, the nakedness, and self-deception of self-righteousness. He writes:

THE EMPEROR'S NEW CLOTHES

Many years ago there lived an emperor who thought so much of new clothes that he spent all his money in order that he might be very fine. He did not care for his soldiers, nor for going to the play, or driving in the park except to show his new clothes. He had a coat for every hour of the day, and just as they say of a king, "He is in the council-room," so they always said of him, "The Emperor is in his dressing room."

The great city where he lived was very gay (merry, airy, jovial, sportive, frolicsome. Webster's Dictionary–1828); and every day many strangers came there. One day there came two swindlers; they gave out that they were weavers and said they could weave the finest cloth to be imagined. Their colours and patterns, they said, were not only exceptionally beautiful, but the clothes made of their material possessed the wonderful quality of being invisible to any man who was unfit for his office or hopelessly stupid.

"Those must be wonderful clothes," said the Emperor. "If I wore such clothes I should be able to find out which men in my empire were unfit for their places, and I could tell the clever from the stupid. Yes I must have this cloth woven for me without delay." And he gave a lot of money to the two swindlers in advance, so that they should set to work at once. They set up two looms and pretended to be very hard at work, but they had nothing whatever on the looms. They asked for the finest silk and the most precious gold; this they put in their own bags and worked at the empty looms till late into the night.

"I should very much like to know how they are getting on with the cloth," thought the Emperor. But he felt rather uneasy when he remembered that he who was not fit for his office could not see it. He believed, of course, that he had nothing to fear for himself, yet he thought he would send somebody else first to see how matters stood. Everybody in the town knew what a wonderful property the stuff possessed, and all were anxious to see how bad or stupid their neighbors were.

"I will send my honest old Minister to the weavers," thought the Emperor. "He can judge best how the stuff looks, for he is intelligent, and nobody understands his office better than he."

So the good old Minister went into the room where the two swindlers sat working at the empty looms. "Heaven preserve us!" he thought, and opened his eyes wide. "I cannot see anything at all," but he did not say so. Both swindlers bade him be so good as to come near, and asked him if he did not admire the exquisite pattern and the beautiful colours. They pointed to the empty looms and the poor old Minister opened his eyes wider, but he could see nothing for there was nothing to be seen. "Good Lord!" he thought, "can I be so stupid? I should never have thought so and nobody must know it! Is it possible that I am not fit for my office? No, no, I cannot say that I was unable to see the cloth."

"Well, have you got nothing to say?" said one, as he wove. "Oh, it is very pretty—quite enchanting!" said the Old Minister, peering through his spectacles. "What a pattern and what colours! I shall tell the Emperor that I am very much pleased with it."

"Well, we are glad of that," said both the weavers, and they named the colours to him and explained the curious pattern. The old Minister listened attentively, that he might relate to the Emperor what they said; and he did so.

Now the swindlers asked for more money, more silk and gold, which they required for weaving. They kept it all for themselves, and not a thread

LEGALISM, ITS FRUITS, AND THE TRUE GRACE OF GOD

came near the loom, but they continued, as hitherto, to work at the empty looms.

Soon afterwards the Emperor sent another honest courtier[1] to the weavers to see how they were getting on, and if the cloth was nearly finished. Like the old Minister, he looked and looked, but could see nothing, as there was nothing to be seen.

"Is it not a beautiful piece of cloth?" said the two swindlers, showing and explaining the magnificent pattern, which, however, was not there at all.

"I am not stupid," thought the man, "is it therefore my good appointment for which I am not fit? It is ludicrous, but I must not let anyone know it," and he praised the cloth, which he did not see and expressed his pleasure at the beautiful colours and the fine pattern. "Yes, it is quite enchanting," said he to the Emperor.

Everyone in the whole town was talking about the splendid cloth. At last the Emperor wished to see it himself while it was still on the loom. With a whole company of chosen men, including the two honest councilors who had already been there, he went to the two clever swindlers who were now weaving as hard as they could, but without using any thread.

"Is it not magnifique?" said both the honest statesmen, "will your Majesty see what a pattern and what colours?" And they pointed to the empty looms, for they imagined the others could see the cloth.

"What is this?" thought the Emperor. "I do not see anything at all. This is terrible! Am I stupid? Am I unfit to be emperor? That would indeed be the most dreadful thing that could happen to me."

"Yes, it is very fine," said the Emperor. "It has our highest approval;" and nodding contentedly, he gazed at the empty loom, for he did not like to say that he could see nothing. All his attendants who were with him looked and looked, and although they could not see anything more than the others, they said, like the Emperor, "It is very fine." And all advised him to wear the new magnificent clothes at a great procession which was soon to take place. "It is magnifique! beautiful, excellent!" went from mouth to mouth, and everybody seemed to be delighted. The Emperor gave each of the swindlers the cross of the order of knighthood and the title of Imperial Court Weavers.

All through the night before the procession was due to take place, the swindlers were up, and had more than sixteen candles burning. People could

---

1 The labels "honest old minister" and "honest courtier" are "tongue-in-cheek" and should not be taken as derogatory about age nor honesty. There is no hope for a civilization that relegates its oldest and wisest into categorical irrelevance.

see that they were busy getting the Emperor's new clothes ready. They pretended to take the cloth from the loom, they snipped the air with big scissors, they sewed with needles without thread, and said at last, "Now the Emperor's new clothes are ready!"

The Emperor with all his noblest courtiers then came in; and both the swindlers held up one arm as if they held something and said, "See here are the trousers! Here is the coat! Here is the cloak!" and so on. "They are all as light as a cobweb! They make one feel as if one had nothing on at all, but that is just the beauty of it."

"Yes!" said all the courtiers, but they could not see anything, for there was nothing to be seen.

"Will it please your Majesty graciously to take off your clothes?" said the swindlers. "Then we may help your Majesty into the new clothes before the large looking-glass!"

The Emperor took off his outer[2] clothes, and the swindlers pretended to put the new clothes upon him, one piece after another; and the Emperor looked at himself in the glass from every side.

"Oh, how well they look! How well they fit!" said all. "What a pattern! What colours! That is a splendid dress!"

"They are waiting outside with the canopy which is to be borne over your Majesty in the procession," said the chief master of the ceremonies.

"Yes, I am quite ready," said the Emperor. "Does not my suit fit me marvelously?" And he turned once more to the looking-glass, that people should think he admired his garments.

The chamberlains, who were to carry the train, fumbled with their hands on the ground as if they were lifting up a train. Then they pretended to hold something up in their hands; they dare not let people know that they could not see anything.

And so the Emperor marched in the procession under the beautiful canopy and all who saw him in the street and out of the windows exclaimed, "How marvelous the Emperor's new suit is! What a long train he has! How well it fits him!" Nobody would let others know that he saw nothing, for then he would have been unfit for his office or too stupid. None of the Emperor's clothes had ever been such a success.

"But he has nothing on at all," said a little child. "Good heavens! Hear what the little innocent says!" said the father, and then each whispered to the other what the child said. "He has nothing on—a little child says he has nothing

---

2 The word "outer" has been added to the original

LEGALISM, ITS FRUITS, AND THE TRUE GRACE OF GOD

on at all!" "He has nothing on at all," cried all the people at last. And the Emperor too was feeling very worried, for it seemed to him that they were right, but he thought to himself, "all the same, I must keep the procession going now." And he held himself stiffer than ever, and the chamberlains walked on and held up the train which was not there at all.

"Which was not there at all." Is not this the deceptive tragedy of self-righteousness, that it is "not there at all?" It is a tragedy, because as long as we claim to see what we don't see, we shall remain blind. And it is a tragedy, because if we only confessed that we don't see what we don't see, confessed our undone nakedness then—and only then—does Jesus Christ draw near and clothe us with His own Righteousness, which he appropriated for us by His death and resurrection.

For righteousness in our own strength is an impossibility. As impossible as it is to weave cloth with threads that are not there at all. When God says, "there is none righteous, no, not one." (Romans 3:10) He does so from His own eternally honest and upright perspective, judging us from His own righteous and eternal Law. It is this Law under which we either try to justify ourselves in our self-righteousness, or we break, repent, and humbly come to Jesus for forgiveness, cleansing, and renewal. To Jesus Christ, who "is made unto us wisdom, and righteousness, and sanctification, and redemption: That, according as it is written, He that glorieth, let him glory in the Lord." (I Corinthians 1:30-31) He is everything to the Believer, through His Holy Spirit He imparts Godly understanding—wisdom—to the heart and mind. He imputes righteousness to us through His shed blood, His death on the cross, and His resurrection; He imparts sanctification from the inside out, through the in-dwelling of His Spirit, which is the imparting of His Life; He is our redemption now and in the future, as we look forward to that final redemption of our bodies when He comes again to receive His own unto Himself.

The true grace of God has its fruits. 1 Peter 5:12 speaks of the true grace of God. It is the kind that teaches us that "denying ungodliness and worldly lusts, we should live soberly, righteously, and godly, in this present world." (Titus 2:12) That is the true grace of God. It is the grace by which we are justified. "Being justified freely by his grace through the redemption that is in Christ Jesus." (Romans 3:24) "For the grace of God that bringeth salvation hath appeared to all men." (Titus 2:11) "That being justified by his grace, we should be made heirs according to the hope of eternal life." (Titus 3:7) Grace sufficient for all our needs. "And he [God] said unto me, My grace is sufficient for thee: for my strength is made perfect in weakness." (II Corinthians 12:9) Grace by which we are empowered, as in the rest of verse 9, "Most gladly therefore will I rather glory in my infirmities, that the power of Christ may rest upon me."

Grace is gifted to us by Christ. (I Timothy 1; Ephesians 2:8, 4:7) Grace is gifted to us through faith in Jesus' blood. (Romans 3:24-25)

Faith is believing the witness and testimony of God through His word. (Romans 4; Hebrews 11)

Faith is a gift from Christ. (Ephesians 2:8, 6:23)

Faith comes by hearing the Word of God. (Romans 10:17)

The goodness of God leads us to repentance, as in Romans 2:4, "Or despisest thou the riches of his goodness and forbearance and longsuffering; not knowing that the goodness of God leadeth thee to repentance?"

By faith in Jesus' sacrificial offering of Himself, we are perfected; we have His laws in our hearts and written in our minds, our sins are not remembered, we may enter into the holiest; Jesus is our High Priest, we may draw near in full assurance of faith, and hold fast the profession (acknowledgement, covenant) of our faith without wavering.

On the subject of legalism I think it good to give a little disclaimer of what legalism isn't; Legalism is not a righteous man who feels good about what he is doing. When the Pharisee stood in the temple and prayed thus with himself, "God I thank thee that I am not as other men are—extortioners, adulterers or even as this publican," Jesus didn't commend him for his righteous living. When the Pharisee continued on to pray "thus with himself," and I think it noteworthy to stop and notice that Jesus called it praying "thus with himself." The Pharisee prayed saying "I fast twice in the week. I give tithes of all that I possess." Jesus didn't commend him for his "fasting and tithing." It was never acknowledged in the scriptures that he was a godly man or that he was a righteous man. Rather, at various times, Jesus rebuked the Pharisees for being good on the outside for the praise of men, for doing some right things to be noticed by others, but their hearts were full of excess and bitterness. And they robbed widows' houses. Much wrong was going on behind the scene, but they had a cloak of religion (which was "not there at all.")

While there is goodness on this earth, it is all a result of God's Goodness and should be recognized and acknowledged as flowing from His Grace, as He is longsuffering with His patience. Without God's grace and forgiveness we are undone, for we are not by nature holy, we are unholy, much as we would try to persuade ourselves and "the onlookers" otherwise. When we ascribe any good to ourselves, as if we were its origin, we are yet—from God's perspective—spiritually "naked" (Revelation 16:15) and the shame of it, evident to His Omniscience, will one day be evident to all. (Luke 12:3) May we see before it is too late—as the two swindlers so aptly demonstrated—that pandering and flattery are a form of self-serving, as they are self-protective, expecting reciprocity, and lead into deception.

God doesn't flatter. He convicts and redeems. Conviction is never flattering and redemption is a humbling experience. True humbling is a proper clothing (I Peter 5:5) for the covering of spiritual nakedness, (Revelation 3:18) as it leads the soul to Christ and the Cross. "Blessed are they whose iniquities are forgiven, and whose sins are covered." (Romans 4:7)

PROPER CLOTHING

The Emperor's new clothes, were exceedingly fine,
And light as a cobweb, the two swindlers opined.
With persuasive flattery, they coerced him t' yield,
Ensnared by vanity, he allowed them to lead,
Him into deception, into thinking he's clothed,
Though with bareness of loom, the "cloth" they had weaved.

In pompous procession, the Emperor paraded,
On the streets of the town, as the townspeople watched.
That he couldn't see cloth, he didn't dare to admit,
Lest he's not fit for office, or hopelessly stupid,
So he paraded along, though uneasy at best,
The townspeople exclaimed, what a wonderful fit.

The Emperor's new suit, was an instant success,
"What a beautiful long train, how finely he dressed."
Though none could see aught, none cared to admit it,
Each privately thought, they were too stupid t' see it,
Though formerly anxious, t' see how stupid their neighbor,
Now were anxious 'bout themselves, though outwardly sure.

"He has nothing on at all," said a child to th' father,
"Hear what the child says," exclaimed dad to another.
The crowd then was freed, from self-blinded stupor,
"He has nothing on at all," they all cried together,
The Emperor then was feeling quite worried, tho vain,
And walked stiffer, as th' chamberlains upheld th' fake train.

Self-righteousness really, is not righteous at all,
Th' more refusal t' admit, th' more condemned by the law.
For reality shows, all are naked in spirit,
With desire to be clothed, we're tempted to fake it,
Though deep down we know when we're real and we're honest,
The clothes really aren't there, unless clothed by Christ's Spirit.

Gottes sege dazu winscha
(May God add His blessing)

14

LEGALISM, ITS FRUITS AND THE TRUE GRACE OF GOD

Part 2

What is legalism, or self-righteousness; where did it begin? Legalism, or being righteous by the law as it is held out in the scriptures, gives us the idea that there is a righteousness that man goes about to establish and that there is a righteousness of God. The two are separate; they are not the same. In Genesis 2:15-17, we see where it began. "And the Lord God took the man, and put him in the garden of Eden to dress it and to keep it. And the Lord God commanded the man, saying, Of every tree of the garden thou mayest freely eat: But of the tree of the knowledge of good and evil, thou shalt not eat of it: for in the day that thou eatest thereof thou shalt surely die."

And in Genesis Chapter 3 we read of the serpent that came. "Now that serpent was more subtle than any beast of the field which the Lord God had made and he said unto the woman, Yea, hath God said ye shall not eat of every tree of the garden. And the woman said unto the serpent, we may eat of the fruit of the trees of the garden, but of the fruit of the tree which is in the midst of the garden God has said we shall not eat of it. Neither shall ye touch it lest ye die. And the serpent said unto the woman, ye shall not surely die, for God doth know that in the day ye eat thereof then your eyes shall be open and ye shall be as gods knowing good and evil. And when the woman saw that the tree was good for food and that it was pleasant to the eyes and a tree to be desired to make one wise, she took of the fruit thereof and did eat and gave unto her husband with her and he did eat. And the eyes of them both were opened and they knew that they were naked and they sewed fig leaves together and made themselves aprons."

And we read on, that these aprons were not sufficient, there was not enough covering them; therefore God slew an animal to create a clothing for them to clothe their nakedness. It took the shedding of blood to cover them, which was a foreshadowing of the blood of Christ being shed to cover our sins which are "naked and open unto the eyes of him with whom we have to do." (Hebrews 4:13)

Here we have the beginning of man deciding for himself what is right and wrong. They were forbidden to eat of this tree of the knowledge of good and evil. But when she gave in to the tempter, and he to the temptress, their giving in became a decision—though perhaps unaware of the extent—to make wise decisions on their own, apart from God's restraint and direction. To decide right and wrong for themselves, the disaster of which we live with, and suffer for, even to this day.

What does this tree of the knowledge of good and evil represent for us today? They were told they were not to eat of it. But the serpent came and cast doubt upon God and God's word, and he said "yea hath God said" thereby casting a question on God's word and what God had said. And Eve, when she looked on the tree, began to see things a little different than she had before. When God had first told them not to eat of this tree, there was no problem. But when the serpent came and tempted her, he got her attention on this tree of the knowledge of good and evil, and she turned, looked at it, gazed upon it, and began to question God. When she saw that the fruit was good for food, and a tree desired to make one wise, she reached out her hand, took of the fruit, ate of it, and gave to her husband and he did eat. And their eyes were opened; they were no longer directly under the control and guidance of the Lord God. But they had partaken of the tree of the knowledge of good and evil and they began from there to decide for themselves what is good and what is evil.

Is this not the essence of self-righteousness? Of the meaning we ascribe to legalism? God has continually given His commandments and His word. He gave His commandments to His people in the Old Testament and they were to live by them, they were to do them and live by them, but they found it impossible to live a righteous and upright holy life according

LEGALISM, ITS FRUITS AND THE TRUE GRACE OF GOD

to the commandments of God. And so they had two choices. One was to cast themselves upon the mercy of God, as many of them did. Another was to bring down the law of God to a level that they could reach on their own strength. And by the flesh. And that is the continual struggle from then until now, is it not? That we tend to bring down—to reinterpret—the law of God in some way that it can be attained to in the flesh; and that is, in accordance with Scripture, partaking of the tree of the knowledge of good and evil; deciding for ourselves what is right and wrong.

The tragedy, of course, is that all the "bringing down," all of the "deciding," will never move God's holy and righteous law, but, that is also the stability, the strength, the beauty, and the trustworthiness of it. It is without partiality, and the Holiness of its Lawgiver makes it immovable, and Him, trustworthy.

The word of God tells us that "not he that commendeth himself is approved, but whom the Lord commendeth." (II Corinthians 10:18) And Jesus rebuked the self-righteous in Matthew 23. He said the scribes and Pharisees did sit in Moses' seat. "All therefore whatsoever they bid you observe, that observe and do; but do not ye after their works: for they say, and do not." (Matthew 23:3) They weren't a people who were living a righteous life, and their only problem was that they were feeling good about themselves. They were a people who had used religion for a cloak. And they had partaken of the tree of the knowledge of good and evil deciding for themselves what is right and wrong. But Jesus told the people, yes they say the right things; observe those things, but do not do as they do. Do as the righteous. He that doeth righteousness is righteous. A righteous man is not a legalist. I John 3:7 tells us, "Little children, let no man deceive you: he that doeth righteousness is righteous, even as he is righteous."

Righteousness is a fruit of the spirit and the righteous should feel good about what they are doing. It feels wrong to a child to do something that he or she has been forbidden to do. It feels good for that same child to be obedient and to do what is right. And so it feels to us if we are obedient to the Lord, it feels good and it is right and it should feel good. We should feel good about what we are doing.

However, history and the scriptures make it very clear that feeling good about what we are doing is not a safe gauge. We can feel good about something wrong just simply because we have gotten used to it. Or because we have been taught it as being good. Drift away from God is driven by excusing, and thereby getting used to things we should never get used to. We are commanded to have our senses exercised to discern both good and evil. (Hebrews 5:14) Our senses need to be exercised in the word of God, not in our own thoughts. Not in our own reasoning and in our own justification, not in our own ways. The word of God has the answers.

Self-righteousness—legalism—takes on many forms, which are being pushed upon us by the subtlety of the devil, with his demonic plans. There are seven forms (though by no means exhaustive) that I think it good to address here. They are:

Atheistic Legalism
Humanistic Legalism
Modernistic Legalism
Besetting Sin Legalism
Self-willed Legalism
Religious Legalism
Liberal Legalism

Atheistic Legalism. It openly denies the spirit realm and opposes itself against the knowledge of God. At its helm is dialectical materialism with all its reasoning and rules of conduct. It denies having anything to do with Laws that God has woven into the fabric of nature; being guided by the vacuum of its own thinking. And we may call it a vacuum, methinks, because Atheism is a constant consumer of the graces and blessings of God, yet staying hungry and dissatisfied, which it deems to be a good thing. Ever refusing the spiritually nutritious in-filling offered by God Himself, because the initial taste is not to its liking, for its taste buds are trained into being pleased only by materialism. In its denial of any higher authority than mankind, atheism is negative at its core, for it relies on denial of inner knowledge about God, and relies on the control of negative actions through the fear of negative consequences.

There was a time in the history of Israel when "every man did that which was right in his own eyes." (Judges 21:25) That, in the long run, is practical atheism, its logical and final conclusion being Anarchy, as it bears with it the uneasy question of final Authority. Since Atheism proclaims its own rightness in forming its own laws, having no higher authority than its own, we may call it self-righteous, or Legalistic, at its core, at its very foundation. It partakes of the tree of the knowledge of good and evil on a spirit level, deciding for itself what is right and what is wrong.

Humanistic Legalism. Believing that mankind is basically good, it trusts in its own inner goodness to become—and to be—the good person of its imagination. In its belief in its own goodness, it is a denial, whether overt or covert, of the Authority of Almighty God, taking that Authority to itself. Imagining that the laws God has woven into the fabric of nature exude from itself, it endeavors to present humanity as The Answer to its own problems, rightly recognizing humanity as the problem, but wrongly believing that the need can be overcome by simply nourishing mankind's basic inner goodness.

But God gives us a diametrically opposite description of the inner reality of men and women in our natural state of heart and mind. His Word, besides telling us in plain words not to trust in ourselves that we are righteous, also gives us many examples—from the Crucifixion of Christ to the exile of John—of what happens to Christians when Government is given over to trusting in themselves for righteous judgment. There are many examples in history of what happens when Godless governments try to cleanse their own system. Muddy waters cannot be cleansed by adding more muddy water. As the uneasiness of the Emperor could not be cured until properly clothed, so the uneasiness of mankind cannot be cured until we cease to decide right and wrong for ourselves, repent of our "nakedness" and are clothed upon with the righteousness of Christ. By faith, not by deception. In relying upon its own goodness—which it believes in—Humanism refuses the Goodness of God—which it does not believe in—thereby establishing itself upon its own self-righteousness. Deciding for itself what is right and what is wrong.

Modernistic Legalism. Modernism, at its core, is a denial of the supernatural, also believing that mankind is basically good and given the right programs, teaching, and circumstances, will be good and do good things. So persuasive were they in their supposed pursuit of goodness, that churches, especially those of the northeast, were infiltrated by their message of the evolving goodness of mankind. In churches accepting this message, their "belief" in social evolution caused them to reject all supernatural miracles. The miracles, being a threat to their materialistic worldview, were reasoned around, marginalized, and explained away. When miracles happened in the Bible, they supposedly were the result of natural phenomena or of the goodness of good people. In Modernistic thought, when Jesus miraculously fed 5,000 people, the listening crowd had become so softened and inspired by Jesus' teaching that their hearts opened to each other and all loved each other so much that they all shared their lunch. And since they shared, there was plenty for all, even twelve baskets of leftovers.

Well, that may be a nice story, but it's not the Bible; it is again, mankind exalting itself above God and His Word.

We do have reasoning powers. But we are not to reason with ourselves. We are to reason with God. Or rather to allow Him to reason with us, on His terms. "Come now, and let us reason together, saith the LORD: though your sins be as scarlet, they shall be as white as snow; though they be red like crimson, they shall be as wool." (Isaiah 1:18)

Besetting Sin Legalism. This is the legalism that lives in sin, cannot overcome sin, and just continues in sin. There is a besetting sin in the life and one cannot overcome it. We have met many of these, I have been there myself, and have found a common strain in all who do not repent and receive the Lord Jesus Christ. Who do not commit their ways to the Lord. There is a common thread that runs through all of such. And I have been one of them. I was there. I justified myself for many years in my sins, caught up in the rock 'n roll rebellion of the 70s.

Even the drunkard has many reasons for being where he is. He has had so many things go wrong in his life. Nobody loves me. He has all kinds of reasons that he has fallen back into drink again. The husband who falls into adultery, blames it on his wife; his wife is a nag. Or the woman whose husband is too busy for her, and her heart turns away from him and she turns to other things or people or another man. All sinners, that do not find the mercy of God by faith in Jesus Christ, find justification for their actions and form their own rules and beliefs of right and wrong. We by nature do that. No one can live with a sin for very long, realize that he is lost, know what lost is, and continue living and being comfortable with himself. All sinners find justification for their actions. I've met sinners in prison, and in ministering to them, all have some justification for their actions, except the ones that are repentant and have a heart open to receive the word of God. And that is the place where all of us need to come to and stay there, not just once, but always.

Self-willed Legalism. Self-willed Legalism has a will for what it wants; saying, I want, therefore I get. In the heart one knows that there must be a good reason for what is done, so there is a searching and reasoning going on in the mind to justify those things desired.

There are things that feel good to the flesh that we need to avoid and not create an appetite for, as we can feed that appetite to the point where it grows beyond reason, beyond our ability to control it. We need to stop where we can stop and make a choice to have our ways committed unto the Lord. That first little sin, that first step away from God, whatever it might be in your life or mine—that first little step may be a small step, but it is still a step— is a step toward the tree of the knowledge of good and evil. And we may be able to make a choice on that first step or that second step. The grace of God may not immediately leave, but as we continue that choice away from God, eventually the flesh and the appetite take over and man loses control of himself. Sin has no convenient stopping place.

There is a stopping place, however. At the foot of the Cross, where we cease to go about establishing our own righteousness and, in humility, submit to the righteousness of Christ, receiving His forgiveness and His cleansing.

Religious Legalism. This is the self-righteousness that Jesus confronted in Matthew 23. Deeply settled and ingrained in the human psyche is the need for Highest Authority, for Law and Order, a Standard of Conduct that mankind looks to, and submits itself under. Even in Anarchy, where persons supposedly become their own highest authority, there is an inner knowing, an inner guide, (whether it be natural law, God, or demons of rebellion) guiding the thought patterns into persuasion of mind, thereby becoming religious in nature. God will have the final say, the last word, and traces of Him can be found in all religion, though one may be hard pressed to find them in some more than in others.

The Apostle Paul said that as a Pharisee he was "touching the righteousness which is in the law, blameless," and yet there is the record of him, as Saul, consenting to the stoning of God's messenger, Stephen, searching for more Christians, apprehending them, and committing them to prison. (Philippians 3:6, Acts 8:1-3) Breathing out threatenings and slaughter against these Christians, he desired of the high priest letters to the synagogues at Damascus "that if he found any of this way, whether they were men or women, he might bring them bound unto Jerusalem." (Acts 9:2) Saul believed in what he was doing, and believed he was doing the will of God. When Jesus spoke out so vehemently against the scribes and Pharisees in Matthew 23, he was speaking to a people caught up in their own righteousness, and thus, caught up in the blindness of unbelief in Him. They had been, and were still, rejecting His teachings. Jesus was speaking to a people who knew the Law of God, and in their desperate sincerity to keep the Law had interpreted it in ways that made it more doable in the flesh. They may have been sincere, but they were sincerely wrong. And such was Saul on his way to Damascus, concerning zeal, persecuting the church, (Philippians 3) determined to stop this encroaching "new" religion that did away with ceremonies so dear to the sincere Jewish mindset. And God saw that this sincerity, once turned, was to be a valuable asset in the Kingdom of Christ. It was not their sincerity that Jesus spoke out so vehemently against, but their self-established rightness, or legalism, if you will.

Is not this the temptation and weakness of us all? That we have this innate and deceptive tendency to turn from the God of our religion to religion itself? And thus religion becomes an idol, a sort of god of the mind, as we resort to sorting out right from wrong in our own minds, becoming less and less dependent upon God for direction as we become less and less dependent upon His Word. We are religious by nature and our mind will always grapple with desire to connect with a higher good, a higher law than ourselves.

Saul met Jesus, of the Christian Religion, on the road to Damascus and became the Paul that we today know through his Spirit-inspired writings contained in God's Holy Word. When Saul met the God of Religion in Jesus Christ, the god of religion that he had been serving crumbled, and his life was transformed from Saul the Persecutor to Paul the Persecuted. Whereas guided and strengthened by the god of religion, his life had been one of threatenings and taking life; now, having met the God of Religion in Jesus, and being guided and strengthened by His Spirit, his life became a life of serving and offering life. May all of us be thus transformed. (Romans 12:1-2)

Liberal Legalism. Liberal legalism busies itself legalizing that which is right in its own eyes. Having desires and goals, wanting the world and what it has to offer, it busies itself step by step—however little or big—legalizing what it really wants and thereby partakes of the tree of the knowledge of good and evil. Choosing right and wrong for itself; with excuses and reasons it keeps its bases well covered to the eyes of man, forgetting—or at least wishing to—that there is no escaping the eyes of Him with whom we have to do.

Balaam, who loved the wages of unrighteousness, (II Peter 2:15) was a liberal legalist. He just could not accept "no" from God. He kept pushing and kept pushing until God let him go, and then he went; and even then all he could do was bless the children of Israel. But the Bible tells us very clearly that his heart was not with God. And then he found a way to get around what God was telling him that he could not do. And that was to curse Israel. He found his own way to curse Israel, finding a way around the law of God, the word of God. And in doing so He taught Balak to put a stumbling block before the children of Israel in sacrificing to idols. Josephus, the Jewish historian, writes that Balaam taught Balak to send the young Moabitish women into the Israelite camps to seduce and to win the hearts of the young men, and teach them to serve idols.

Balaam had been "rebuked for his iniquity: the dumb ass speaking with man's voice forbade the madness of the prophet." (II Peter 2:16) I am hard pressed to imagine which would be the most disturbing; the donkey talking to the man or the man answering the donkey, but whatever the case may be, history keeps giving us stubborn facts about the degeneracy of Godless cultures; and yet the liberal keeps pushing against Godly influence and tradition.

The rules change for the liberal legalist. He keeps pushing, taking small steps, always in one direction. Outward things change and inward things change. A person does not begin to wear wolves' clothing without becoming a wolf. He becomes a wolf. And sheep do not wear wolves' clothing. We have the warning that wolves wear sheep's clothing, but inwardly they are ravening wolves. We don't have any warning of the opposite way; that a sheep will begin to wear wolves' clothing and deceive all those around him. God's work of redemption is from the inside out, changing lives by changing hearts and minds.

"For there are certain men crept in and unawares … turning the grace of our God into lasciviousness, and denying the only Lord God, and our Lord Jesus Christ." (Jude 1:4) Turning the grace of God into licentiousness, or a license for sin. When Eve reached forth her hand and took of that fruit of the tree of the knowledge of good and evil, she plucked it off and she ate of it and gave to her husband and he did eat, deciding for themselves what is right and wrong. When we legalize what God doesn't, we deny our Lord God and our Lord Jesus Christ. That is what these men did when they crept in unawares and they turned the grace of our God into lasciviousness. They denied the only Lord God and our Lord Jesus Christ. When the liberal legalizes what God doesn't, he becomes a liberal legalist, setting up his or her own self-righteousness.

Legalism has its fruits. It has its fruits in the atheist who has no absolutes. It has its fruits in the sinner who keeps on in his sins. It has its fruits in the self-willed who keeps on in his self-will. It has its fruits in the modernist, the humanist, has its fruits in the religious as he continues in his wrong thinking, and often sincerely so. It has its fruits in the conservative. And in the liberal. All need the gospel. But at the bottom, where we have no self-righteousness left, is where we meet Jesus at the foot of the Cross, and there we, being naked and undone, are forgiven and clothed upon by Jesus with His white clothing of righteousness.

We just lately experienced a split at a church in town. There were two of this denomination, now there are three. The church had merged some years ago with a main body of churches, a denomination with standards lower than their own. The main body accepted homosexuals into church membership, but they told the local church at that time that they didn't have to change their standards to be like the main church body. Let's just join, they said, let's merge, be together; we are brethren, brothers and sisters, we are one.

Well, over a ten year period there was more and more pressure on churches to not only merge as a body, but to also merge in thinking and in standards. Pressure was put on local churches to change to the Episcopalian understanding of God. And so the ELCA, as a body, capitulated and they gave in. They began to accept homosexuals into the church and now into the ministry, and that's what the split in our town was about. There were

LEGALISM, ITS FRUITS AND THE TRUE GRACE OF GOD

those within the local church who could no longer endure the lower standards and they split away.

During this liberal versus conservative split, I had an eye-opening opportunity to join in a conversation with a small group representing both sides. Those that I spoke with who stayed with the main body quoted humanism, not the word of God, not the true grace of God. Until that time I was still naive enough to think they would at least try to use isolated Bible verses, but none did. There was a need to first establish a Biblical basis for discussion. With Christians.

I have an old friend in Kentucky who wears a long beard, has worn a long beard for many years. Ever since I've known him he has had a long beard. They were in a church more or less alone for many years. There was another church close by and the ministers from the other church wanted to merge, wanted to join fellowship, wanted to join hands; so they met together for a meeting. I was not there but had an, admittedly, one-sided fill-in later. He said it seemed to go fairly well except when he shared concerns about some outward things, their answer was that we should not judge by outward appearance, but judge righteous judgment. And so his concerns were not heeded. In the course of conversation, he did not keep pushing his concerns, but he didn't back down from them either ... and they began to accuse him of being a legalist. When he asked, "What have I said, or what have I done, where is your concern, I need to know so that I can change or repent if I am being a legalist," they responded with "Well, look at your long beard. Look at yourself, look at your long beard." They had just finished telling him not to judge by outward appearance when he brought concerns about them.

Legalism tends to do that; it judges arbitrarily. We need to remember that what is good for the goose is good for the gander. In this writer's finite opinion, the post-modern form of liberalism being pushed upon us these days should properly be called legalism, or even more properly, self-righteousness. For right and wrong is subjected to man's opinion and becomes so ambiguous as to be applied one way to the goose (conservative) and another way to the gander (liberal). An extreme example of this is the LGBTQ outcry against the Baker for standing by his beliefs while they (the gander) were supposedly right to honk loudly about their own. In attempting to push Mr. Philips against his own conscience—a matter of conscience, by the way, that has a solid and enduring foundation in God's Word, The Holy Bible—they demonstrated their belief in the right to push against Biblical agenda while promoting their own agenda. Even to the hurt of others, deciding for themselves what is right and what is wrong. In so doing, they demonstrated their own lack of being gracious to those whom they accuse of being ungracious, challenging them for being intelligent enough to allow God to be the One making the rules. God's rules that have God's grace embedded in them.

The true grace of God teaches us that "denying ungodliness and worldly lusts, we should live soberly, righteously, and godly, in this present world." (Titus 2:12) Romans 12:2 speaks of the transformed mind "that ye may prove what is that good, and acceptable, and perfect, will of God." There is a will of God that God has for us that is good and perfect. He knows what it is. We don't always know. And we need to remember that so we don't go to this tree of the knowledge of good and evil and decide for ourselves what is right and wrong. We need transformation by the renewing of our minds. That transforming of the mind comes from having our attention towards God, having our attention on the Word of God and praying; desiring the spirit of God to lead us in our lives, desiring the conviction of God. And when something doesn't seem right in our lives, that we open our hearts and minds to the Word of God. We open our minds to know what is right from someone outside of ourselves to receive inner knowledge, from God and the Holy Spirit, and from our brothers and sisters in the Lord. A transformed mind is of utmost importance to escape this trap of justifying ourselves. The man in Romans Chapter 7 is struggling under the law for a long time it seems. At least he went through many thoughts and many struggles until he came to the place where he surrendered it all. "O wretched man that I am! who shall deliver me from the body of this death?" and then he said, "I thank God through Jesus Christ our Lord. So then with the mind I myself serve the law of God; but with the flesh the law of sin." The reality settled upon him that even though he puts his mind to serving the law of God, even though he has a mind to do it, there is a law within him that works against the law of his mind and brings him into captivity to the law of sin which is in his members. So he finds in himself that even his mind is not strong enough to overcome sin, because though he has the mind to serve the law of God, yet with the flesh he serves the law of sin. In verse 24 he comes to the end of himself. And then he finds the answer in Romans 8:1. "There is therefore now no condemnation to them which are in Christ Jesus, who walk not after the flesh, but after the Spirit."

Or not after the confidence in the flesh, not after the tree of the knowledge of good and evil, deciding for oneself what is right and wrong, but walks after the spirit. "For the law of the Spirit of life in Christ Jesus hath made me free from the law of sin and death." (Romans 8:2)

And that could be my testimony, I could share my testimony, and it would be very much like that. Though I consented to right, I consented to the word of God, I did not find in myself the power to overcome sin. The law could not give power over sin, but the law of the spirit of life in Christ Jesus has made me free from the law of sin and death. The life in Christ Jesus is the overcoming power for what the law could not do, in that it was weak through the flesh, my flesh. The law could not bring righteousness, because of the weakness of my flesh. There is nothing wrong with the law, but it is myself that is the problem. The law is holy, just, and good. But I am carnal, sold under sin, as a sinner. And Romans 8:9, "But ye are not in the flesh, but in the Spirit, if so be that the Spirit of God dwell in you. Now if any man have not the Spirit of Christ, he is none of his."

The Spirit of Christ has fruit; fruits by which we can understand if it is the spirit of Christ or not. The fruits are very clear: "love, joy, peace, longsuffering, gentleness, goodness, faith, meekness, temperance: against such there is no law." (Galatians 5:22-23) These are fruits of the spirit of Christ. "If Christ be in you, the body is dead because of sin; but the Spirit is life because of righteousness. But if the Spirit of him that raised up Jesus from the dead dwell in you, he that raised up Christ from the dead shall also quicken your mortal bodies by his Spirit that dwelleth in you." (Romans 8:10-11)

Proverbs 3:5-7 says "Trust in the Lord with all thine heart; and lean not unto thine own understanding." Don't look toward that tree of the knowledge of good and evil and pluck from it. "Lean not unto thine own understanding. In all thy ways acknowledge him, and he shall direct thy paths. Be not wise in thine own eyes: fear the LORD, and depart from evil." Jesus said the way is narrow. This narrow way cannot be lived in the flesh—not in our own strength—we need the power of God. We need to be quickened by the Lord. The law is the end of our own way. The law cannot produce righteousness. It is not possible to live a righteous life under the law by self-determination, nor by determining for ourselves what is right and wrong. It is not possible to understand the law of God, to endeavor to live by it and do it in the flesh. We need the spirit of Christ.

The way is narrow. After initial salvation we need to keep that humility. At times all of us need to come to a place where we understand that we have done wrong, and repent and turn back to Christ and allow Him to lead us in the way of righteousness. All of us have those times. We don't live a life that is perfect all the time. If any man sins, we have an advocate, Jesus Christ, the righteous. Making a mistake is not as damnable as not admitting it. They who will not learn from the mistakes in history are destined to repeat them. When we make a mistake, when we fall, when we go out of the way, it is God's call to come back to the straight and narrow way. To nip sin in the bud before it becomes a full-blown flower. The Biblical Conservative is God's helper in the garden of life and is involved in preparing the soil, planting, watering, cultivating, and weeding in accordance with God's Conservation Program given to us through His Holy Spirit. "There is therefore now no condemnation to them which are in Christ Jesus, who walk not after the flesh, but after the Spirit." (Romans 8:1)

In walking in the Spirit, we are to be diligent workers in the Kingdom of Christ, according to the Great Commission He gave to all Believers after His resurrection and before His ascension to Heaven. "And Jesus ... spake unto them, saying, All power is given unto me in heaven and in earth. Go ye therefore, and teach all nations, baptizing them in the name of the Father, and of the Son, and of the Holy Ghost: Teaching them to observe all things whatsoever I have commanded you: and, lo, I am with you alway, even unto the end of the world." (Matthew 28:18-20)

We are called to be workers with Christ in His Kingdom, leaving final judgment of people to God, according to instruction that Jesus has given in His Sermon on the Mount when He taught, "Judge not, that ye be not judged. For with what judgment ye judge, ye shall be judged: and with what measure ye mete, it shall be measured to you again." (Matthew 7:1-2) He went on to give the example of getting a mote (splinter) out of a brother's eye while having a beam in one's own eye, implying that to set oneself up as Judge, as if one was Omniscient, is akin to having a beam stuck in one's eye. First get the beam out, He said, and then you can see clearly to help your brother. (paraphrased) The brother may still need help with his splinter, he may not even be sure that it's still in there, or he may know but needs help to get it removed. Either way, it is noteworthy that Jesus gave the eye as a metaphor in His lesson, for the eye is a very sensitive organ, even while it is the only organ being exposed to the elements. The warning is to be gentle, be careful, be caring, in removing the obstruction to our brother's vision, his ability to spiritually see being obstructed.

We are, however, called upon to judge things, as in I Corinthians 2:15. "But he that is spiritual judgeth all things." And to discern between good and evil, as we become spiritually mature enough to no longer be cuddled

LEGALISM, ITS FRUITS AND THE TRUE GRACE OF GOD

at the church's breast, but our system can take on and digest the meat of life, having a strengthened faith, and able to teach others also. (Hebrews 5:12; paraphrased) To be this discerning our spiritual senses need to be exercised, because exercise strengthens. "But strong meat belongeth to them that are of full age [mature], even those who by reason of use have their senses exercised to discern both good and evil." (Hebrews 5:14)

Self-righteousness labels those whom God does not. (Acts 17:6) Righteousness judges all things (I Corinthians 2:15), and discerns both good and evil. (Hebrews 5:14)

DIVINE RESPONSE

THE MASTER GARDENER

Said the liberal to the conservative,
I would really like to know,
Why you're so anxious about these little things,
Look ahead and worry so?

Said the conservative to the liberal,
To the thistle pay no mind,
And it will send a thousand seedlings,
To the wind, then to the ground.

And each little seedling, when it takes root,
Will produce a thousand more.
Please now take heed this little lesson,
For sin can take you down for sure.

You may think I'm overly concerned,
'bout little things that stir up strife
But like the metaphor of the thistle,
Sin'll grow and choke out life.

Let us look to the Master Gardener,
All gardens need His touch,
Who said, "he that is faithful in the least,"
"Will be faithful also in much."

We may think it's just a little thing
But to God it isn't small
For He sees more than floating seedlings,
He sees thistles big and tall.

We need to heed the Master Gardener,
Gardening is what He does best
We'll always have to deal with thistles,
Till we're in eternal Rest.

God grant us, of Thy Holy Spirit,
So we can always faithful be,
Our senses exercised with discernment,
Ever drawing close to Thee.

Gottes sege dazu winscha
(May God add His blessing.)

15

CULTURE AND THE BIBLE

THERE IS A COMMON Pennsylvania Dutch saying that means "we have to hear what a German means, not just what he says." That is good advice anytime, for we need to listen to the heart of the matter in order to communicate well, no matter the nationality.

But to say as some have said, that words are subjective to their context, is too broad and sweeping a statement. Many words have objective meanings and to say otherwise is to bring more confusion into an already confused and confusing world. To invite another Tower of Babel confusion.

While some words such as, but not limited to: *run, runs, running, tape, fall, lot,* and yes, *culture,* are subjective to the context; there are those words that do, and need to, remain objective if we wish to continue speaking the same language. Dictionaries are very useful for this purpose; and on the subject of culture, to "touch base" on what well-established dictionaries give as a definition or definitions for this word, seems a good place to begin. The word does have a dual meaning, though the one could well be a word picture for the other.

Some words, such as *hot, cool, awesome, goodness, freezing,* and *word,* should remain as objective and consistent as possible for two reasons; one, to avoid confusion and be able to effectively communicate, and two, to avoid sinning. Let your yea be yea and your nay be nay, "for whatsoever is more than these cometh of evil" (Matthew 5:37) is what the Word of God says about the misuse and abuse of words.

As Robert Bates, our bishop in Ghent, Kentucky, would say; "We should say what we mean and mean what we say."

Divine Response

So, what is meant by *culture*? And what does it have to do with the Bible? The Encyclopedic Dictionary has this to say about culture; "the sum total of the attainments and learned behavior patterns of any specific period, race or people, regarded as expressing a traditional way of life subject to gradual but continual modification by succeeding generations." Another definition is "the development of microorganisms by prescribed means."

The first part of the first definition, of course, is the one pertinent to this study. Actually, all of the first definition except the part about being subject to gradual but continual modifications by succeeding generations. Which, sadly, has often been the case, especially when Christians have gotten their focus off the Bible as the inspired Word of God to be lived out and obeyed and have begun to view their lifestyle as a "culture" on a par with other "cultures." When this happens, and especially when it is taught—either subtlety or openly— the ensuing result, as can be expected, is to lose identity as a Christian separated unto God. Romans 12:2 which says "And be not conformed to this world: but be ye transformed by the renewing of your mind, that ye may prove what is that good, and acceptable, and perfect, will of God", loses its meaning to such, and they become swallowed up and eventually disappear into the surrounding culture, no longer proving what is that good and perfect and acceptable will of God.

While we believe that the Bible does and will affect culture and actually creates a culture of its own, we also believe that it is a tragic fallacy to move the focus from the Bible as the Word of God to be lived out and obeyed, to culture and its accepted norms. We believe that the Bible is the Word of God, to be lived out and obeyed, and as such its truths are timeless and relevant, in every age and to all people.

Timeless, because it is the Word of God and God is God of the past, the present, and the future.

Relevant, because as God of the past, the present, and the future, He has full authority over us, and not only us, but to every generation preceding or following us.

Therefore, it is of utmost necessity and importance that we lay a foundation, set a direction, a pattern of living, in the reality of that timelessness and relevance of God's Word. And understand our need for subjection and obedience to Him in all things, for ourselves and for those following us.

In addressing this subject, my thoughts turn to missions and some of the controversies of the past and the present. For we cannot escape the fact that there have been significant controversies, which have resulted in some

CULTURE AND THE BIBLE

groups turning against missions, to the point of not wanting to be involved. And this, from a people whose very existence as a church fellowship is a testimony of the power of the gospel to spread through the preaching and teaching of willing workers. Those who gave their lives for this very cause, namely the spreading of the liberating Gospel of our Lord Jesus Christ. It is this writer's finite observation that this turning against missions has been unnecessarily fueled in some groups as they note the absorption of missionaries by the culture in which they serve. Am I wrong?

And in addressing this subject the thought does not escape my attention that I could be embarking on a subject that could create controversy with some whom I love and respect deeply. While I regret even the possibility of such, my love for the church of Jesus Christ and its purity in practice and doctrine, compels me to address a subject that I see as a threat to such purity and doctrine.

Webster's dictionary gives the meaning of culture as the act of developing the intellectual and moral faculties, especially by education. While the secular mind may stop there, as if that information is complete enough in itself, it is right for us who are believers in the origin of man being from God to not be satisfied with such vague and incomplete information. But to ask the question; yes, but from where does intellect and morality come, from where does it originate? The Word of God gives us the answer to that question, which is one of the most necessary of all questions and unavoidable for any real seeker of truth.

For what we believe to be truth becomes the doctrine we live by, becoming habits that form character, this character influences others, becoming tradition that forms culture, which in time forms an identity. There are certainly lies that spread in the form of gossip that sabotage character, giving a negative false identity to upright persons, as there are also deceptive attempts at causing the fallen to appear upright, but we speak in a general sense about the shaping of societies.

We may think we are an individual and therefore exempt from outside pressures and influences, but taking that thought to its logical conclusion would mean that we are complete in ourselves from birth to the grave. (Is not this the epitome of pride?) For so saying would mean that we were, and are, self-conceived, self-born, self-sustained, self-raised, self-corrected, self-taught, self-guided, complete in ourselves and therefore in control of our own destiny. And the death, burial, resurrection, and ascension of Jesus would (God forbid) become meaningless.

Divine Response

Nay, when we become so self-important and full of ourselves and lose our sense of dependence, then we also lose all sense of direction and our destiny is already sealed. The destiny of those dependent upon Jesus Christ is also sealed. "For God so loved the world, that he gave his only begotten Son, that whosoever believeth in him should not perish, but have everlasting life." (John 3:16)

"He that believeth on him is not condemned: but he that believeth not is condemned already, because he hath not believed in the name of the only begotten Son of God." (John 3:18) Two responses to Jesus the Christ. Two destinations. Dependent upon our responses to Jesus Christ. Ultimately dependent upon our Lord Jesus Christ.

When we give up on ourselves and become fully dependent upon Jesus Christ for our salvation, then we become keenly aware of our reliance upon Him. For the sustenance of life here. And for the sustenance of life eternal. And for the sustaining of truth. For He is Truth itself. In response to Thomas' question of "how can we know the way," Jesus said unto him, "I am the way, the truth, and the life: no man cometh unto the Father, but by me." (John 14:6)

And in being Truth itself, He sustains truth. And believing in Him, we believe in His Truth. This belief becomes the doctrine we live by, becoming habits that form our character. This character influences others, becoming tradition that forms culture, identifying us as Christian. Both now and on the Day of Judgment. (Matthew 5, 6, 7 & 25) Then said Jesus to those Jews which believed on Him, "If ye continue in my word, then are ye my disciples indeed; And ye shall know the truth, and the truth shall make you free." (John 8:31-32)

Do we desire to be free?

Then desire to be free from self-dependence.

Desire to be free from self-indulgence.

Desire to be free from passivity.

Desire to be free from aimlessness.

Desire to be free from destructive passions.

Desire to be free from selfish pursuits.

Desire to be free from the pressures of an ungodly culture.

Desire to be free to continue in Christ's word, to be His disciple indeed.

Desire for Christianity to influence and form a Godly culture.

Desire to not allow ungodly cultures to influence and form Christianity.

For Christianity so formed will doubtless not remain Christian. For it is no secret that not all being called "Christian" has been Christian, and should be judged as not Christian. "...he that is spiritual judgeth all things."

CULTURE AND THE BIBLE

(I Corinthians 2:15) While we are not to judge people (Matthew 7:1), we are to judge "things." Things that are, things that happen, things that are done, and things that are not done, to discern both good and evil. But, we are to do it in meekness, lest we also be tempted. (Galatians 6:1) For when we look down our noses at others, we cannot see clearly to help another because of the beam, (nose?) in our own eye. (Matthew 7: 3-5) Thus the damage may well increase.

Damage, however, according to the Word of God, can also be inflicted upon the church from within when sin is overlooked and disunity festers. "For this cause many are weak and sickly among you, and many sleep." (I Corinthians 11:30) The call to be united by the Spirit of Christ was Jesus' prayer in John 17 and is echoed in I Corinthians Chapter 11. For "Christians" (in the broad sense of the name) have been united by other causes besides the Spirit of Christ.

Bloody wars have been fought between "Christian" denominations opposing each other. The bloody crusaders who stormed and conquered Jerusalem taking it from its Muslim defenders were "Christians." "Christians" have persecuted Christians in an attempt to extract a particular "confession of faith" from them. "Christians" have executed Christians in cruel, inhumane, and gruesome ways for daring to stand apart from the local form of "Christianity." And even in this New World, the land of opportunity, in the land of freedom, we are disgraced by the infamous "Salem Witch trials" of 1692 in Salem, Massachusetts. A city, incidentally, that today has the Satanic Temple, the headquarters for satan worshipers, within its limits.

But in all this disgrace, the true Christian can still lift his head and say "but ye have not so learned Christ." For the example and teachings of Christ through the Apostles, are "love, joy, peace, longsuffering, gentleness, goodness, faith, meekness, temperance: against such there is no law." (Galatians 5:22) That is, and remains, the teaching of Christ in condensed form; and is, and remains, consistent with His character and Spirit no matter what "Christians" say and do to the contrary. Whatever else may be said of the bloody wars, the bloody crusaders, the bloody persecutions, the bloody witch trials, and we add etc., this much we know; by the example and teaching of its founder Jesus Christ, that "ye have not so learned Christ."

The most recent of the above-mentioned happenings, the Salem "witch trials" were not a result of Christian influence, but were a result of "Christianity" run amok. The fruits of the Spirit of Christ were surrendered to the enemy of our souls and fear and superstition took over, permeating the culture to such an extent that by the time some of the more sensible of the city's authorities came to their senses and sounded the alarm, 19 innocent persons had been "tried" by the courts and executed (most of them hung) for witchcraft. And exonerated of the charge several years after their deaths. Deaths brought about by fear and superstition with the only evidence being spectral, without any real substance.

Nay, whatever else may be said of these bloody events in history, it can only be grossly dishonest to ascribe them to the teachings and example of Jesus Christ or to His faithful followers. For true Bible Christianity has had a calming, peaceable influence on cultures and societies whenever it has been embraced and adhered to. An honest study of history will reveal that where revival fires have burned, the chaff has been consumed, the gold has been refined, and the dross removed. And had a decidedly positive effect on the culture.

We cannot claim that this country's founders and the framers of its Constitution were all Christian, and therefore this country is a Christian country, without being dishonest about its history and about the teachings of Jesus Christ. Yet, this country's founding, its laws, and its culture were initially—and reap benefits still—heavily influenced by Judeo-Christian beliefs, taught and adhered to by a Bible-believing populace. To deny it would be just as dishonest about history and the teachings of Christ. "This constitution," said John Adams, upon the signing of that venerable document, "has been written for a moral and religious people, it is wholly inadequate for the government of any other." For when a people are governed by their own conscience, they become constrained to do good and not evil by an ever-present authority governing their life from the inside out. This always was, and always will be, the safest society in which to live.

This is the calling of every Christian individually, and of the church corporately, to be governed from the inside out. And if need be, to form a culture within the culture. To allow Jesus Christ to form our beliefs through the Truth of His Word, allow His truth to be the doctrine we live by, becoming habits that form good character, influencing others to Godly traditions that form Godly culture, identifying us as Christians.

On the subject of the development of the intellectual faculties of mankind in the definition for culture, the Word of God makes some profound and all-encompassing claims. It tells us in Psalms 111:10 that "The fear of the LORD is the beginning of wisdom: a good understanding have all they that do his commandments: his praise endureth forever." And wisdom is our God-given heritage, available to us for the asking. As in James 1:5, "If any of you lack wisdom, let him ask of God, that giveth to all men liberally, and upbraideth not; and it shall be given him." In Verse 6, however, a condition is laid out for us if we are to be given God's wisdom. "But let him ask in faith, nothing wavering. For he that wavereth is like a wave of the sea driven with the wind and tossed." Waves are very unstable as they are subjected completely to the elements, having no protection from the winds to be tossed hither and yon, depending on which way the wind is blowing. We are not to waver when asking. And wavering necessitates two opposing forces. Just as the waves necessitate them as well, namely, the water which is stable and stays in its place without an opposing force and the wind which is not stable. It comes from any direction, dependent on the movement of cold and warmth, their collision, and resulting opposing forces.

What are these two opposing forces that we are not to waver between? It is of utmost importance that we get to the bottom of that question, for the condition is reinforced in Verse 7. "For let not that man think that he shall receive any thing of the Lord."

Verse 8 is another reinforcement of the point, "A double minded man is unstable in all his ways." What is double-mindedness? Let us again consider the points already given.

1. God alone has wisdom and that wisdom is ultimate.
2. We are to ask Him for that wisdom, when we lack, for all wisdom comes from God.
3. When we ask it shall be given, liberally, without scolding for our lack.
4. However, there is a condition to this receiving.
5. That condition being a singleness of heart and purpose.
6. If we are given to change in this, we will not receive.

What is this singleness of heart and purpose that we are not to deviate from? This condition that we must reach if we are to receive the wisdom that we seek and ask for?

Is it not, first of all, that we must give back to God the authority that was denied Him in the Garden of Eden? The authority that God Himself put on the line when He created us to be creatures of choice? A people that will, of their own volition and common sense, serve Him as the ultimate in knowledge, and as such, the perfect and only dependable lawgiver?

We are not to waver, then, between our wills and God's will.

Someone has said that wisdom is what we would do in any given situation if we had all the information surrounding it. We don't know everything, but if we are Christians, then we know Someone who does, and whom we can trust to always have our eternal welfare in mind and on His heart. There is a lot of information concerning eternal things that are withheld from us for this time, which withholding we don't understand; but we can trust Him who withholds it, and gives it as we need and ask for it. That is, asking out of the true need for it, and also not asking amiss, from a wrong motive. (James 4:3)

The first and great commandment, Jesus said, is to "love the Lord thy God with all thy heart, with all thy soul, and with all thy mind ... And the second is like unto it ... [to] love thy neighbour as thyself. On these two commandments hang all the law and the prophets." (Matthew 22:37-40)

The first, to love the Lord thy God, is not just a verbal saying so, but a reality that touches us where we live, our lives, and lifestyles. Jesus said, "If ye love me, keep my commandments." (John 14:15) And, in I John 2:4, "He that saith, I know him, and keepeth not his commandments, is a liar, and the truth is not in him." A liar; and liars will "have their part in the lake which burneth with fire and brimstone: which is the second death." (Revelation 21:8) How can we love God if we don't know him? The truth is not a part of such a one. He doesn't know truth. Truth centralizes in God and to not accept His words is to deny any real contact with reality, and consequently with truth. This love for God is characterized by a seriousness about keeping His commandments and the strength to overcome temptation. And in so doing actually be able—by and through the indwelling Spirit that Jesus promised—to live a life that is pleasing to Him. The overcoming power, by and through the Holy Spirit that He promised and did send when He went to the Father, is the proof, in shoe leather so to speak, of love for God. It is the faith that has substance as in Hebrews 11. The faith that has works, as in James 2. Can we rightfully conclude then that what Christians—who take the Word of God literally and have made an honest attempt to obey and live it—do, and have been doing for centuries, is "just culture?" I will answer the obvious: NO. WE CANNOT.

At least, we cannot conclude this and get by with it. We cannot without also reaping the dire consequences that would make our ears tingle if we heard about them all at once. But the devil is a master at conditioning people by getting them used to things that we should never get used to. And in doing it without exposing his master plan. Like cooking the proverbial frog. This is why we need to have our senses exercised to discern both good and evil.

CULTURE AND THE BIBLE

Culture may be good and it may be bad, traditions may be good or they may be bad. It is not safe to assume that either is neutral. At anytime or in anyplace. They may have good origins or they may have bad origins.

Do their origins really matter? someone may ask. Yes, we may answer, it does matter whether something has its origin in the mind of God or in the mind of the devil. It is sacrilegious and disrespectful to suggest anything else. So much so that it seems almost sacrilegious and disrespectful to name both in the same sentence, and I would not do so except that the subject calls for it. Their purposes and long range goals are diametrically opposed to one another.

And we could illustrate it like this; do names matter? What about the name Adolph? Before World War II this name was quite popular, but after the war the name fell into disfavor. Why? Another pertinent example would be that since the betrayal of our Lord by a man by the name of Judas, no more babies are named Judas. Why? The name, by the way, has become synonymous with the word traitor, and no one wants to name their little baby boy "traitor." Some may have a good understanding of why these names have fallen into the category of "no longer used" and others may not. The meaning attached to these names should cause us also to no longer use these names. This is an example where the culture around us should affect our choices. But it should affect our choices because of a Higher Lawgiver. Not despite Him.

This parallel also illustrates the point that we cannot assume something to be neutral on the grounds that we do not understand its meaning. And that culture, like names, often means something, however obscure, to those having grown up and immersed in that culture even though they may be hard pressed to explain the meaning.

But we need to look further. From where did this custom originate, for instance. Can we see its correlation with the Word of God or can we not? If we cannot, then caution should be exercised. "Prove all things; hold fast that which is good" is the instruction to us in the Word of God. (I Thessalonians 5:21)

"Proving all things" does not sound like immersing ourselves in a culture in order to gain a hearing with the people in that culture in which we live. As a matter of fact, it sounds quite contrary to that thought. Romans 12 lets us know that it is possible to know what is that good and acceptable and perfect will of God. And to do it.

Divine Response

"Hold fast to that which is good" we are told, with no instruction on not being offensive to the culture around us. Which does not mean that we should just do what we do without consideration of how it may be interpreted by others. No, we are instructed to "Give none offense, neither to the Jews, nor to the Gentiles, nor to the church of God." (I Corinthians 10:32) We are to be conscious of how our actions will be interpreted by others and whether our actions may embolden them to endanger their own souls as they observe the liberties we take. (I Corinthians 8:9)

We should note, however, that the Word says to "hold fast." Not hold loosely. Not hold tentatively; not hold as long as the culture is in agreement with it. No, hold fast denotes holding on firmly, with desperation even. Hold fast when the odds are stacked against you. Hold fast when the pressure and flood-waters threaten to sweep you away. Hold fast, even when your "friends" endeavor to persuade you otherwise. For they are not your "friends" indeed. Hold fast, for your very life and the lives of all who follow you, are going to spend eternity somewhere. Hold fast, for His name's sake who is worthy. Hold fast, for the Kingdom of God's sake. Hold fast to that which is good.

Are there parts of a culture that should be accepted? The answer to this question should be quite simple. But, understandably it becomes more complicated and tends to lose some of its simplicity when real flesh and blood people are involved. What we need to remember, though, is that it is never God who makes things complicated and no longer simple. It is us who make it that way. Us and our will that runs counter to God's will. God's will is made clear in His word for every honest seeker. Everything in a culture, then, must be brought under the spotlight of His Word and it must be done with our wills nailed to the cross. "God forbid that I should glory, save in the cross of our Lord Jesus Christ, by whom the world is crucified unto me, and I unto the world." (Galatians 6:14)

It is not right for me to take my design for a house in South Dakota into an Asian or African village, nor go to the expense of having it shipped over there. But that doesn't, nor should it, mean that I view their cultures with pagan backgrounds as "just culture" and accept it as normal for a Christian. There are many ways that a culture can and should benefit from Christian influence. While it is true that we need to be sensitive about staying with what is also available to them, we need to be even more sensitive to the Word of God. And to not allow the idea of cultural sensitivity to override our sensitivity to that Word, which stands forever.

CULTURE AND THE BIBLE

Possibly the most misused scripture on this subject is the one in the Acts of the Apostles where Paul speaks to his impromptu audience on Mars Hill. The argument given is that Paul used the writings of the pagan philosophers to persuade them. And in so doing, he set a good example for us, in becoming more culturally like them in order to win them.

There are several problems with this view. One, Paul was not becoming like their culture in order to win them. He, by quoting the pagan philosophers and using the truth in their saying, can only be truthfully represented as believing that even the pagan authors were capable of saying true things and that he saw that truth in their own writings. He was willing to acknowledge truth wherever he heard it and began with a truth that he knew that they already knew.

Two, Paul wasn't referring to just any truth. He was referring to one in which they gave honor to a god whom they themselves said they didn't know. This god did not have a personality nor a set of laws and ethics in the minds of these people. He was, to them, an unknown god. Someone they may have been vaguely aware of, but was not within the scope of their understanding, philosophically nor spiritually. To say that this scripture can be applied, then, to all manner of deities who already have their own set of laws, ethics, and personality, as long as they are referred to as a creator god, is a stretch that would, we believe, grieve Paul and does violence to other scriptures. And it is just as much of a stretch to apply it to other areas of culture and customs.

Thirdly, that same God who said "thou shalt love the Lord thy God with all thy heart, with all thy soul and with all thy mind," also said "thou shalt have no other gods before me." No other gods.

Last, but not least, the question could and should be asked: Who, or what, are we endeavoring to win people from other cultures to? If our focus is to impress them about us and our acceptance of them and their culture, then yes, it makes sense to become like them. But if we are endeavoring to convey to them the utmost necessity of giving in to God while we can do so voluntarily, and the love that God has for sinners who come to Him in repentance, then it becomes questionable at best. And dangerous at worst.

For it has not escaped this writer's attention that at the same time that an emphasis has been growing to accept other cultures in order to better minister "cross culturally," there has also been a growing disregard among some for traditional Christian values because they are, after all, "just culture." Is there a connection? Or is it coincidence? How is it that we need to be careful with pagan cultures so as not to offend, but a culture that has had Godly influence with astounding and long lasting effects on generations of people and society should be disregarded as "just culture"? And carelessly discarded. Does it not seem evident that a love for this present world is driving this arbitrary, blindsided view?

We want to acknowledge here, that there are those who are very sincere in their teaching of "cross cultural ministry." We do not want to hinder them in the good they are doing for the kingdom of God, nor do we wish to misplace blame on them. But we also need to acknowledge that it is being interpreted by some as an encouragement to accept "western culture." Even so, we also need to acknowledge that this may be due to our negligent attitude towards Bible truth and doctrine.

We also need to acknowledge that the growing lack of discernment in digital media and the growing trend toward mainstream culture seem to go hand in hand. The teaching to "cross cultures" only appears to legitimize the desires already being entertained in the minds of so many. And we want and need to again acknowledge the danger of getting our focus and attention so much on culture and tradition that we can disregard a commandment of God. Almost without noticing. As Jesus said to the Jews of His day, that "ye made the commandment of God of none effect by your tradition." (Matthew 15:6) We also need to acknowledge that the emphasis on being cross-cultural could become OUR tradition that makes the Word of God of none effect to us and our children, whether they be spiritually or blood related.

The Word of God is a call to recognition of our fallen, depraved, and wayward nature. And it is a call to love God first and foremost as we bow our hearts and minds to this recognition, thus loving God more than ourselves.

The Word of God is a call to being set free from the bondage and condemnation of sin. To be set free by grace through the faith of our Lord Jesus Christ.

The Word of God is a call for us to love our fellowman as ourselves. Through caring actions. Ultimately through presenting and representing Jesus Christ, the Way, the Truth, and the Life.

Scriptural contextualization presents Christ as the context to which culture must bow.

CULTURE AND THE BIBLE

THE CALL OF THE GOSPEL

This present day problem,
Of Bible dilution,
Is leading so many,
Into worldly delusion.
Being deceived by the masses,
Heading for hell,
And the wolf in sheep's clothing,
Saying all is well.

Tho judgment is coming,
So many don't fear,
For they've stopped up their ears,
Lest they should hear.
For conversion could mean,
Their lifestyle must change,
As they against their own flesh,
In war must engage.

Will we join the masses,
In having their fun?
Or will we stand out,
All evil to shun?
Will we join this pleasure mad
World to its end?
Or will we consider
Where we'll eternity spend?

"Let us blend with the culture"
So many are saying.
Let's blend the world with the church
To keep them from straying,
But, in so doing, the church
Invites the sinner within,
And slowly but surely,
Sinks deeper in sin.

Divine Response

Yes, the form without life,
Is empty and wrong,
Yet, the life needs a form,
To stand straight and strong,
Yes, together they'll stand,
And like a soldier will fight,
With the grace of our Lord,
For the truth and for right.

All life has a structure,
And as a body needs bone,
So the life of our Savior,
Is by our life shown.
And the life-blood that courses,
Thru the veins of the church.
Needs a structure and form,
To function as such.

For the fruit of a Christian,
Proves who he is
Not his lips, nor his doctrine,
Nor well-founded creeds.
Though his doctrine and creeds
Be right all the way,
We cannot be cleansed,
By the things that we say.

Nor are we made right,
By comparing ourselves,
To the sins of others,
Be they ever so gross.
For within the breast,
Of every person that's born
Lies evil potential,
We temptation must spurn.

CULTURE AND THE BIBLE

Our cleansing must be,
As Jesus' blood atones.
Then our doctrine and creeds,
Will help as the bones,
Come together with sinew,
And flesh and skin,
To form a new man,
With Jesus within.

From inside to outside,
This Gospel must work,
Then our doctrine and creeds,
Help us not to lurk,
With evil companions,
That would lead us astray,
As the dike holds the water,
And keeps flooding at bay.

Rise up and be men,
Let's fight and be real,
The devil is busy,
Our children to steal.
He wants the fowls of the air,
To pick the flesh from the bones,
He wants the structure to fall,
Midst our grief and our groans.

Let us do our duty,
And be men who will fight,
The good fight of faith,
As we walk in the light.
Let us not be shirking,
Our duty this day.
But show the world and our families
The Gospel Way

Gottes sege dazu winscha
(May God add His blessing)

16

BEHOLD, THY KING COMETH!

THE YOUNG MAN WEARING the simple work clothes of a carpenter, astride the donkey that looked too young for riding, carried himself with the erect confidence of a nobleman, a king even, who knew what he was doing and where he was going. Yet, He was relaxed and comfortable while the compassion of His heart for the people thronging around Him softened His dark eyes and his strong Jewish facial features.

Though his mount was that of a commoner, his clothing that of a working man, yet there was an invisible aura of kingship about him, the sense of something deeper going on here than met the eye. This sense of something deeper going on behind the scenes was not lost on the adoring crowd of people accompanying him, as they spread articles of their own clothing in the way. Perhaps for the donkey to walk on to prevent its hoofs from kicking up the stifling dust of the roadway. Clothing, and also branches taken from the palm trees nearby, were strewn before the donkey and rider as they descended the Mount of Olives and entered the city of Jerusalem through the gate standing open in the eastern wall facing the Mount.

There was nothing unusual about the appearance of the man and donkey in Jerusalem, as the donkey was a common means of transportation for the common man of the time. And so they now rode and walked. The casual observer may have seen the clothing and branches strewn on the road, wondered what was going on, ignored the scene and moved on.

But for the Jew, properly taught in Tradition, the Law, and the Prophets, this was a momentous moment, a moment prophetically announced by the Prophet Zechariah hundreds of years before. Prophecies that the Jew understood to be announcing the arrival of a King to the capitol city of Jerusalem to permanently deliver the Nation of Israel from the oppression of foreign governments, the present one being Rome. So they understood, and partially misunderstood, the Prophecies. For the ride did not lead to the palace of kings. It didn't end at any capitol building of government prominence. No, this ride's destination was the religious center of Jerusalem. The Jewish religious center. The Temple. God's house on earth. The central place on earth for worship of the one true God. The place where animal sacrifices were offered as burnt offerings to God to cover the sins of the people, as an example and shadow of heavenly things. (Hebrews 8:5)

The temple was a fitting destination for the coronation of priests. Or a High Priest. But a King? Hardly, unless … unless this king was the King prophesied by the Prophet Zechariah, by the inspiration of God. "Rejoice greatly, O daughter of Zion; shout, O daughter of Jerusalem: behold, thy King cometh unto thee: he is just, and having salvation; lowly, and riding upon an ass [donkey], and upon a colt the foal of an ass." (Zechariah 9:9) The fulfillment of this prophecy is recorded for us in Matthew 21, Mark 11, Luke 19, and John 12.

Excitement ran high. Here was a spiritual teacher. One who healed the sick! And raised the dead! Now fulfilling yet another prophecy! Would He at this time restore the kingdom again to Israel? Surely, for prophecy must be fulfilled! And so their excitement burst forth with a loud voice rejoicing and praising God for all the mighty works that they had seen saying, "Hosanna to the Son of David: Blessed is he that cometh in the name of the Lord; Hosanna in the highest." (Matthew 21:9) "Blessed be the King that cometh in the name of the Lord: peace in heaven, and glory in the highest." (Luke 19:38)

These children of Israel, the children of Abraham, God's chosen people, these children of Promise, did not always understand the Promise of God to them. The promises about God blessing them with material prosperity in response to their obedience to His laws and statutes—they understood very well. And, they also understood very well the withholding of His blessing in response to their disobedience. What would happen to them if they turned to the gods of their heathen neighbors, had been a painful lesson to learn and relearn. Until Babylon. After that infamous captivity the Jewish mind was set. Never again. Never again would they fall for the deceptive gods of the heathen. And they didn't.

Divine Response

But while they diligently protected the front door of their hearts, homes, and places of worship, the devil, in his subtlety, was slipping another god in the back door. A god of the mind. But for today there was rejoicing and praise. And the aura of excitement seemed in contact with the heavenlies themselves as God Himself smiled upon this fulfillment of prophecy.

Prophetic utterances were very much a part of Jewish experience and tradition; the Law and Prophets being taught, memorized, and recited from school-age on. Rightly believed to be the very word of God, the prophecies and the Law were the central focus of Jewish study and worship. Though hard to understand, and maybe at times as a result of it, many a Jew was drawn into study because of a deep desire to understand God. A deep desire for God's blessing upon himself, his family, his community, and nation. A deep desire to see and experience the fulfillment of Prophecy.

Prophecies hidden in the Law and in prophetic utterances. Hidden. Why hide them? We may ask, and our hearts respond with understanding to the exclamation of the disciples when they said, "Lo, now speakest thou plainly," in response to Jesus telling them that: "I came forth from the Father, and am come into the world: again, I leave the world, and go to the Father." (John 16:28-29) Jesus had also told them, "These things have I spoken unto you in proverbs: but the time cometh, when I shall no more speak unto you in proverbs, but I shall shew you plainly of the Father." (John 16:25) Though they tried, the disciples likely did not understand that Jesus spoke of Pentecost and onward when their understanding became illuminated by the Holy Ghost taking up residence in their hearts and minds. As He continues for all of us as we become repentant and accept the reality of our fallen condition, and of God's Divine response, through Jesus Christ, to the desperation of our need.

But why speak in proverbs? In obscure prophecies? In even more obscure types and shadows woven into the Law of ceremonies so much a part of Jewish life and practice? Why not speak plainly? God will speak for Himself one day, and plainly give us the reason why, but in the meantime He gives us some hints, though admittedly obscure, in His Word.

In I Corinthians Chapter 2, the Apostle Paul, by the inspiration of God, tells the Corinthians that he did not come to them with the excellent nor enticing words of man's wisdom but that he spoke the wisdom of God in a mystery: "Which none of the princes of this world knew: for had they known it, they would not have crucified the Lord of glory." (I Corinthians 2:8) It is clear then, that neither the devil nor his minions knew what they were doing, the devil not knowing that he was bringing about his own defeat and destruction, the High Priest didn't know he was ushering in an eternal Priesthood, and the king didn't know he was setting up a King and Kingdom that would claim a country without boundaries, and be everlasting in its scope. It follows that prophetic meaning was hidden from the devil, who then became a "vessel of dishonor" (Romans 9:21) in God's plan for salvation in the war for man's soul.

Considering the devil's limited knowledge it also follows that he cannot read minds as God can. God has retained that ability for Himself. While the devil can hear and see what is said and done and arrange his strategies accordingly, he cannot hear our thoughts nor argue with us in our minds. Those arguments are the result of our "thoughts the mean while accusing or else excusing one another" (Romans 2:15) and are to be brought captive "to the obedience of Christ." (II Corinthians 10:5) For Praise the Lord! God even tells us how to think! We are to think on those things that are true, honest, just, pure, lovely, of good report, if there be any virtue, and if there be any praise; think on these things. (Philippians 4:8)

The devil is limited to outward observation. God alone is Omniscient; All-Knowing. He knows us. Even better than we know ourselves. Which means that He knows how best to answer our prayers, for He understands what we need before we ask. The prayer and the asking is for communication, connection with God, and to bring us into unity, a proper union with God.

There are then, several logical reasons for God to speak in obscure, prophetic language; one, so as to keep the "mystery" hidden from the enemy of our souls. And, two, so that understanding could be by revelation of God's Holy Spirit, when the heart and mind are prepared and open. Which happened at Pentecost and continues to happen to each individual personally upon repentance and receiving the saving knowledge of Christ. It must be by divine revelation to the heart and mind, because "the natural man receiveth not the things of the Spirit of God: for they are foolishness unto him: neither can he know them, because they are spiritually discerned." (I Corinthians 2:14)

In seeking to understand prophecy, we need to consider the indictment of history upon the Old Testament children of promise, the Jewish people. Who were so persuaded of their own interpretation of prophecy, its meaning so cemented in their collective minds, so persuaded that the Promise pertained to an earthly kingdom, that they murdered the Lord of Glory, the very Son of God, for not agreeing, but rather rebuking them.

Divine Response

And we need to consider the indictment, and consequent conviction, of history so we can learn from history and not repeat its mistakes. Possibly the deeper purpose of prophecy is to help us understand what is going on as events unfold, thereby strengthening our faith and purposeful resolve to go on with God, despite the downward pressure seeking the eternal destruction of all. The Jewish mistake was not in their deep desire to understand prophecy. The heathen culture of Rome made that mistake, as they uncaringly ignored prophecy and all else not having the ability to fulfill the lustful desires of the flesh and of the mind.

No, the caring and the deep desire to understand prophecy was in itself good. The Jew, caring about spiritual things, caring about God, His Law, and being right with Him, resulted in the Church Age—which we now live in and benefit from—being ushered in by Jews. Jesus was born into a Jewish family, raised Jewish, was taught in the synagogues. His disciples were Jews and His message was recorded for us in the Holy Bible by Jews. As a Gentile, I benefit from Jewish history, Jewish zeal, and the tenacity of Jewish desire to serve God. Hebrews 11 records the most prominent of the Old Testament faithful, and we trust there were many more of whom we have no record.

The Jewish failure was not lack of caring about God. Rather, his failure was in allowing his own desires to obscure and eventually darken the understanding, his resistance obstructing light and the illumination of God's Spirit. Believing he understood, he called light darkness and darkness light. (Matthew 6:23) Not understanding God, but believing he did, he formed a new understanding of God—a sort of god of the mind—and unwittingly turned again to serving a heathen idol. An idol of the mind.

We have the warning of history. We are no better. We are of the same stuff. We have the same temptations, the same weaknesses. We also are spirit, soul, and body. We also are fallen man. We also need Jesus.

Yet, in our deep desire to understand and be blessed, we need to also recall to mind the words of God through the Apostle, "For now we see through a glass, darkly; but then face to face: now I know in part; but then shall I know even as also I am known." (I Corinthians 13:12) Perhaps as we face the limitations of seeing "through a glass darkly" we should be more diligent in being familiar enough with the Book of Revelation that when these things come to pass, we may be of those blessed who "heareth the word, and understandeth it." (Matthew 13:23) And thus our faith be strengthened.

BEHOLD, THY KING COMETH!

To study the Old Testament Messianic prophecies and their fulfillment is a faith-building exercise that is broad in its scope; and from the advantageous perspective of hindsight, startling in its detail. It is this writer's belief that as we become, and stay, familiar with end-time prophecy, we will be amazed and strengthened at the Prophetic detail in the Book of Revelation to John, as events unfold in due time.

God's promise of a coming Deliverer begins in the Garden of Eden when God spoke of the "seed" of the woman bruising the head of the serpent. (Genesis 3:15) Jesus was not born after the seed of Adam, but was born of a virgin, being the "seed of the woman." Being conceived of the Holy Ghost (Luke 1:35) He yet received His physical form of the woman who bore Him full term and then gave birth. He lived a faithful life of love from birth to crucifixion where He bore "our sins in his own body on the tree, that we, being dead to sins, should live unto righteousness: by whose stripes ye were healed." (I Peter 2:24) Jesus effectively and forever bruised the head of the serpent, when the devil's destructive intent was turned upon himself through the birth, life, crucifixion, burial, resurrection, and finally ascension of our Messiah, Jesus. The One foretold by the Prophets. The Fulfillment of Promise. The One typified by the saving of Noah and his family by the Ark into which they entered, escaping the catastrophic world-wide flood that destroyed everything and all not found within. Following the instructions and plan that God laid out for him, Noah spent 100 years building the Ark that was to carry life from the existing world into the next, escaping the judgment befalling the unbelievers left behind, who became believers, but too late.

We are warned of another, still in the future, catastrophic world-wide event, when "the elements shall melt with fervent heat." (II Peter 3:10) When all who are not in Christ will be lost forever. (Matthew 24:36-39)

Some say that the Ark is a type of the Church and emphasize the need to be a member of the Church in order to be saved. Rightly understood, this view is a Biblically correct one, as each member individually and all together are in Christ. However, the danger in this view is the shift in emphasis from being "in Christ" to being "in the Church." And when being "in the Church" takes precedence over being "in Christ," we get "the cart before the horse." This is a dreadfully awkward position in this life and a dreadfully fearful one in the next. As God tells us through the Apostle John, "He that believeth on the Son hath everlasting life: and he that believeth not the Son shall not see life; but the wrath of God abideth on him." (John 3:36)

DIVINE RESPONSE

The wrath of God. Unto this day we know Jesus, or know of Jesus, as the Babe in a manger, as the King who rode a donkey, as the Great Healer, as the Master Teacher, as the Miracle Worker, and finally as the sinless One nailed to a cross, dying in our stead, rising again the third day and ascending to Heaven, where He is "King of Kings and Lord of Lords." (Revelation 19:16)

We do well to know of Jesus historically, but I "would to God" that we all know Him as our Personal Savior, who has redeemed us and cleansed us from our sins by His own blood on the tree. That our sins have, in spirit, been unloaded at—and nailed to—that emblem of suffering Love, the Cross.

The Cross is the Biblical account of Redemption that gives hope, assurance, protection, and power to overcome each present-day tactical obstruction to a victorious life and to future glory that the devil, with subtle hatred, tempts us with. And the rest of the story awaits us. It is yet in the future. Someday the future will become today, today will be history, and the future "today" will become history. We have one life to live, one chance at Glory. "Today, if ye will hear his voice, Harden not your hearts, as in the provocation, in the day of temptation in the wilderness: When your fathers tempted me, proved me, and saw my works forty years. Wherefore I was grieved with that generation, and said, They do always err in their heart; and they have not known my ways. So I sware in my wrath, They shall not enter into my rest." (Hebrews 3:7-11)

Then God, through the author of Hebrews, by giving a warning still relevant to the present day, also gives us a glimpse into why the Israelites did not know His ways, and could not enter into His rest; by warning us in verse 12: "Take heed, brethren, lest there be in any of you an evil heart of unbelief, in departing from the living God."

Unbelief is a serious offense to God, and we venture to say that it is because of the clear direction God has given between right and wrong; directly at times by the Father and by Jesus Christ, also by the Law given to Moses, by natural law woven into nature by His creation, by the written Word, and by the Living Word, the Holy Spirit. Does God not say as much in the next verse when He gives the warning after giving the directive to exhort one another? Verse 13: "But exhort one another daily, while it is called Today; lest any of you be hardened through the deceitfulness of sin." For sin, when not repented of, darkens the understanding and then, under the cover of darkness, deceives. Its deceptions are manifold but its basis is all the same; an attempt to find fulfillment in something or someone other than God. Something or someone that is easier on the flesh, less rigid, with less requirements. Something or someone that will give us the liberty to "do our own thing" and still feel good about ourselves at the end of the day.

But while they promise them liberty, they themselves are the servants of corruption and brought into bondage. (II Peter 2:19) How can someone in jail promise liberty to his cellmate when he himself is incarcerated? He cannot; he does not have the authority nor the power to do so; therefore, if he is foolish enough to make such a promise, we readily and rightly would understand it to be empty and vain. In mankind's innermost and most deeply felt emotional, spiritual, and even physical needs, the often alluring promises of sin are just as—and even more so—empty and vain. Not to say that there is not enjoyment; for yes, sin can be sensually enjoyable. For a time. And for a short time only, because physical life is short; and even if it were a long one, unbridled sensual indulgence desensitizes one to the enjoyment of sensual pleasure, leading to an ever more desperate feeling of need for more of it. Hence the soul becomes ever more wound into the hard cords of bondage. Thus the promising feelings of liberty actually allure and lead the soul into ever deeper bondage and fear of death. (Hebrews 2:15)

But there is a way out. It is the way of the cross. It is not the way of chariots, horses, armor, nor the show of military might. It is the lowly way of One riding a donkey, it is the lowly way of one serving others, the lowly way of our life being "crucified with Christ, nevertheless living, yet not us but Christ living in us; and the life that we now live in the flesh, we live by the faith of the Son of God, who loved us and gave Himself for us." (Galatians 2:20 paraphrased) Our King Jesus was coronated with a crown of thorns and a purple robe of mockery. He was given a kingly title, but only upon being nailed to a wooden cross as if He were a criminal deserving of capital punishment, upon which cross a superscription was placed above Him that read: "This is the King of the Jews." (Luke 23:38) If this was an attempt at mockery, it was a failed attempt to mock, for it was an accurate and prophetic statement. As all will one day acknowledge, and openly believe, and confess. Every eye shall see Him. Every knee shall bow, every tongue shall confess that He is Lord, to the glory of God the Father. (Philippians 2:10; Romans 14:11)

The Almighty has decreed this coming event and has mercifully communicated it to us through His servant John on the Isle of Patmos, where he had been exiled upon the rejection of his message, and consequently of himself, by the Roman government of that time. And to that lonely Isle

God came. John records the events of that encounter by beginning with, "I was in the Spirit on the Lord's day, and heard behind me a great voice, as of a trumpet." (Revelation 1:10) We understand "the Lord's Day" to be the day when Jesus rose from the dead, having fulfilled the prophesies of His first coming in minute detail. Having defeated the gates (counsels) of hell. (Matthew 16:18)

Then John records what the voice said: "I am Alpha and Omega, the first and the last: and, What thou seest, write in a book, and send it unto the seven churches which are in Asia; unto Ephesus, and unto Smyrna, and unto Pergamos, and unto Thyatira, and unto Sardis, and unto Philadelphia, and unto Laodicea." John turned to see who spoke and saw "in the midst of seven candlesticks one like unto the Son of man, clothed with a garment down to the foot, and girt about the paps with a golden girdle." John describes this Son of man further and then says, "And when I saw him, I fell at his feet as dead. And he laid his right hand upon me, saying unto me, Fear not; I am the first and the last: I am he that liveth, and was dead; and, behold, I am alive for evermore, Amen; and have the keys of hell and of death." (Revelation 1:11, 13, 17-18)

The keys of hell. The keys of death. Jesus has them. He has outgrown the manger, dismounted the donkey, been removed from the cross, has resurrected from the grave, and ascended to Heaven. He has not only shown us how to overcome the forces of evil through humility and love to our fellowman, He has gone on to become, and be, that overcoming Power for us as we yield and submit our own wills to His.

And having fulfilled the mission of His first coming, He now has a second, and last, Divine appointment with the earth as we know it. An appointment that is impossible for any of us to avoid. Time is not our servant, but His. And when time comes to an end, eternity begins. In this life—in this realm of time as we know it—we have some control over events, either causing them to happen or not to happen, for we are given this decree by God, the Creator of the Universe as He gave it to our first parents, Adam and Eve. "And God blessed them, and God said unto them, Be fruitful, and multiply, and replenish the earth, and subdue it: and have dominion over the fish of the sea, and over the fowl of the air, and over every living thing that moveth upon the earth." (Genesis 1:28)

By this decree from the Almighty, mankind has built marvelous buildings, has increased mobility upon the earth, is able to travel through the air propelled by thundering jet engines, has the ability to be thrust into outer space, is able to return to earth again from outer space, is able to project images, text, and voice through space, can receive those images, text, and voice through little hand-held gadgets, has learned to subdue all manner of animals, and has trained them in ways to cause one to stop, to watch, and to marvel.

In eternity we are given no such decree. Which is a good thing, considering how we mess things up here; for as we continue to seek more comfort, faster travel, better food and drink, a life of ease and entertainment, we are also plagued with pollution, diseases, and obesity. And pollution of the mind. No sooner is a new thing invented than someone uses it to perpetuate sin, which we have the evidence for in two global wars fought in the same century, that because of inventions still new in their time, were unprecedented in their ferocity and in the world-wide scope of their territory and destruction.

And for which we have evidence in the devastating culture wars being fought in our time. Facts and morality are in jeopardy, as are the minds and very basis of an entire civilization. It is a known neurological fact that brains need exercise for strength, proper function, and health. No such study has been done on the human thumbs. Although, of course, some coordinational skills may be acquired by using them and the brain simultaneously.

But in order to acquire the every-day life skills so necessary for the survival of civilization, we need the entire body to become, and remain, proficient in its coordination with the brain. I became painfully aware of this in 2011, upon suffering severe brain damage after a fall from a roof that resulted in the loss of practically all of my motor skills. I had to relearn how to move my limbs, how to walk, to brush my teeth, to bring food to my mouth, to properly chew, even to swallow, and a myriad of other functions that we take for granted, and do, innumerable times in a day. We, myself included before that traumatic experience, take for granted the marvelous brain and body coordination needed for the body to function in these every-day things we do naturally to sustain ourselves.

While these motor skills are, for the most part, involuntary in a properly functioning body, the voluntary skills that we gain must be acquired through much practice and only become a skill when the brain and body coordinate seamlessly; though we must, of course, give room for human error.

One place where we don't like to give room for human error is on the operating table, as one mistake may cost our life. About six months after the fall from a roof, I was again in the hospital, this time because of gall stone

Divine Response

problems. Upon being prepared for the operating room, I was introduced to the surgeon who would be doing the surgery who then explained to me the surgery, the anesthesia, and the associated dangers. My heart went out to him as I thought about the stress of his job, knowing every day when he performs a surgery that there is another life in his hands. And that a life, once lost, can never be regained. If the life is lost because of a surgical mistake, there is no undoing, no going back and redoing it. No "do overs." So I spoke to the good doctor, compassionately assuring him that I understand mistakes because I am a carpenter and make mistakes. I can then take my mistake apart and redo it, but I understand he might not have that luxury. I assured him that if I die on the operating table, I want him to know beforehand that I forgive him. He seemed to appreciate it; but then as I was being wheeled in for surgery, I thought, "What did I just do? Why did I say that? What if he gets careless because, after all, I've forgiven him before it happens?" I confess that being in the hands of a doctor, even a good one, didn't feel very safe at that moment. I committed myself into the hands of God then. In God's hands, after all, is the only safe place to be. And I'm confident that the doctor, whom I'm still able to call a good one, would agree. And I lived to be thankful that the good doctor had honed more skills than brain and thumb coordination. I am thankful that he wasn't "all thumbs."

Yes, it is a marvel how well mankind has fulfilled God's decree to "subdue the earth and have dominion." It is also a marvel how sloppy and careless mankind can be about the second coming of Jesus Christ. He is coming again. King of Kings and Lord of Lords. His coming is prophesied in the Book of Revelation. To those who doubt His coming, consider how much prophecy He has already fulfilled. And then consider the risk of procrastination and neglecting preparation through repentance and salvation. "What shall a man give in exchange for his soul?" (Matthew 16:26) Are the weak, beggarly, fleeting, and temporary elements and pleasures of this world worth the risk?

From a proper perspective, which is eternal reality, the Believer's answer is a joyful and resounding, NO. To the Unbeliever facing reality, the answer is a painful, but just as resounding, NO. In facing and accepting reality though, the unbeliever has the blessed privilege to become a Believer. Because facing reality draws the soul to repentance for sin at the cross of Christ, and to salvation through His shed blood, His death, and Resurrection. These events of the first coming of Christ were prophesied and have been fulfilled. We now await His second coming and final judgment of the earth, including all of us individually, both dead and living. As has been prophesied by Jesus when here on the earth (Matthew 13:30-50, 16:27, Chapter 25) and in the Book of Revelation. (Revelation 19)

Indeed, as we consider that the entire Bible, both Old and New Testaments, revolve around the Creation, the Fall of man, the Divine response to that fall, the second coming of Christ, and the final Judgment, we can perhaps get a glimpse into understanding the reason throughout history, and even unto this day, for the fascination concerning this Book of all books. There is a certain fascination with fiction books and movies, but the fascination is always tempered by knowing the eventual need to have our minds again transported from the dream world back to the real. While our minds can and do become addicted to the thrills and excitement of fiction, yet, for those who care anything for reality, there is always that deep down unsettling conviction of reality awaiting.

I enjoy flying via commercial airlines. The lift-off when the wheels leave the runway is a thrill every time. Being in the sunshine above the clouds or having a panoramic view of the earth from around six miles up is exhilarating. But, as with fiction, the thrill and exhilaration is tempered with the reality check of "what goes up must come down." So we hope, and if you're like me, pray for a safe landing.

Unlike fiction of course, a safe landing is accompanied with the feeling of having safely arrived; whereas the feeling of "coming back to earth" after a fictitious book or movie is one of sinking let-down for one to whom reality feels less than perfect. We don't live in a perfect world and the emotions that ascend into the clouds of fantasy must eventually descend to a landing among this imperfection. Is not this the attraction of the horror movie; that the feeling of let-down when coming back to earth becomes replaced by a feeling of relief and safety? From this perspective, horror stories are quite useless. Good fiction, though, may—and can—portray good lessons. However, reality is the litmus test of lessons learned.

There is only one legitimate place to feel relieved and safe. That is the place of repentance and humility within the circle of God's acceptance of us because of Jesus, whose pure life, death on the cross, resurrection from the tomb, and ascension into Heaven, has enabled Him to intercede for us and to invite us to join Him in that place of eternal bliss. Does this not give us an even deeper understanding of the continued fascination with the Word of God with its settling knowledge of Reality? A reality that is personally settling or unsettling, depending on how we relate to it? Is not this settling

Reality, in the souls of men and women, that which has given them courage to accept the hardships and butcheries of horrible atrocities meekly, without returning the same, over past millennia?

We believe this to be so, and long for the Reality of that Relief and Safety for all.

BEHOLD, THY KING COMETH

Jesus was born in a Bethlehem stable,
Was dependent like all other babies,
Though He lived from everlasting,
And He is our Prince of peace;
He was born in a lowly place,
And He lived His life that way,
Being an obedient carpenter's son,
Tho He'd made, and divided, night from day.

Jesus met with the doctors of law,
In the temple of His Father,
They all were astonished at His wisdom,
His understanding and His answers;
His parents sorrowed when they missed Him,
As they sought out where He was,
"Wist ye not that I must be,"
He asked, "about my Father's business?"

Jesus taught with real humility,
As He taught the multitudes,
As He healed the sick and dying,
And brought to them Good News;
He is the Way, the Truth, the Life,
He is the only way to God,
The only way and everlasting,
Son of man, and from everlasting, Word of God.

BEHOLD, THY KING COMETH!

And even though He'd made the donkey,
Still He rode it on before,
Surely it behooves us to be humble,
He is our mighty Counsellor;
Jesus rode upon a donkey,
Through His capitol's city gate,
Our King of kings and Lord of lords,
Come in humility, to redeem us, from our fate.

Jesus groaned in deep travail,
In the garden of Gethsemane,
As He struggled with the weight of sin,
That He bore for you and me;
He submitted to our Father,
When he said, "Thy will be done,"
He voluntarily bore our sin,
And for us the victory, and the crown, has won.

Jesus endured with real humility,
He was stricken, smitten and abused,
The chastisement of our peace laid upon Him,
And by His stripes we are healed;
We hid, as it were, our faces from Him,
He, being railed on and reviled,
Had a crown of thorns pressed on His head,
Was mocked, cruelly scourged, and crucified.

Jesus died and Creation shook,
As the rocks were rent apart,
The graves of many were opened,
And in day the sun turned dark.
Jesus preached to the souls in prison,
As he defeated the gates of hell,
The enemy could not stop Him,
Could not His power, nor His purpose, quell.

Divine Response

Jesus rose with mighty power,
With victory over grave and death,
The enemy could not stop Him,
Jesus has power over breath.
Tho His rising seemed obscure to most,
Many witnesses have we,
And the prophets have described Him,
It is sure, there is no doubt, this is He.

And there's an inner way to know,
That He is risen from the grave;
He stills the stormy inner tempest,
He calms the roaring crashing waves.
But first of all we have to hear Him.
When confronted with our sin,
We must bow down to His Lordship,
He has won, He does win, and He will win.

Jesus will come with awesome power,
Not on a donkey but a white horse,
And every eye shall see Him,
Time will be halted from its course;
Every knee shall bow before Him,
Every tongue shall now confess,
Sinners quake and fear and tremble,
Our dependence, the faith of saints, put to the test.

Jesus the Christ has awesome power,
Dear sinner won't you come right now?
Submit and bow your knees before Him,
And live for Him, He'll show you how;
He is pleading, He is gentle,
He is loving and forgiving,
He will reveal Himself to you,
As yourself, your all, to Him you bring.

BEHOLD, THY KING COMETH!

Let us voluntarily accept,
And so acknowledge our guilt,
Let us tear down, remove the walls,
That we've deceptively built;
For we need to humble ourselves,
And bow our knees to His name,
When He calls and reveals to us,
Our deep need, our guilt, and our shame.

Jesus the Christ has awesome power,
As He puts His life in us,
When He takes the stony heart out,
He puts in us a heart of flesh;
We must be diligent to keep Him,
First and foremost in our life,
For we'll lay these bodies down,
Stay conscious, but leave this world, of sin and strife.

And the graves will someday open,
Seas give up the dead in them,
The saints will rise to be with Jesus,
As body and soul unite again;
The saints still living caught up with them,
In the clouds, there to meet the Lord,
In the air, so to ever live,
We shall stay, we shall be safe, with our Lord.

Then forever we will praise Him,
In the glory He has prepared,
With all repentant of their sin,
And with whom His life He shared;
Hallelujah praise and glory!
Praise to the Lamb that was then slain,
JESUS has AWESOME POWER,
Through time, and all eternity, JESUS REIGNS.

Gottes sege dazu winscha
(May God add His blessing)

17

MEANWHILE BACK ON THE EARTH

Part 1

"Your old men shall dream dreams, and your young men shall see visions," said the Prophet of old as he spoke the Word of the Lord to the people of that time, and speaks to us still, even these many years later, through the written Word of God. (Joel 2:28)

The disciples, on the day of Pentecost, experienced the fulfillment of this prophecy when about a hundred and twenty were together in one place. (Acts 1:15-21) On this day of Pentecost, multitudes of people were together at Jerusalem. Pentecost was a day of celebration, a time of Thanksgiving; seven weeks, or the fiftieth day after Passover, and at the time of wheat harvest. It was a day of laying aside work, a day of gratitude to the Lord, symbolized in the offering of two loaves of leavened, salted bread, baked according to precise instructions.

Ten days ago the disciples had seen Jesus, their Lord and Master, ascending from Mt. Olivet, and a cloud receiving Him out of their sight. And while they looked steadfastly toward Heaven, two men in white appeared and stood by them. Which also said, "Ye men of Galilee, why stand ye gazing up into heaven? this same Jesus, which is taken up from you into heaven, shall so come in like manner as ye have seen him go into heaven." (Acts 1:11)

And now they remained at Jerusalem because their Lord had commanded them not to depart, but to wait for the promise of the Father which he had told them of. Jesus had also told them, "For John truly baptized with water, but ye shall be baptized with the Holy Ghost not many days hence." (Acts 1:5) So in Jerusalem they tarried, at this time of Pentecost, at this time of harvest, and as yet unbeknownst to them, to also take part in the most rewarding, the most fruitful, the most bountiful harvest of all time. A spiritual harvest. A harvest of which Jesus had spoken when He said, "Say not ye, There are yet four months, and then cometh harvest? behold, I say unto you, Lift up your eyes, and look on the fields; for they are white already to harvest." (John 4:35) "The harvest truly is plenteous," He had said, and sent them forth, "as lambs among wolves." (Luke 10:3)

And now at Jerusalem they tarried. In the very city where their Master had been falsely accused, brought before the Tribunal at the Judgment Hall, condemned for treason and whatever else came to frenzied minds, taken out of the city, and crucified on a hill as a criminal. Crucified with common criminals as a bad man himself. Being lifted up, as the brass serpent on a pole. (Numbers 21:9) Fulfilling the prophecy he had prophesied of Himself in John 3:14 when He told Nicodemus that, "as Moses lifted up the serpent in the wilderness, even so must the Son of man be lifted up." So also was our Master lifted up, vilified as the common serpent.

And now in Jerusalem the disciples waited. Waited for the Promise. But they did more than wait. Peter expressed the need to replace Judas who, being one of the twelve and having betrayed his Lord, committed suicide in his abject desperation over what he had done. Peter, having denied his Lord not once but three times, turned to his Lord again in repentance and was forgiven his transgression; but Judas turned to himself, and finding no answer for his misdeed, his horrible sin of betrayal, went out and hanged himself. (Matthew 27:5)

The others agreed to the need for a replacement, as expressed by Peter, "And they gave forth their lots; and the lot fell upon Matthias; and he was numbered with the eleven," (Acts 1:26) bringing the number again to twelve specially chosen disciples. "Have not I chosen you?" Jesus had asked the former twelve, and then He also chose this one, through the lot.

"And when the day of Pentecost was fully come, they were all with one accord in one place. And suddenly there came a sound from heaven as of a rushing mighty wind, and it filled all the house where they were sitting. And there appeared unto them cloven tongues like as of fire and it set upon each of them. And they were all filled with the Holy Ghost, and began to speak with other tongues, as the Spirit gave them utterance." The sixteen nationalities of people gathered together at Jerusalem were amazed when they heard the disciples speaking in tongues. For each nationality heard them speak in their own language. Some searched aloud for some meaning to this. Others mocked and accused the disciples of drinking problems.

But Peter, standing up with the eleven, assured the crowd of people that what they were seeing and hearing was not a result of drunkenness as they supposed, "but this is that which was spoken by the prophet Joel; And it shall come to pass in the last days, saith God, I will pour out my Spirit upon all flesh: and your sons and your daughters shall prophesy, and your young men shall see visions, and your old men shall dream dreams: And on my servants and on my handmaidens I will pour out in those days of my Spirit; and they shall prophesy." (Acts 2:16-18)

And then Peter preached the sermon that shook the Jewish mindset. Contained in it was the message that has ever since been shaking the self-righteous, insulated-from-the-Spirit of God mindset and preparing hearts and minds to crack open to receive the Truth of God's Word and the Gospel. Contained in this sermon is the message that has shaken earthly kingdoms and rulers of this world ever since. Here was a King and a Kingdom that rendered useless all material means to overcome and bring into subjection. Here is a King and a Kingdom that the sword, the spear, and the bow cannot touch. Here is a King and a Kingdom that cannot be overcome with any of the weapons of carnal warfare, whether they be ancient or the modern weapons of mass destruction in the form of atomic energy releasing bombs that permanently changed the way nations relate to each other since the conclusion of the second World War.

This King, whose name is Jesus, is always ready, through his subjects, to speak up in defense of this Kingdom's boundaries. Its boundaries cross the boundaries of Nations, Races, Cultures, and Seas. But it has boundaries which are moral, ethical, and spiritual. Its boundaries are moral for The King clearly tells us in His Word, and through inner conviction, what is right and what is wrong. Knowledge of right and wrong is built into the very fabric of nature, for we instinctively know that there must be right and there must be wrong to avoid anarchy and the descent into total chaos that would be sure to follow. And we instinctively know—if we wish to that is—when we are doing wrong and when we are doing right, unless our minds have been corrupted from original simplicity. For original simplicity recognizes original sin. This Kingdom has moral boundaries that put a much needed restraint on the lower nature of mankind.

MEANWHILE BACK ON THE EARTH

The Kingdom of God has ethical boundaries. The King tells us in His Word and through inner conviction how we should conduct ourselves toward, and how we should treat our fellow human beings. He tells us "whatsoever ye would that men should do to you, do ye even so to them," (Matthew 7:12) to "recompense to no man evil for evil," (Romans 12:17) to turn the other cheek and be ready to give the very clothes off our back. (Matthew 5:38-42)

This King gives instructions for the defense of His Kingdom's boundaries and then He also gives instructions for taking the offense in gaining ground for His Kingdom. For He is a King of conquest and His agenda is to have every soul on the face of the earth become a citizen of His Kingdom.

The following of His instructions concerning fellow human beings have directed the course of history, as the world has experienced the lasting impact of The King's directive to His subjects to be on the offense. "All power is given unto me in heaven and in earth," He said. "Go ye therefore, and teach all nations, baptizing them in the name of the Father, and of the Son, and of the Holy Ghost: Teaching them to observe all things whatsoever I have commanded you: and, lo, I am with you alway, even unto the end of the world. Amen." (Matthew 28: 19-20) And He sent them into spiritual battle "as lambs among wolves." (Luke 10:3) Instructing them to be "wise as serpents, and harmless as doves." (Matthew 10:16) As He does even to this day. For a thorough study of history reminds one of Stephen's indictment of his own people and how the conclusion of the sermon cost him his life. "Which of the prophets have not your fathers persecuted?" he asked, "and they have slain them which shewed before of the coming of the Just One; of whom ye have been now the betrayers and murderers: Who have received the law by the disposition of angels, and have not kept it." (Acts 7:52-53) This is the judgment call on their actions that cost Stephen his life. For they gnashed on him with their teeth, cast him out of the city, and stoned him till his body succumbed to the stones being furiously hurled by furious men.

And this is the type of judgment call on the actions of wolves, which have then killed, or incited other wolves to kill, innocent lambs ever since. While Christians are called to leave final judgment of people to God (Matthew 7:1), we are just as clearly called to judge actions and things, (I Corinthians 2:15) for actions and things have everything to do with the boundaries of the Kingdom of God. And judging actions and things have everything to do with maintaining those boundaries.

Divine Response

If the public disposition is opposed to torture and physical killing, then the livelihood and/or good name is attacked. From the stoning of Stephen, to the world trying to force its values—or rather the lack of them—on the Hobby Lobbys, the bakeries, and on individuals, even in this country with its Constitution, its Bill of Rights, and its Statue of Liberty; attempted persecution of Bible-believing Christians continues. (Besides the physical persecution being enforced in some countries.) For the mark of a wolf is that it kills and devours, while a mark of lambs is that of being attacked for no other reason than to satisfy the hunger of wolves. And in practical terms, refusing to move the boundaries of the Kingdom. Which he or she has, by the way, no authority to do. To make a show of doing so is a farce, and makes him or her guilty of deceiving those they profess to love.

For in the end, abiding in Truth will be the vindicator of love. If we see our neighbor's house is on fire at night, we suspect they are asleep in it, but dread disturbing them, so we just go back to bed and arise in the morning to discover that they perished in the fire, our insistence that we loved them too much to disturb them last night would, and rightly so, incur the wrath of all loving neighbors. Can we then know the Truth and refuse to stand for it—to the eternal detriment of those whom we profess to love—without incurring the wrath of Almighty God? This is a question the Word of God has already answered. (Ezekiel 33)

The Kingdom of God has spiritual boundaries. As Jesus said, "The kingdom of God cometh not with observation: Neither shall they say, Lo here! or, lo there! for, behold, the kingdom of God is within you." (Luke 17:20-21) A kingdom within!? One begins to feel for Nicodemus who, in response to Jesus' teaching about the new birth, wondered aloud how he could re-enter his mother's womb and be born the second time? (John 3)

But this is a spiritual Kingdom. A Kingdom of Truth, as Jesus said, "the words that I speak unto you, they are spirit, and they are life." (John 6:63) The words that Jesus speaks are spirit, and "the Spirit is truth," God tells us through His servant John. (1 John 5:6)

"What is truth?" (John 18:38) asked Pilate in seeming exasperation at the Jews and the predicament his own position had forced him into. He had no heart for the judging of this innocent man, whom he was persuaded had been delivered to him for judgment because of envious Jews. Though what he knew in his head did not keep him from caving in to their demands upon the covert threatening of his position, yet the question was a worthy question if only asked from the proper perspective of really wanting to know. A wanting to know—despite the pain that knowing might cause. And is it not the initial pain of knowing the truth about ones self that was causing the frenzied outcry against this man who was the physical embodiment of truth itself? We believe this to be so. And can we not all identify with having those times when truth was painful? So painful that we did not want to face up to it? If we then draw religion around ourselves, as a protective cloak of fig leaves that we rest and have confidence in, and the two-edged sword of the Word of God begins its work to expose the Truth, it is of utmost necessity for the sake of our never-dying souls that we receive and accept the Truth and not react against it simply because it initially doesn't feel good. "It's right if it makes me feel good" is not only a modern-day attitude, but seems to have been very much alive in Jesus' time. When such an attitude becomes interwoven into the fabric of religion, men will go to great lengths for fig leaf protection, especially when it is all we see and know. But when we voluntarily surrender our cloaks of self-protection at the prompting of God's Holy Spirit and receive the covering of Christ's righteousness, then we have the calm assurance of His grace. And the frenzied outcries of self-protection seem foolish indeed—because they really are.

We now live in a day and time when we are again being bombarded by the outcries of frenzied minds. If the left-wing liberals of our day have their way, there will be no recourse left to resist the frenzied outcries against the restraint of mankind's lower nature. No recourse left, that is, except the recourse of the fear of man. Of which fear the Bible says, "the fear of man bringeth a snare." (Proverbs 29:25) One wishes that the liberals would consider the historical record of governments and cultures who departed from the fear of God and of necessity became dependent on the fear of man. How those governments and cultures have morphed otherwise sane men into brutes and mice. And how the brutes have hounded the lives of those who, refusing to become mice, wished to retain their own sanity by upholding the fear of God, both in their own lives and in the cultural times in which they lived.

While Old Testament history of God's judgment on nations by other nations is at times admittedly brutal, the brutality is always rightly understood to be God's direct or indirect judgment upon the sins of individuals or of nations. Old Testament history helps to give us a better understanding of the severity with which God views sin. And how severely it has been, and will be, judged. Upon writing of God's goodness to the repentant and His severity against the unrepentant, the writer of the book of Romans begins his conclusion with this exclamation, "Behold therefore the goodness and severity of God." (Romans 11:22) And truly, they are both attributes of God that need to be accepted, thus awakening the fear of God by first awakening our understanding.

Mercy and truth (judgement) are met together, righteousness and peace have kissed each other, wrote the Psalmist by the inspiration of God. (Psalms 85:10) The demands of righteousness and judgment were satisfied by Jesus Christ on the cross of Calvary, thus when we allow ourselves to be judged by the righteous demands of God's righteousness, mercy is extended to us, because Jesus lives! And peace rests upon and in us as Jesus Christ, who is the Prince of Peace, by His Spirit, takes up residence in us. And calls and empowers us to right actions.

Dr. Martin Luther King Jr. was a man of the 20th century who dreamed of righteous change being brought about through peaceful means. He dreamed of racial desegregation and consequently the integration of blacks into a white-dominated social structure, that despite the Emancipation Proclamation and a Civil War, still repressed—and in many ways rejected—blacks based on their skin color. The injustices commonly practiced by the whites of those days who believed in Aryan race supremacy seem incomprehensible to those of us who were raised in the later era of integrated freedom we enjoy today.

A black man himself, married and having children, Dr. King, having been raised in the deep South, was painfully familiar with the injustices. He could have reacted with bitterness, as some others did, and stirred up bitter violence against the white establishment. But Dr. King didn't, because he was a Christian Believer with a dream.

It seems that the world needs these people with dreams. These people willing to stand up, and to speak up, against unbiblical social norms; and to present a Biblical dream to a world steeped in darkness, while yet trusting that many still grope for the light. For Scriptural dreams become visions that motivate action. And action, when empowered by our Lord Jesus Christ, has Holy Scripture as its basis and the Holy Spirit as its Power. The battle, then, is the Lord's. And the battle, when the Lord is in it, does not depend on you, me, or anyone else individually. If we pass from the scene, the Lord finds someone else to fill our place, for we are not alone but together, under one banner following one Lord, one Master.

Ironically, Dr. King's dream for peaceful integration brought about by peaceful means through the Prince of Peace, cost him his life. On April 4,

1968 Martin Luther King Jr. died for that dream and for the goal emerging from his dream. Shot and killed in Memphis, Tennessee, his dream lived on, gaining momentum toward the goal. A goal looking attainable if only not thwarted by ironic and almost devastating violence by a minority of people having the same skin color as he, but not being of the same heart.

The suppressed bitterness erupting in too many ghettos in too many cities in the mid-1960s came closer to derailing the momentum towards equality than did the force employed by the white establishment of the South. Whose attempts to suppress marchers and demonstrators for equality by means of dogs, clubs, and even guns at times by white police officers, whose posses sometimes included members of the Ku Klux Klan, only served to arouse the compassion of a slumbering giant—American society as a whole—fostering many more marches and demonstrations throughout the nation.

Martin Luther King Jr., while seeking for a peaceful resolution to the problems brought on by a racial caste system, ironically found himself caught between the violence of white resistance to change and the violence of a minority of his own skin color who used the exposure of racial injustice as an opportunity to violently express their hitherto suppressed outrage over the discrimination, and their impatience at the pace of the non-violent movement going away from it.

His became a life of being a "lamb among wolves," though he dreamed of the peaceful integration of his people into a desegregated social structure. A dream that Martin Luther King Jr. lived for. And died for. But before he died, his dream was cemented into the American national mind.

On August 28, 1963 the park between two memorials in Washington DC thronged with over 200,000 people, including many whites who had joined the cause. Only the rectangular pool several hundred yards out from the front of the Lincoln Memorial stood out in dark contrast to the sea of people covering the rest of the park.

As Dr. King reached the top of the long flight of stairs, stepped onto the Lincoln Memorial porch with its huge white columns, and turned to face the sea of faces, he was also fittingly facing the Washington Memorial across the way at the far end of the park. His speech was measured and deliberate as he spoke of ground gained and ground still to win; but then became measured and impassioned as he spoke of his dream. In a clear voice ringing with sincerity, he spoke with the staccato but measured strength of controlled passion. He stood straight and confident behind the podium, with a small number of guards and supporters standing in a semi-circle behind him. His voice swelled across the responsive crowd through the public address system, as the sea of people were infused with like-minded passion. For some, this passion was borne from years of repression, and for others, from a sympathy for the repressed.

Dr King spoke of his own happiness in being part of this great demonstration for freedom, taking place in the symbolic shadow of the man who, 100 years before, had signed the Emancipation Proclamation. He spoke of that decree being a great beacon of hope, a joyous daybreak, as millions of blacks were freed from the injustice of their captivity. Then he went on to draw attention to the shameful condition of segregation and discrimination.

And indeed, it was a shameful condition. Whether it was Abraham Lincoln's untimely death, the wearied bureaucracy, or both, the Emancipation Proclamation was hindered from delivering its promise of equality to full fruition. Though the slaves had been freed from the bondage of being thought of as someone else's property, made to work and serve as if he or she were either a sound—or not so sound—beast, Mr. King was right; Blacks were still not free. The laws, known as the Jim Crow laws, sanctioned the sanctimonious practice of segregation between blacks and whites, categorizing each in a class by themselves. Providing an environment of opportunity, and even wealth, for whites, while simultaneously and heavy-handedly keeping blacks in subjective poverty.

Despite the repression however, there were those such as Dr. King, who became educated and understood the deep and far-reaching discrepancies between the repressive Jim Crow laws and the freedom promised in the U.S. Constitution. While not promising equality of outcome, the Constitution does provide for equality of opportunity. This is what Dr. Martin Luther King Jr. understood on August 28, 1963, as he stood before that vast throng of people and so eloquently presented his case to them, and to the world at large. While his people had been freed from slavery, yet their God-given creative gifts were as yet shackled and denied expression. The opportunities that whites were so free to pursue were denied them by the bureaucratic machinery of their white contemporaries.

Dr. King understood the pain of repression; he had been raised in a social order steeped in it. He understood the promising provisions in the U.S. Constitution. He also understood the teachings of our Lord Jesus Christ, and addressing the crowd and all who would hear, he solemnly exhorted them to not be guilty of wrongful deeds. To not attempt to satisfy their thirst for freedom at the cup of bitterness and hatred. To face their circumstances, yes, but to continue striving toward the goal.

Dr. King spoke that day of traveling blacks being denied a place of lodging in the motels of the highways and the hotels of the cities, of being confined to living in ghettos. Of being robbed of dignity by signs stating "For Whites Only." Of being denied the right, nor given a reason, to vote.

He spoke to those who had suffered jail time for their non-violent attempts to desegregate the prevailing culture. For suffering police brutality. A suffering they had not, nor should they in any way earn. "Continue in the faith," he encouraged them, "that unearned suffering is redemptive." Nowhere did he encourage physical resistance, whether armed nor unarmed, to law enforcement. Nay, the movement of yesteryear appears as the antithesis of today, as police in liberal cities suffer threatening, at times violent, mobs on the one hand and repression from liberal politicians attempting to appease the mobs by giving in to them, on the other.

He encouraged them to continue in unearned suffering as they went back home. To not wallow in the valley of despair, but to hold onto the truth that all men are created equal.

And he spoke of his dream that the children of former slaves and children of former slave owners could one day sit together at the table of brotherhood. He dreamed that his four children could one day live in a nation where they would not be judged by the color of their skin, but by the content of their character. His dream that one day black children would be able to join hands with white children as sisters and brothers.

And then with resounding clarity, peculiar to the free in spirit, he spoke of freedom. Freedom that he desired would ring across America. Of peaceful change, which would result in America becoming a nation of peaceful equality.

The generations born in the '70s and beyond have no memories of segregated schools, stores, eating establishments, and ideally, not of churches. While integration of varied skin colors in the same church are very much a part of the Gospel of Jesus Christ, in practical terms it has not always been that way, and change has been slow in coming. But overall the integration of blacks has been so successful that our great country now has skilled black workers in all trades, black entrepreneurs, executives, lawyers, doctors, pilots, judges, and has had one elected to the highest office in the nation. In some cases it even seems as if the tables have turned and whites become suspect because of their skin color.

Divine Response

In Sioux Falls, SD, on August 24, 2020, as I stepped out of Barnes & Noble and walked to my pickup in the parking lot, I spotted a group of youth picketers standing at the intersection of 41st St and Louise Ave.

Wondering, as I got into my pickup truck, if BLM-ers had come to Sioux Falls, I was curious enough to exit the parking lot so as to drive past them.

Sure enough, as I approached the intersection, the first picket sign I read said "Black Lives Matter." The next said something about Blake, whom I had not heard of as yet. I stared, trying to understand what I was reading, while aware of the need to keep moving. As I made the turn, I did so to a chorus of female screams and male yells of "Racist! Racist!" Me? A racist?! For being a bit near-sighted? For not tooting my horn?

I continued on, but I was deep in thought. I didn't know Blake, but I knew enough about BLM to be troubled about my lack of response. Several vehicles' horns had been mildly tooted to the enthusiastic cheering of the protesters, but I had driven past without speaking out for Truth.

Feeling compelled to respond, I circled back through town and approached that intersection again. Lowering the passenger side window I pulled to the curb and stopped in front of the first person, a young white lady, holding a "Black Lives Matter" sign and hollered loud enough that hopefully all the picketers could hear, "Amen! And the last I checked in with the Lord, unborn babies' lives also matter!"

The picketers had been raucous so I didn't know what to expect. Would they hurt me? Would they damage my truck? Or worse?

Maybe it was the mask on the young lady's face, but her voice sounded subdued and respectful as she responded with, "Okay." Silence reigned with the rest as I resumed driving. As I turned the corner I heard one solitary female voice cry out, "I hope you're not racist, sir!"

The "sir" caught my attention. And the respectful tone of the voice, despite being rather shrill. Then there was the respectful response of "Okay" from the girl behind the mask. And the impression of respect in the silence of the rest.

So I drove away with a little more hope for this segment of the younger generation then when I drove away the first time. Maybe deep down there was still an inner sense of Biblical right and wrong.

Maybe these young people had more values than a mere fanatical protection of blacks.

Maybe they still cared about the character beneath all skin colors.

Maybe they still cared about the big picture.

Maybe, when alone, they still ponder about Life matters.

Or, maybe I'm the one who doesn't have the big picture.

Maybe they are being dumbed down, indoctrinated, and then agitated by dark networks behind the scenes that have also, for decades, been infecting our learning institutions with their liberal, Marxist, and then violent ideas.

The name and violent segment of Black Lives Matter, and other similar movements, draws attention to skin color more than character. Thus, undermining the work of Dr. King Jr., who expended the last decade of his life successfully emphasizing that attention to character leaves skin color irrelevant.

To quote Nesaim Nicholas Taleb, "In a complex world, intelligence ignores the things that are irrelevant." So let us lay aside the irrelevance of skin color for now and respond to a relevant wake-up call; that we again live in a day and time of attempted repression, a repression of values and of character. A direct attack against the Word of God, the Bible. A repression of the Ten Commandments and prayer in, of all places, our public schools where the minds, and consequently the lives, of a majority of this nation's youngsters are being formed. While home still has influence, most school-age children spend more waking hours being influenced at school than at home. And if the liberals have their way, that influence will continue to be godless, even become more so, with even open sin being renamed as "alternative lifestyles." The liberals have not been satisfied with removal of the Bible and prayer from our schools, but now they wish to inject the poison of their own values, or lack thereof, into the very life-blood and future of this entire nation beginning in the hearts and minds of our children. Again, one wishes the liberals would consider the indictment of history upon the so-called "freedom" they wish to introduce and to make a part of our national identity.

For where individual conscience is no longer encouraged, and is even repressed and punished, there, of necessity, the force of human nature takes over. Where the fear of God is repressed, the fear of man takes up the slack. And because man is neither omniscient, omnipresent, nor omnipotent, the switch is futile and ultimately self-destructive. The ancient Roman Empire, the Dark Ages, the Nazis, the Communists, and others have repressed and destroyed Christians, Jews, or both for the simple reason of the faithful wanting God first and man second. There have always been, and appears there always will be, till the end of time that is, men and governments deceived into thinking they play second fiddle to none. Even God. And then find themselves in the impossible position of ruling the minds of men by the use of force. This is impossible because "the man persuaded against his will is of the same opinion still." There is no force so potently powerful as an ideology forming in a man's mind, persuading him to an extent that the thought pattern becomes such an integral part of them that it molds and forms that person's character. Christianity does that and does it thoroughly, because not only is it built upon a foundation of truth, it also has a persuading witness as the Holy Spirit impresses that Truth upon the heart and mind of each individual, and thus, the church corporately. That is, when it is Truth. Let a Christian depart from Truth and the Holy Spirit no longer bears witness to him or her, nor to their words. Make no mistake, the Holy Spirit does witness to Truth. The Truth irritates, infuriates, intimidates, convicts, softens hearts, draws the sinner to Christ, empowers the life, and persuades minds. And when the mind is persuaded, the Holy Spirit becomes as a guiding compass in that mind, ever pointing to higher ground. Which higher ground so transcends the laws of man that the fear of man becomes a hindering encumbrance as it seeks to draw the soul away from the fear of God from whom all blessings flow. And from whom all true Biblical Truth and conviction comes.

While Darwin, Marx, Wellhausen, Dewey, Freud, Keynes, Kierkegaard, and others have had their ideologies that formed and persuaded men's minds, the resulting character traits of their followers, and in at least some of their own lives, have been far less than desirable, to the extent that the more persuaded the less desirable. While the name Christian can conjure up images of undesirable individuals and even churches, one must admit that the more a person is persuaded of New Testament Truth and empowered by its Life, the more he/she can be trusted to stay within the lawful bounds of Governments. As long as that Government stays within its own bounds of God-given jurisdiction, which clause must be included so as to keep the conscience healthy and alive to God, for God will be second to none.

While dictators and tyrants may attempt to be second to none, the attempt is futile and defeated before the struggle even begins for God was, is, and will be, second to none. He is God. He is the only true and lasting security. "Perfect love," God tells us in I John 4:18, "casts out fear."

MEANWHILE BACK ON THE EARTH

PERFECT LOVE

Are we afraid of Governments?
Are we afraid of Kings?
Are we afraid of Darwin?
Who inspired Karl Marx,
To promote Socialism,
In his doctrines without God?

Are we afraid of Wellhausen?
His Modernistic views,
Teaching that the Bible,
Doesn't say what it means,
Thus emboldening Dewey,
To guide schools away from God?

Are we afraid of Sigmund Freud?
Praised as psychology's whiz,
Ungodliness proclaimed wise,
In understanding the mind,
Emboldening Society,
In its doctrines without God?

Do we fear the world of finance?
"Keynesian" economics,
"We just owe it to ourselves,"
But the debt went out to others,
Thus causing inflation,
To spiral out of control?

Are we afraid of Kierkegaard?
His Existentialism,
Where truth is nowhere solid,
Just like Evolutionism,
Thus causing low morals,
To spiral out of control?

Those who reject God in Doctrine,
Will reject Him in life,
Causing depravity 'n sin,
To spiral on downward,
'Til God is given again,
Our lives, to control 'n to cleanse.

Divine Response

Are we afraid a World Ruler,
Will force and rule the whole world,
As if man had no soul?
There's much reason to fear,
There must be something solid,
There must be purpose and goal.

So let us,…turn astonied gaze,
To Scripture, God's Holy Word,
Where Truth is understood,
To be solid, where God says,
That our very existence,
Is dependent on Him.

Depending upon Jehovah,
We shall fearlessly stand,
Upon His Rock Solid Word,
Spoken to us by God.
Written by Prophets 'n Moses,
Culminated in Jesus.

Men who stand and speak fearlessly,
Having Godly conviction,
Are the Godly backbone,
Of all God-fearing culture.
There is no fear in love,
Perfect love casts out fear.

We love Jesus, He first loved us,
In Him is love made perfect,
The fear of man is not,
Made perfect in love,
Because fear hath torment,
Perfect love casts out fear.

In God's strength, we'll not be fearful,
Of this world and its doings,
Let us turn in reverence,
And holy fear, to God's Word,
From there to reach out in love,
Giving God's invitation.

MEANWHILE BACK ON THE EARTH

There's no other answer given,
For the needs of the soul,
Than Jesus, our foundation,
He calms and soothes the fearful,
Provides for us, in Heaven,
A city, not made with hands.

It's obvious, we're not here t' stay,
Whether wealthy or poor,
We all go to the grave,
We'll carry nothing there.
But, living in Jesus' love,
Perfect Love casts out fear.

Gottes sege dazu winscha
(May God add His blessing)

18

MEANWHILE BACK ON THE EARTH

PART 2

HE IS GOD. JEHOVAH is God. That may sound to some of us like a bland and obvious statement. Like having a keen sense of the obvious. But it is a statement that, down through the ages, has often been misunderstood and misdirected. We know this to be true by reading God's Word, for while the Bible is history of the founding of the Christian Church, history of Israel as God's children, and the origin of man; it is also a history of confusion about who God is. Or whether he exists at all.

For reasons that God alone best understands, He has chosen for this time not to reveal Himself to us in physical form. The closest He has come to doing so is Jesus appearing to His disciples and followers after His resurrection. The Bible is clear that He wants our hearts and minds to be persuaded by faith in Him, as He said to Thomas after allowing that doubting disciple to feel his nail-scarred hands and His spear-pierced side. "Be not faithless, but believing … Thomas, because thou hast seen me, thou hast believed: blessed are they that have not seen, and yet have believed." (John 20:27, 29)

That is us. We are to believe the historical record of those who did see Him after His resurrection and before His ascension into Heaven; where Stephen, as he was being stoned and martyred for his faith, saw Him "standing on the right hand of God." (Acts 7:56) And we are called to believe the Holy Spirit's witness to our hearts and minds. As He convinces us of sin, of righteousness and of judgment. (John 16:8) And, as He is the Comforter to us that shall come. (John 14:26)

This constitutes a relationship between us and God. A relationship that is dependent upon Him for He is all powerful. A relationship that is also dependent upon our response to Him for our all-powerful God has given us the freedom of choice. We cannot curse God and still have a good relationship with Him. Nor can we ignore Him and still have a good relationship with Him. Nor ignore His commandments. A good relationship with God is dependent upon Him and also depends upon our response to Him when He convicts, rebukes, chastens, comforts, and loves on us. A father/child relationship is to be a reflection of our relationship with God. A relationship of love flowing rich and deep. This father/child relationship, and our ensuing accountability to Him, does however cause an awareness in us of the ongoing tension between Good and Evil. The tension that inwardly tears us apart when the awareness of our Father's will conflicts with what we want.

Is not this the appeal of idols? And of false gods? For an idol is the work of our hands, the false god a figment of our imagination. And when we worship our own creation, can we not make our own rules? And demand that others do the same? Does not the game designer also write the rules of the game?

Idols do appeal to our lower nature and Old Testament history attests time and again how quickly, after being blessed by God, mankind can fall from His grace to the worship of idols. But if we think of idols only as those ancient carvings and engravings of wood and of stone such as Baal, Ashtoreth, Buddha, or many others; we miss the heart of what idol worship is and may well be caught up in it ourselves. For an idol is first of all, a work of man's hands. And so are the things that we build and use every day. Including houses, barns, shops, offices, cars, trucks, airplanes, and the digital electronic devices becoming so prevalent everywhere. Or a myriad of other things. The way we relate to these things has everything to do with whether we worship them or not. They must not be what we turn to for courage. They must not capture our devotion. And if they capture our "free time," have they not also captured our devotion? If they capture our minds and hearts, have they not also captured our bodies? And thus are we not wholly given over to worshiping something other than God? And if our bodies become given over to the lust of the flesh, the lust of the eyes, and the pride of life, have they not become a tool of our devotion to whatever our heart and mind is focused upon? Possibly our bodies, or pictures of them, have become the very idol itself? "Little children [newborn Christians], keep yourselves from idols." (I John 5:21)

God will not share His Glory with another. God will have first place in our lives or not be there at all. (I Corinthians 1:29-31) There is no selfishness in this demand, for if God were not to retain first place, then all creation would immediately implode upon itself; because all creation is upheld by the Word of His Power. (Hebrews 1:3)

And someday, the Bible warns, it will not be upheld, as the elements themselves shall melt with fervent heat. (II Peter 3:12) In this past century, science (as in observable repeatable science) has clearly shown this not to be an empty threat, as a close study of the elements has revealed what the 20th century genius, Albert Einstein, labeled as $E=MC2$. That equation changed the course of history and now helps us to better understand that if God were to release the latent energy in the mass of our world, there would indeed be an instantaneous world-wide meltdown. For what is it that keeps protons and neutrons spinning around the nucleus instead of shooting straight out, which produces heat beyond measure? This is a question that Scientists who do not believe in God have yet to answer, but go on searching for what some of them have ironically referred to as "the god particle."

There is One who has given Himself for our sins and wants to rescue us before this final meltdown. His name is Jesus. The One who saves us from our sins. And saves us from future destruction. And saves us unto eternal life. Eternal bliss, peace, and comfort. Never-ending. Forever. God has created us creatures of choice, which means our rescue needs to involve our cooperation. Not a cooperation of saving ourselves, for we cannot, but a cooperation of being available for rescue, allowing ourselves to be found. Which doesn't always feel good. Especially not initially as He brings His Authority to bear upon our life. But when we allow ourselves to be found, then we find Him, and find that He is indeed gracious, merciful, and comforting, as He forgives and receives us as one of His own.

But, while yet here in this life, we have an enemy of our souls, the devil, continuously trying to keep us lost. Or to have us leave the protecting Authority of Jesus, for the beggarly elements of this present world, after we have been found. There is nothing new under sun, God tells us through the writer of Ecclesiastes. (Ecclesiastes 1:9) Yet, the devil is finding ways in these last days to make the old temptations of the lust of the flesh, the lust of the eyes, and the pride of life, more readily available. Easier to access.

MEANWHILE BACK ON THE EARTH

God tells us through the Prophet Daniel that, "many shall run to and fro, and knowledge shall be increased." (Daniel 12:4) As we observe the unprecedented accumulation of knowledge encompassing this past century and a half, beginning with the steam locomotive, one ceases to wonder if we live in the last days of which Daniel speaks. The accumulation of knowledge shows no sign of letting up at this time, and indeed seems to have become a sort of god of the mind. While the brain is an organ that is strengthened by exercise and becomes more capable with use, it is not strengthened nor made more capable by information flashing through in bits and pieces that find no lodging there.

The brain is a fascinating organ that becomes stronger as it is exercised and becomes flabbier when it is not, as neurologist Peter Miller informed me when I was in recovery after my head injury in 2011. So I exercised it by doing math in my head, recalling previously memorized Bible verses, doing English, doing spelling, recalling names and faces of people I knew. But best of all was the memorizing of Bible verses, for this memorization also has a spiritual benefit. "Finally, brethren," God tells us through the writer to the Philippians, "whatsoever things are true, whatsoever things are honest, whatsoever things are just, whatsoever things are pure, whatsoever things are lovely, whatsoever things are of good report; if there be any virtue, and if there be any praise, think on these things." (Philippians 4:8) Praise the Lord! God even tells us how to think! I find that thought liberating as it gives direction.

A method for memorizing scripture that I've found helpful is to write the verse or verses for the day, several days, or for the week, on a piece of paper; underline or circle the first word of each part of speech or phrase preferably in red, and then memorize those first words in sequence as a list. When that list can go through the mind at will and a fast pace, I find that the rest of the verse can be memorized with ease. Memorizing a list of words may seem like a waste of time at first, but by the time I have mastered the, at first seemingly unrelated, list of words, I have also practically mastered the verse. We may think of it as building a grape arbor and planting a grapevine in anticipation of enjoying the fruit of the vine. Is it not anticipation of the fruit that encourages the husbandman to keep pressing on even if, or when, the going gets tough? It takes diligence to press on with memorization, but if we press on, it has the benefits of "the washing of water by the Word," knowing and applying the Word of God in everyday life, strengthening of the brain through exercise, and giving our thoughts direction through discipline.

Divine Response

The temptation to allow thoughts to wander into useless meanderings is never far away, but a spiritually fit mind is akin to a physically fit body in that once it is fit, the fitness feels so healthy that unhealthy habits become more and more undesirable and healthy habits more and more desirable.

One of the most unhealthy mind habits is also the one habit that is most prevalent in this 21st century that we live in. It is the habit of relaxing the mind in front of a screen. Critiquing information is not in vogue these days. Discerning right from wrong should be a continual exercise in our hearts and minds, (Hebrews 5:14) and instead, so much time is spent and minds wasted through uncritically absorbing the combination of visual and verbal information that has become so much of our daily national diet.

In *The Next Story*, a thought-provoking book on the subject, author Tim Challis gives the results of a 2008 study. He begins by asking, "Just how much are screens an essential part of life in the 21st century?" In 2008 the Council for Research Excellence decided to find out. They worked with Nielsen to carry out a broad research project that would monitor media usage for 476 Americans. Using a small data-collecting device, running specialized software, an observer monitored each of the subjects for two full waking days, yielding a total of three-quarters of a million minutes of observation time measured in ten-second increments. Here are a few of the more significant results of their study.

- Adults ages forty-five to fifty-four accumulate the greatest amount of screen time, totaling nine hours and thirty four minutes per day. The average daily screen time for eighteen year-olds is slightly less at eight and a half hours. Screen time for those under eighteen lacks thorough studies at the moment, but it's thought to be at least equal to that of eighteen year-olds.

- About a quarter of that screen time is "combined time" meaning that during these periods people are using more than one screen at once; perhaps watching TV while surfing the internet, or watching a movie while texting and checking e-mail. The accumulated screen time is about two hours more than the actual screen time.

- Time in front of the television screen, whether watching television, watching a DVD, or playing a console game still makes up the largest amount of time; about five hours for the eighteen year-old and a bit more for Mom and Dad. It rises very sharply as Mom and Dad become Grandma and Grandpa. Those who are age sixty-five and older average well over seven hours per day of TV time.

- When we analyze these screen times, we realize that the average American spends approximately one hour per day watching television commercials and other promos.

Considering that these were average Americans, such exorbitant amounts of screen time, if there is no critiquing of content, is in itself harmful; as it amuses the mind into a state of sleepy numbness. As does any form of thoughtless meandering disconnected from reality, when the brain and mind are not exercised by Godly principles.

"While I was musing the fire burned," (Psalms 39:3) wrote the Psalmist of old as he described the inner stirrings of reflecting on the deeper truths and realities of life. And death. Musing, according to Strong's Concordance, is a form of meditation. Webster's Dictionary (1828) simply says, "meditation; contemplation." It also gives this definition for "*museful*: thinking deeply or closely; silently thoughtful." Hmmm. Silently thoughtful. Thinking deeply. Is it not more necessary, in these clamorous times, to find a quiet place? A place of quiet communion with God. A place of reflection. A place to ponder the Word of God and to allow it to reflect upon our lives. A quiet place to study God's Word and to pray. A place to unload our cares about the present and our worries about the future on Him and to leave them there.

In considering the visual and verbal presentations of the lust of the flesh, the lust of the eyes, and the pride of life, with even murder being displayed on screens in glamorous context, is it any wonder when selfishness and violence rule the day? While the makers of lust filled, violent movies are being exonerated and even praised by many law-abiding citizens, the NRA and the Second Amendment are being challenged when a shooting occurs because they own or defend ownership of guns.

Guns do not kill people, for guns are inanimate objects. People kill people. And people use guns to kill people. People also use cars to kill people. And pick-up trucks. And butcher knives. And baseball bats. And steel pipes. And anything they can or cannot get their hands on; for even bare hands are known to have killed people. In fist fights, by strangling, by pushing off high places and probably a myriad of other ways I cannot, nor want to, imagine.

With a little bit of sound logic, then, it becomes obviously futile to remove every object that may or may not be used to destroy a fellow human being. Because murder is an expression of the human heart, when first inward and then outward restraints have been cast off. Either restraints against drunkenness, restraints brought on by a sense of the sanctity of human life, or, as in most cases, ceasing to restrain hatred. Jesus said it best when He said, "That which cometh out of the man, that defileth the man. For from within, out of the heart of men, proceed evil thoughts, adulteries, fornications, murders, thefts, covetousness, wickedness, deceit, lasciviousness, an evil eye, blasphemy, pride, foolishness: All these evil things come from within, and defile the man." (Mark 7:20-23)

As a nation, are we not amusing ourselves to death? For while musing is the deep pondering of reality, to be amused is to have the mind disengaged from critical thinking, or discernment. Entertainment of the mind. What is presented on the screen in movies is not to be understood as real life. So if it is not real, is it not entertainment? And how can we possibly allow ourselves and our children to be entertained by varied lusts and graphic violence without reaping the dire consequences, especially in our hormone-driven teens, as we detach from reality and our heart and minds are re-programmed by the overpowering influence of what we see and hear on the screen, while we watch from our comfortable chairs with our tasty snacks and beverages? What our hearts (emotions) and minds feed on, we eventually develop an appetite for.

While the so-called "enlightened" thinkers and their "children", the "progressive" thinkers, vainly herald the evolution of a better and better tomorrow, the idea of having evolved from a Big Bang or whatever else comes to the imagination of desperate minds, is actually, at its root, the belief in the abject degradation of mankind. The Bible presents man as being "made in the image of God." He is not to worship that image, he is to worship God only; but he is to respect and care for what God has made, especially that which God has made in His own image.

A woman who was called "pond scum" as a small child tells of believing that degrading lie and the long-term devastating effect that lie had on her opinion of herself. Instead of accepting the Truth that she was "made in the image of God," that God cared and had such an intense interest in the salvation of every soul that Jesus came and gave His life for the sins of the whole world, that every soul was precious in His sight and that she herself was one of those "precious souls" that Jesus gave His life for, intensely desiring her salvation, she instead believed The Lie that she was worthless, like "pond scum."

Does this Lie not sound familiar? "Pond scum" is not "made in the image of God." God did not breathe into "pond scum" "the breath of life." "Pond scum" has no sense of eternity in its heart. "Pond scum" has no sense of right and wrong. God did not send His only begotten Son into the world for the love of "pond scum."

While it is true that our own righteousness is as filthy rags before God, (Isaiah 64:6) that is, in comparison to His Divine Holiness; yet it is also true that He has provided all the resources for us to be remade, to have our spirit and soul be more and more "conformed into the image of Christ" after being reborn. Born again, old things being passed away and all things becoming new. (II Corinthians 5:17) We are not in need of more "self-esteem," we are in need of more appreciation for God's creation and His plan for our salvation.

Whether we like it or not, the lie of being pond scum is very like the "Primordial Soup" lie of Evolution, that unscientific curse on humanity that reduces human life to the level of "pond scum." Or a Big Bang that happened, though we are clueless as to how; or where matter came from in the endless regions of outer space, eons or millions of years ago. Somehow through untold millions of evolving mutations, we are who we are and who knows what we will become?

Children by the millions are being taught, under the guise of "Science," that their very existence happened by chance as an accident of nature; that they then evolved into a creature sensible of its own existence, immersed in a "survival of the fittest" struggle against death.

Upon this foundational teaching of "survival of the fittest mutations," a denial of the existence of God becomes the logical next step. And if there is no God, there is also no higher law than the decisions and consensus of mankind. And if there is no higher law than the decisions and consensus of mankind and the foundation of our very existence is "survival of the fittest," is it not logical that fitness is proven by survival? And if fitness is proven by survival, then should not I, who have the best idea, survive? Nay, these ideas militate against the finest of human instincts, of which are compassion for the down-trodden, the hurting, the handicapped, and the elderly. The finest of human instincts are impressed upon us by natural law that God has purposefully woven into the very fabric of nature; and once these are rejected and denied upon the foundation of the fittest surviving, it is only logical that many will, and do, slide into Nihilism, and eventually Anarchy.

Divine Response

So now there are hundreds of thousands of disillusioned young people believing as they've been taught; that their very existence began with an accident, (and is what began as an accident, not an accident still?), that they are who they are because the fittest survive, and that because all this is true the world is becoming better and better and mankind is becoming more and more able and wise. And yet, even natural law is convincingly showing them the diametrical opposite.

Into this seething cauldron of confusion comes a seemingly endless supply of graphically violent movies and video games that draw the unwitting young untrained mind into the story and the simulated violence. And the more the mind becomes immersed in the unreal world of animated cartoons, of graphic violence, of simulated horror, of fairy-tale romance, of beautiful houses with gorgeous gardens, of haunted houses with possible horror lurking at every turn, and all this on an animated screen with accompanying conversation and sound effects, the more blurred the lines become between the Real and the Unreal.

Between truth and falsehood. Between right and wrong. And the idea of peace remains only that, an idea, blurred and unattainable, always seeming within reach but always just out-of-reach. On the other hand, the Bible, through Jesus Christ, gives a solid basis, a solid foundation to discern between right and wrong, between true and false, between what is real and what is unreal. A solid basis and foundation that is the same "yesterday, today, and forever." It never changes, because God never changes—it is the very word of God.

Though not as titillating through instant gratification in this present time, the Bible directs our attention forward, when what is now future will become "this present time." And when that "present time" arrives that we may be ready to be transported and received into eternal glory and bliss, made all the more blissful by the reassurance that the safety, security, and glorious bliss we are now experiencing will never change; it will now always be, this way. Between now and then may our minds be clear, our hearts clear, and peace reign; because our hearts are assured before Him. (I John 3:19)

While the task of keeping our minds and hearts clear is a daunting one in our day, it actually has always been this way because of the lust of the flesh, the lust of the eyes, and the pride of life that have been a part of the makeup of mankind since the Fall in The Garden. "There is no new thing under the sun." (Ecclesiastes 1:9) But with six thousand years of experience behind him, the devil seems to become ever more wily in his methods of offering the same old temptations; and now with the advent of digital technology, his offerings have taken on a glamorous hue hitherto unknown to mankind. Who can deny it? It is especially obvious to those of us born in a different era, in an older generation. While we may have been teens in the '50s, '60s, or '70s, and our bodies tempted to twitch with the pounding music that was still new in those days; and while the TV and movie theaters had already been assimilated into the culture, yet the ability to have dominion over and control the screen before us, as it is today, was only the stuff of science fiction back then.

If someone had told us back then what all we would be able to see and accomplish with the slim pocket-size devices we call smart phones, would we have believed him? I don't think so. Absolutely not, is probably more like it. And yet we have a generation growing into adulthood now who accept it as a part of life, much in the same way that we, back then, accepted that the movie theater and TV were a part of life as it is. Though some of us were raised without it being acceptable, yet we knew it was there, available, and therefore it was a part of life as we knew it.

While the expensive and cumbersome car phone of the '70s was only as mobile as the car it was wired to and had just two functions, one being making phone calls and the other receiving phone calls; the devices of today fit in the palm of our hands and cannot only do phone calls, but can send and receive printed text, take pictures, send and receive pictures, show maps, pinpoint our own location and the location of others that have Smart Phones. It can record and send moving pictures with accompanying voice recordings. It can tell us the time of day, the temperature and the weather forecast. It can access the Internet and view its endless offerings. Using a credit or debit card number, it can buy and sell. And more. As we consider this panorama of apps and functions, can we do aught but wonder, what next? Are we nearing the end of the invention road? Or not?

And as it functions as our servant, ever offering us more tools and mobility, will its myriad offerings eventually bring us into bondage to it? Are we in bondage even now? Already functioning as a medium between friends, family, news, seller to buyer, buyer to seller, will it eventually become the only medium between buyer and seller? Will it be the medium to bring the Mark of the Beast, also called by the number 666 in Revelation Chapter 13, upon an unsuspecting society, slowly being conditioned even as the proverbial frog? That frog whose body temperature adjusted slowly to the rising temperature in the pot of water over the fire, until he could no longer jump out—as he could once have easily done—instead becoming thoroughly cooked.

Or is the Smart Phone the forerunner of an implanted microchip that will become an identification tag? Reducing those who receive it to the status of cattle, with a one world Dictator as their Ultimate Authority and Master? Leaving those who give in with no hope beyond this temporary life. Will the microchip be the new and only medium between buyer and seller? Will God, in the last days, tweak the air waves and confuse the language of our post-modern-day tower of Babel, the World Wide Web? Will we no longer be able to communicate with its www language? Causing the kings of the earth to lament and bewail her, standing afar off for the fear of her torment, saying "Alas, alas, that great city Babylon, that mighty city! For in one hour is thy judgment come. And the merchants of the earth shall weep and mourn over her; for no man buyeth their merchandise any more." (Revelation 18:10-11) This prophecy will come to pass, the only question is how? And when?

These are questions that time will answer, for God has given us only hints in Prophecy, to help those who are spiritually awake to identify the signs of the times. And God will awaken those who turn to Him and acknowledge Him as their ultimate Authority. There have always been those dictators wishing to crush Christianity, because Christianity bows its knees to God only, esteeming His Authority to be sacred and above that of Dictators, Tyrants, or any other authority; for all are under Him. God has Ultimate Authority. He tells us in His Word, by His Ultimate Authority, how we should relate to earthly authorities, both church and civil. And how church and civil authorities should relate to those being led by their leadership. He gives the scope and limits of authority both Church and Civil. He helps all of us, whether over or under, to find and to stay in our God-given roles in life.

Consider the following diagram:

The Word on Authority Structure

"Nevertheless not my will but Thine [the Father's] be done." (Luke 22:42)

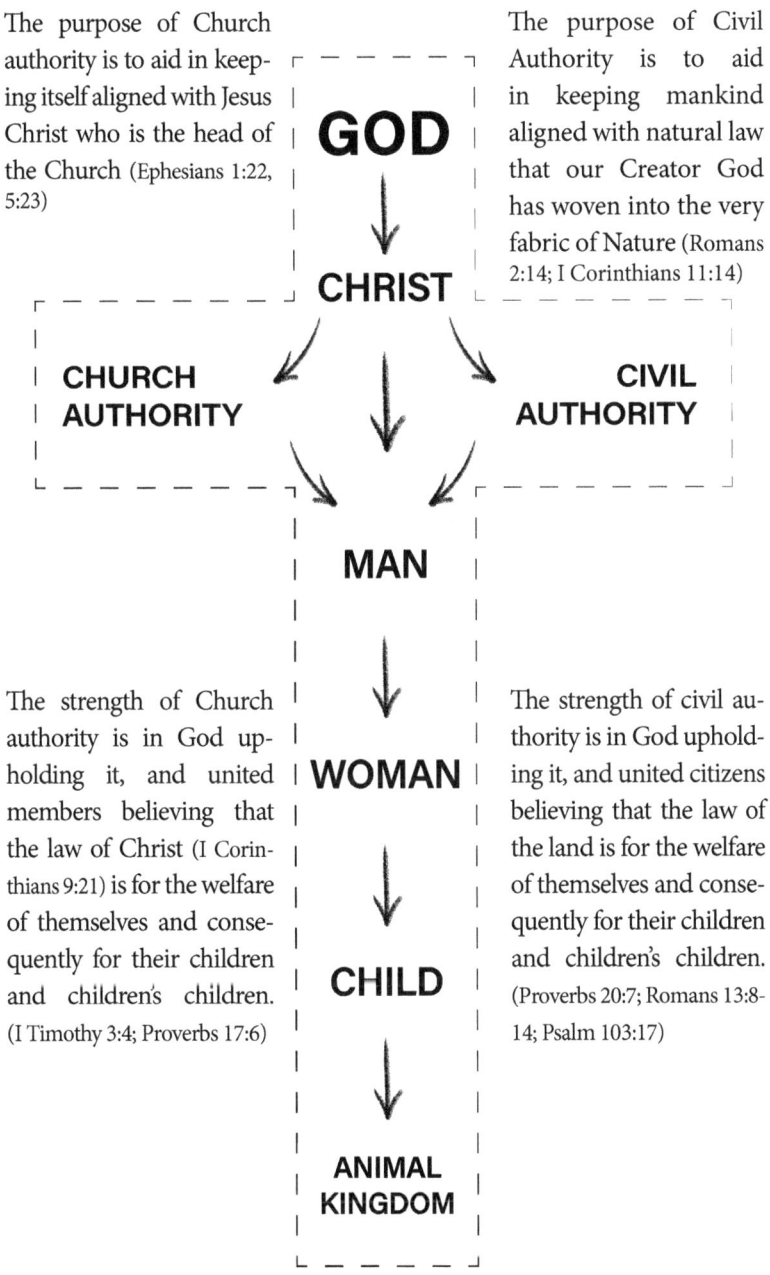

The purpose of Church authority is to aid in keeping itself aligned with Jesus Christ who is the head of the Church (Ephesians 1:22, 5:23)

The purpose of Civil Authority is to aid in keeping mankind aligned with natural law that our Creator God has woven into the very fabric of Nature (Romans 2:14; I Corinthians 11:14)

The strength of Church authority is in God upholding it, and united members believing that the law of Christ (I Corinthians 9:21) is for the welfare of themselves and consequently for their children and children's children. (I Timothy 3:4; Proverbs 17:6)

The strength of civil authority is in God upholding it, and united citizens believing that the law of the land is for the welfare of themselves and consequently for their children and children's children. (Proverbs 20:7; Romans 13:8-14; Psalm 103:17)

- The purpose of the church is to teach all things that Christ commanded, doing so by word and example, thereby being a conscience for those who are lacking and keeping the world and itself accountable to our Creator God. (Matthew 28:18-20)
- Both church and civil authority have their jurisdiction given and established by God. (II Corinthians 5:1, 4-20; I Timothy 4:12-16; Romans 13:1-7)
- Both church and civil authority have their jurisdiction limited by God-established boundaries. (II Corinthians 1:2, 4; Galations 1:10; Luke 12:45-46)
- To avoid deception and/or tyranny, both church and civil leaders are accountable to God, both directly and through the people they serve. (Deuteronomy 13:1-5; Ephesians 4:14; Titus 3:10; Acts 16:37, 20:29, 22:24-29, 25:16, 24:18-21)
- God's Power and Authority are Ultimate. (Isaiah 26:4; Matthew 19:26; Revelation 19:6)
- Therefore we pray: "Thy kingdom come. Thy will be done in earth, as it is in heaven." (Matthew 6:10)

We may, and all of us likely do, have many questions about the future. At the rapid rate of inventions and change in these last few decades, what will the next few decades be like? Will we reach a plateau or will inventions and change continue? And if inventions and change continue, how will they affect our lives? The lives of our children?

But the foundational and over-arching question that literally engulfs all other questions, is the question of authority. Who is—who will be—our ultimate Authority? The Christian has already answered that question. So has the Humanist. The Christian says God is Ultimate; the Humanist says man is. Between these two polar opposites are many "floaters," who by life, beliefs, or both, reveal confusion about this question of all questions. Adding to the cauldron of confusion are those attempting to pull those polar opposites together onto a middle ground of compromise. Be not deceived. There is no compromise. While the devil, through Humanism, or anything in the "floating" realm, may appear to compromise, he is not actually compromising; for his goal is, and always has been, to draw God's children into his own realm of authority. His goal is deception. (Matthew 4:1; John 8:44) God's goal is Reality. And because God lives in Reality, He is Truth itself. He cannot deny Himself. (II Timothy 2:13) There is no compromise. There is no middle ground.

Compromise and middle ground ideas do sound appealing to the natural mind and have their place at times in natural and political negotiations, but on this question of Ultimate Authority there can be no compromise—for Truth is not open to question. There is no point in talking about compromise to a burning house or an activated time bomb. The best we can hope for is to take action and thereby to lessen or avoid the damage. Only a fool denies and ignores the presence of a time bomb. Only a fool denies a burning house. Only a fool denies and ignores the Ultimate Authority of God. For eternity will reveal God being the Ultimate Authority. Authority that shows itself even now in His creation and in the way He upholds it. Authority that shows itself even now through the Holy Spirit, convincing us of sin, of righteousness, and of judgment. An Authority that shows itself even now through the Comforter, the Holy Spirit, that has come.

God, through His Holy Spirit, desires to put His spiritual mark of ownership upon all, and Jesus gave His life for all, making it all possible. This spiritual mark is received into the inner man by believing on Jesus, the One whom the Scriptures and the Holy Spirit witness of. "He that believeth on the Son hath everlasting life: and he that believeth not the Son shall not see life; but the wrath of God abideth on him." (John 3:36) This spiritual mark of God, the indwelling Holy Spirit, changes the life from the inside out. "But if the Spirit of him that raised up Jesus from the dead dwell in you, he that raised up Christ from the dead shall also quicken your mortal bodies by his Spirit that dwelleth in you." (Romans 8:11)

The devil, on the other hand, being the "god of this world," (II Corinthians 4:4) of necessity works from the outside in. Through the lust of the flesh, the lust of the eyes, and the pride of life, the Enemy of our souls endeavors to captivate the desires of the body, subtly drawing the affection of the heart to the senses of the body, thereby entangling and ensnaring the mind. As these body, soul, and spirit tactics of the devil are from the outside in, should we not expect his mark of ownership to be a mark on the outside, in the physical, material realm? Revelation Chapter 13 refers to the devil's mark as the number 666, the number of a man; informs us that all who do not receive it will be barred from buying or selling; and warns that all who do receive it will be barred from salvation when Jesus comes. So this warning is nothing to trifle with and seems to refer to a one-world monetary system being enforced through financial pressure.

And Beware. There is a nameless new religion gaining ground. It lacks an organization and it lacks a name, but from this writer's perspective, is most accurately called "The First Birth Religion;" its first Rule of Conduct being: "It's right if it makes me feel good." While the "Hippie Movement" of days gone by, in obvious rebellion against the status quo of the "Great Society" said, "if it feels good, do it," this new "religion" comes cloaked in religious overtones, speaks of "right" and "wrong" in words sophisticated enough to catch the Biblically unlearned off guard.

If ever there was a need—which there is and always has been—for Bible believing Christians to draw and to stand together forming a Christian Coalition, being a kingdom within a kingdom, that time from all appearances and from Prophecy, is now. May God give wisdom and raise up Christians with the giftings needed to help each other form and lead the Kingdom of God on earth.

Bible believing Christians, Unite! Break off the chains of sin, fear of man, and of pride. Through the indwelling of Jesus Christ by His Spirit. He is our Master. In this 21st century with digital technology a part of life as we know it, can we avoid its dangers and pitfalls? Will we allow man, through mediums such as Alexa, Siri, and Wikipedia to be the final authority on truth? While these mediums retain much of the facts and wisdom gained by the research of former generations, still, Alexa speaks lies in the same tone of authority as she does provable facts; and Wikipedia is open in continual flux to the multitude of opinions. Facts are in jeopardy.

The Bible is very clear that the question of final authority will be cleared up at the final Judgment. Jesus will be the Victor! He is the Victor. He is Truth.

We are, we must be according to Prophecy, nearing the end of time when Jesus will come to receive His own unto Himself.

The war has been won in Heaven. It is over.

The battle continues here on the earth. It is not over.

Yet.

But it will be.

We have the privilege to be on the winning side. To be safe.

Secure.

Forever.

Even so, come Lord Jesus.

Dr. Martin Luther King Jr. had a dream and the momentum of his dream lives on. Compared to Dr. King I feel small and insignificant. Compared to God, even more so.

But my dream isn't small. For I also have a dream ... and in that dream Jesus Christ is allowed His rightful place of being Head of the

Church. May I say that we—Bible-believing Christians worldwide—have a dream?

We have a dream ... of the Church moving forward under the banner of Jesus Christ. We have a dream ... of each member in the Church being equipped with the whole armor of God. We have a dream ... of the Church united in battle against the Enemy of our souls. We have a dream ... of the Church doing exploits against the Enemy and setting his prisoners free by pointing them to Jesus. We have a dream ... of churches planting churches who plant churches and the church-planting continues to the end of time. We have a dream ... of the glory of the Lord purifying the Church. We have a dream ... of a sanctified Church having a sanctifying effect on culture.

We have a goal ... of ourselves, our children, our grandchildren, our great-grandchildren and so on to the end of time being faithful, and with all the faithful, being salt of the earth influencing culture and leading other souls into the Kingdom of Christ.

We have a purpose ... of the Church of Jesus Christ being so filled with the glory of the Lord that it cannot be contained. We have a purpose ... of God's glory, through Jesus Christ, filling the whole earth. We have a purpose ... of a people from every nation, kindred, and language being caught up together in the clouds, "and so shall we ever be with the Lord." (I Thessalonians 4:17) We have a purpose ... that these dreams become visions motivating actions And those actions, when empowered by our Lord Jesus Christ, win the battle.

If you or I were the last Christian left on earth and we were to lead one soul to Christ once a year, and then every convert thereafter, including ourselves, would lead one soul to Christ once a year, in 33 years over 8.5 billion people would be Christians; and the next year would again double if there were that many people on the earth. Consider the estimate of 9 billion people on earth by 2050 and then consider the following numbers.

If the top right number on the left column were you and it also represented the number of Christians left on the earth (which is not the case, by the way), what would you do? Consider the following numbers and consider what would happen if every Christian led one soul to Christ once a year.

DIVINE RESPONSE

Year	# of Christians
0	1
1	2
2	4
3	8
4	16
5	32
6	64
7	128
8	256
9	512
10	1024
11	2048
12	4096
13	8192
14	16,384
15	32,768
16	65,536
17	131,072
18	262,144
19	524,288
20	1,048,576
21	2,097,152
22	4,194,304
23	8,388,608
24	16,777,216
25	33,554,432
26	67,108,864
27	134,217,728
28	268,435,456
29	536,870,912
30	1,073,741,824
31	2,147,483,648
32	4,294,967,296
33	8,589,934,592

Bible-Believing Christians, Unite! From a proper perspective, which is eternal, you have nothing to lose but your chains! And everything to win! For Jesus Christ is your King, your Friend, your Counselor, your Joy, your Consolation, the Prince of Peace, your Comforter, your Guide, your security, both now and forever. May He, the Way, the Truth, and the Life, draw us together in these last days.

God is calling us to reality, to an understanding of time and eternity from His perspective, from that which is. Never forcing anyone into mindless obedience, He nonetheless calls us to a reality that may at times, especially at the outset, feel heavy with the reality of our own nature of sin, and ensuing inclination toward it. While leaving the push for mindless obedience to the leadership of carnal men and demons, God calls us to love. And He calls us through love. While facing reality may not always feel like love (Revelation 3:1-9), it is in the realm of reality that we find Jesus. And He, who is the Way, the Truth, and the Life, meets us there. In real time. In real life. With love that can be sensed. With love that transforms minds. With love that reflects back to Him, (I John 4:16-19) and to others. (I John 4:20-21)

The choice is ours.

In the realm of time.

To serve deception, darkness, and bondage.

Or, to serve Truth, Life, and Liberty.

Let Freedom Ring!

MEANWHILE BACK ON THE EARTH

While we temporarily live down here on the earth,
And go about doing the things that we plan,
We should say, "if the Lord wills we will do this or that."
We have no real control over most of what happens.
Our strength has limits.
God's strength has none.
We need to recognize, acknowledge, our limitations.

Most of our limitations remain all the same,
All of us have twenty-four hours each day.
In each twenty-four hours much good and much evil is done,
And it depends on whether God or man has his way.
When God has His way,
He's seeing beyond,
To where time slips away to eternity's realm.

When God has His way, He's doing what is best,
For humanity, in light of eternity.
We may need to give up much leisure and comfort,
But God will give the comfort of the Holy Ghost.
God's way is best.
'N when time slips away,
We'll see clearly as at the dawn, night yielding to day.

So as we temporarily live here on the earth,
And go about doing the things that we plan,
We should say "if the Lord wills, we will do this or that."
How the most can be saved resides in His sovereign mind.
God has no limits.
But has given us choices.
Our eternal welfare is always on His mind 'n in His heart.

God said to have dominion over the earth and subdue it,
He created mankind in His own image.
While we're here we should care for 'n do our best on this earth.
God wove natural law into the order of things.
He is all-knowing.
Man's wisdom fails.
May God, through His Holy Spirit and Word, in each life prevail.

Looking forward to that day when the saved of every kindred and tongue, people of every tribe and nation, being integrated with the heavenly host of angels, shall worship God with fullness of freedom and joy.

Let Truth prevail! Let Freedom ring!

THE PRESENCE OF GOD

In our highest joy, God is there;
In our deepest sorrow, God is there;
In every moment, God is there;
God is there, for He is here.

www.ingramcontent.com/pod-product-compliance
Lightning Source LLC
Chambersburg PA
CBHW051855160426
43209CB00006B/1314